# Too *Marvellous* for Words!

JULIE WELCH

# Too Marvellous for Words!

**SIMON &
SCHUSTER**

London · New York · Sydney · Toronto · New Delhi

A CBS COMPANY

First published in Great Britain by Simon & Schuster UK Ltd, 2017
A CBS COMPANY

1 3 5 7 9 10 8 6 4 2

Simon & Schuster UK Ltd
1st Floor
222 Gray's Inn Road
London WC1X 8HB

www.simonandschuster.co.uk
www.simonandschuster.com.au
www.simonandschuster.co.in

Simon & Schuster Australia, Sydney
Simon & Schuster India, New Delhi

A CIP catalogue record for this book
is available from the British Library

Hardback ISBN: 978-1-4711-5478-2
eBook ISBN: 978-1-4711-5480-5

Typeset in Bembo by M Rules
Printed and bound by CPI Group (UK) Ltd, Croydon, CR0 4YY

MIX
Paper from
responsible sources
FSC® C020471

To Jonah and Bretch,
in affectionate memory

# Contents

# INTRODUCTION

When I tell people I went to boarding school, they always ask two questions. Was it just like Malory Towers? And did you have midnight feasts?

As it happens, I can answer both these questions and more, loads more, because I remember so clearly everything that happened to me at Felixstowe College in the early 1960s, when the world was quite different from how it is now. When school was a place of weird and wonderful rules and happenings that seemed perfectly normal at the time: when the headmistress and the Head of Science raced each other on public roads in their sports cars; when fire practice involved abseiling down the walls; when having meringues for your birthday tea instead of plain cake was branded 'disgraceful'.

This is a story not just about me but about some of the girls who were there with me, who have equally vivid memories of a life of dorms, bizarre slang, frumpy uniform, mad teachers, pranks, pashes and *no boys whatsoever*.

Felixstowe College was a beautiful school set by the sea on England's east coast. Four main boarding houses were centred round a nineteenth-century school block, its focal point a library with a fairytale glass roof. Felixstowe is now one of Europe's largest container ports but, when the college was founded in 1929, it was a wealthy seaside resort developed in Edwardian times as a British rival to Nice and Biarritz. Mrs Wallis Simpson made it her base while waiting to marry the Prince of Wales.

The school was based in the Old Town, where retired colonels and rich widows lived – the kind of characters who get murdered in Agatha Christie whodunits. Along the seafront and clifftops were vast luxury hotels, as well as the privately owned villas and mansions that, by the time I joined the school, had been taken over by the college. While the world beyond its borders was exploding into a starburst of music, fashion and sexual freedom, we played local lacrosse derbies against St Felix School, Southwold, attended compulsory classical music concerts and wore thick, Nora Batty-type stockings. We were taught how to hold a plate and glass, and an umbrella. Each week there was a set period for Public Speaking – because one day we would be the women who gave votes of thanks at church fêtes and, if we met someone important, we'd know what to do. And then, in 1965, huge excitement percolated through the entire school when Radio Caroline was moored offshore. Hurrah! That really started to drag us out of the Victorian age. (You may have noticed I've written 'Hurrah!'. One of the weird and wonderful rules was that 'Hooray!' was banned, because it was common.)

In this extraordinary world of jolly japes with your chums, terrifying prefects, twice-a-day Chapel and 'House spirit', we were taught by spinsters, made intense, passionate friendships, learned how to curtsey to the Queen, and were forbidden by

'Jonah', our formidable headmistress, from wearing satchels on our backs because that was what day school girls did. Jonah was absolutely adamant that we should never be mistaken for day school girls. We were better than that – we wore boaters, not berets, and cloaks instead of coats. Your boater was made of stiff grey straw, with a flat, shallow crown – and completely useless as a hat. You might as well have stuck a pile of LPs on your head. If you tried wearing it at a fetching angle, a House mistress would yank it straight.

Over the years we were there we played pranks on teachers, held midnight feasts, had pillow fights, won trophies for our Houses and swotted for exams – just like the characters in Enid Blyton's fictional boarding school, Malory Towers. But then there were the goings-on that Enid Blyton didn't write about: the rather dodgy love-ins in the nine-dorm; the Drambuie kept in shampoo bottles; the smoking on the fire escape; the History and English teachers who lived together – were they or weren't they? And ooh, the scandals. The girl who disappeared abruptly in mid-term (whisper: *she was pregnant*). The other girl who was *actually caught at it* with . . . was it a painter and decorator? An under-gardener? Anyway, they were doing the deed in the chapel garden. Round the back, in a nice secluded garden with a pond.

'It was definitely a gardener,' says my friend Della, 'and he wasn't even very attractive.'

So already you can see that this account of life at Felixstowe College is far more weird and wonderful than any boarding school fiction, but it's also much more realistic and full of emotional ups and downs. Girls ran away or discovered sex; parents died or split up. There was homesickness, anorexia and a mysterious outbreak of stealing. Had they happened today, the things one or two staff members did to us would result in suspension, pending an enquiry.

In a way, too, we lived in privileged deprivation. As another friend, Juno, puts it, 'If I ever went to prison, I'd probably find it quite comfortable.' We slept on hard, lumpy mattresses in crowded dormitories where ice formed on the windows – *on the inside*. We were fed on a diet of institutional food that included powdered egg left over from the Second World War, burnt curry, stew with teeth in it and cauliflower cheese with a big grey caterpillar slumped across the top (probably the most nutritious part of the meal). There was a complete lack of privacy, and we were told what to do from ten to seven every morning to Lights Out at night, which was at seven thirty for juniors and as daringly late as a quarter to nine for the Lower Sixth. Can you imagine, in summer, when the sky was still light and the birds still singing? No wonder some of us got into such creative mischief.

Some of my friends thoroughly enjoyed their schooldays. Often they were the ones who had been given a choice as to whether or not they went, or who could rationalise why their parents had sent them away to be educated. Others found the all-chums-together happy times promised by the Malory Towers books weren't quite so fun-packed and appealing in real life, and one hated it so much that even now she calls it 'that place', and gets very angry talking about it.

'For years afterwards,' says Rona, 'the smell of fish would give me a sinking feeling, conjuring up the freezing platform of Liverpool Street station on to which the trains from the east coast would unload their cargo of fish. And from which the next train would depart with its cargo of apparently jolly, grey-clad girls, fighting back tears at leaving their parents and dreading the sight of those iron bedsteads and horsehair mattresses lined up in the dormitories, waiting to offer us the cold comfort of our first night back at school. And the dreaded awakening the following morning to the clanging of the bell and the start of yet another endless term of Spartan grey living, biting east coast winds and grey skies, foggy, soggy Games pitches, enforced sport, jam and marge for tea, grey uniforms, grey knickers, grey lisle stockings, grey cardigans, grey coats and cloaks, grey hats and gloves, grey Sundays ... and the beginning of yet another chart of grey days to be crossed off one by one.'

But most of the young ladies of my generation, including me, look back with affection on our years at Felixstowe College. How else would I have had the chance to climb out of the dorm window in the dead of night, learn how to pick locks or taste our head cook Mrs Kahn's chocolate sponge with chocolate sauce, her signature dish, the best pudding in the world? And though I have always taken pains to repudiate any suggestion that the place left its stamp on me, I have realised that in one way at least I will always be a boarding school girl. One of my personality traits that people have commented on is my enthusiasm, my gusto, what my mother would call 'vim and vigour'. Jolly hockey sticks!

As children in the days before the self-revelation of social media, we just took everybody at face value, and what these women have told me about their lives inside and outside school has been fresh and surprising to me in spite of the fact that we lived so closely together. I'm amazed at the private dilemmas or struggles some were going through. I've been enchanted by their recollections, and also deeply impressed by how these wonderful women have turned out. Most of us agree that the really satisfying thing was how we made lifelong friendships.

In the words of my friend Gill: 'I think it's a testament to the fact that even if we did go through unhappy times we all supported each other, and our friendships helped us through those times. We can all meet again (some for the first time in more than forty years) and still *know* each other and care about each other; still be able to sit down and talk endlessly, not only about school but about life since. We really did know each other well.'

So this is a group biography and a social history, told through my own personal recollections and those of my friends. I hope it will appeal to all women, of every age, who read boarding school stories when she was a child and dreamed of going there, or who is just curious about what life was like for girls back then, or was actually a boarding school girl herself, with her lax stick and House tie, hiding biscuits under floorboards for midnight feasts, sneaking out of bounds to smoke, having unrequited crushes on an attractive Games captain, shutting herself in the bathroom to swot the night before O Levels, becoming heartbroken because her best friend has dumped her for someone else, or even spending an entire weekend unable to stop laughing because it was all so ridiculous. (It's true. One whole weekend.)

Over the next few chapters you'll meet some of the people who are going to share their stories. Some names have been changed, in a few cases because friends have wanted to preserve their anonymity, but in others because of the annoying tendency of middle-class parents to name their daughters from a very small shortlist. For every unique Shirley, Beryl and Susan-Mary, there was a cornucopia of Sarahs, a job lot of Annes and a positive glut of Elizabeths (the Queen has a lot to answer for). All my Ridley House year group are pseudonymous, one reason being that I have been unable to track everyone down but need to include their part in the tale of our goings-on. Another reason is that, as teenage girls, we were sometimes horrible to each other. So some aliases are useful if you're providing the full lowdown on boarding school life as it was truly lived, but on the other hand you don't want the world to know. I'd change my name if I could, but there you are. But these are real women telling their stories and every single thing I've written about here really happened.

## THE STORY OF FELIXSTOWE COLLEGE

Thanks to Facebook, the now-defunct Friends Reunited and the round-robin email, tracking down the girls with whom I shared school life took only a surprisingly easy amount of detective work. As well as describing, though, how we grew from terrified juniors to sixth-form goddesses I wanted also to write something of our school itself, its origins and milestones and significant figures, not to mention how it came to its end. This was more problematic. I didn't know where to start, who to ask, who knew.

Then, one night in the Groucho Club with my husband, during a get-together with two friends over from Los Angeles, I mentioned that I was writing a book about girls' boarding schools.

'Oh,' said Linda, 'you must get in touch with my sister-in-law. She went to Abbots Bromley and her daughters were boarding school girls too.'

'Where?'

'Oh, it was all a bit traumatic; it closed while they were there. Somewhere called Felixstowe College.'

Can you imagine the odds against that happening? But if you think that's serendipitous, what about this? I had already been lent an almost complete set of school magazines, among them a pamphlet detailing the period between 1980 and 1989. Writing it was the retirement job of my old House mistress, Bretch. There is a nice photo of her on the front cover. She hadn't changed. The specs were still bottle-thick, the smile a little sardonic. Her hair, though grey, was still frizzy, still sticking straight up in the air like that of a cartoon figure whom the artist wants to show surprised. 'WHAT do you think you're doing?' she seems to be saying, as she did back then. 'Settle down now!'

Anyway, that, more or less, was What Happened Next sorted out. What seemed impossible, though, was finding out about the school's origins. With the whole place gone, its records destroyed, and staff and pupils who could have told me about the early years long dead, it was going to be like putting together a jigsaw puzzle from which many of the pieces had gone missing. Then, one day, thanks to one of those round-robin emails, I heard from Sue Robinson, who had been two years below me and was Head Girl in 1967.

It was the year Elizabeth Manners had taken over as head-mistress. Within two years, Maude, as she was nicknamed, had published *The Vulnerable Generation*, an eloquent and prescient bit of tub-thumping about the over-sexualisation and increasingly pressurised life of girls. In its day it created a media sensation and polarised opinion. By the time Miss Manners retired, in 1979, the college had developed a strong academic reputation (famously, she had declined to offer the young Lady Diana Spencer a place, having found her academically wanting); it had its greatest ever number of pupils, and was sending an unprecedented number of leavers to Oxbridge and what are now known as the Russell Group universities. It was also clear that the experience of being Maude's Head Girl had been one of the most positive in Sue's life, at a time when events at home had been distressing.

Then I had a brainwave. I remembered that, in 2007, Miss Manners had appeared on a BBC Radio 4 programme called *The Little Red Book*. Aged ninety-one, she had given a spirited performance. At one stage, when asked for her thoughts on masturbation, her comment was, 'I wouldn't know, I never tried it.'

She had been famous in her time. There would surely have been obituaries if she had died; she must still be around. 'Wouldn't it be amazing if you could meet her again?' I said to Sue.

Through a BBC contact I found out that Miss Manners still lived in Felixstowe, and Sue and I visited her in her small flat overlooking the sea. It was almost the same view as the one she had looked out on from the study she occupied as head-mistress, and great age had failed to diminish her. I thought she was worthy of her own tarot card: Force To Be Reckoned With. Sue provided lunch and I brought the wine.

I told Miss Manners of my difficulty tracing documentary

evidence of the school's history. She directed me to her book-shelves, and at last I had in my hands not just a copy of *The Vulnerable Generation*, but a booklet bound in the college colours of grey and red. *The Story of Felixstowe College 1929–1979*, a complete history, had been published to coincide with its half-centenary in 1979. No author is given, but the assumption is that it is the work of Miss MacKerness, Head of English during the era of Miss Manners.

Crucially, from the point of view of this book, Miss Manners allowed me to take it home with me. I would not otherwise have been able to write from such a detailed and accurate viewpoint. I have it in front of me now and I can only say that it is Too Marvellous For Words.

# 1

# THE YOUNG LADIES OF
# FELIXSTOWE COLLEGE

June 2014. A crowd of well-coiffed grandmas bearing contributions to lunch is gathering on the front doorstep of a large barn conversion in Hampshire. Most wear smart-comfy, on a spectrum from jeans to tweeds; there are high-end runabouts parked in the gravelled drive; iPads and iPhones are being flourished.

The weather is British summer at its best – warm, sunny and dry; perfect conditions, we all agree, for an Old Girls' Reunion. Traditionally, this would have taken place over a weekend in the college grounds, with a School vs. Old Girls tennis tournament and a thanksgiving service in the chapel on Sunday – the full works, with prefects parading House banners and the pews awash with hats. Juniors would give up their beds so former Girls could sleep in dorms again. We would bed down on the common room floor, which was only a bit harder than our mattresses, and creep out for a midnight feast.

Now, however, we don't have a school to meet at any more. Felixstowe College closed in 1994, a casualty of the financial downturn and the trend away from single-sex boarding education. It was just one of the many schools you might describe as 'a Malory Towers sort of place', that shut down from the 1970s onwards, one by one, like light bulbs switching off.

A twentieth anniversary of your school closing? Let's party! A throwaway remark on Facebook has turned into reality. Old Girls have travelled here from all points of the compass and Juno, a Cranmer (I'll explain about that later), has lent her house for the occasion. I'm actually nervous, because although I'm riven with curiosity about how everyone has turned out, I have mixed feelings about my schooldays, when I was one of the rebels and it all ended rather scandalously. And even though I went off to make my name as a journalist on a national newspaper, and should sail in looking fashionable and groomed and confidently metropolitan, I feel a bit black-sheepish, if truth be told.

It ought to be a poignant gathering but, in the huge, open-plan reception area, the decibel level is already rising. To one side is a spacious, elegantly converted annexe in which we can see feverish activity: teenage girls are putting the finishing touches to a long table laid with a white damask cloth and festooned with displays of beautifully arranged flowers. Juno, tall, model-slim and smiling, tells me they are A Level students at the school where her daughter works.

'You're looking great,' I say.

'Fillers, dear,' she says. 'And I've got a plastic boob.'

'There's a lot of it about,' says the person behind me in a no-nonsense voice. I turn to see a diminutive woman in a smart suit. She has a tiny waist and salt and pepper curls, and greets me with delight, by name. My mind goes a complete blank but fortuitously we are enveloped by a swell of new arrivals crying, 'Cherry!' and now I do remember. Cherry was another of the Cranmers, an engaging moppet with tangled fair curls. She was a canon's daughter, and tried so hard not to be naughty, but was always being led astray by Juno.

I head off to find Chrissie, who has been my friend since we were small, tubby, bespectacled newcomers, and is now a lovely, quirky granny. She's the only person from school I have kept in touch with. She's a drummer. Proper African drums, not Ringo Starr things. On the other hand, she's also chair of her parish council. All the other women have been fixed in my mind as they were half a century ago, in grey tunics and House ties, with frightful hairstyles. There is warmth in everybody's welcome but, even so, I feel awkward and don't want to offend anybody else by failing to recognise them. They, it seems, don't have that problem.

'You're exactly the same,' is what everyone says to me.

Is that a compliment? Or do they mean I'm still weird and a terrible show-off?

We were the generation who wore the first miniskirts; the girls sent out into a world about to be changed by the pill, feminism and the 1967 Abortion Act; a world suddenly full of choices that our education either hadn't seen coming or had chosen to turn its back on. We represent a fair cross-section of upper middle-class girls of that era – daughters of mothers who didn't have to earn a living, of fathers who were gentleman farmers, the officer class, execs of multinationals and the ambitious bourgeoisie. An outsider looking at us would assume that our lives have gone in straight, privileged lines: marriage, children, a gradual upgrading of real estate, a decent private pension, granny duties, travel and voluntary work. I would place a sizeable sum of money on my being the only member of the Labour Party present.

Of course, being from a comfortably off background doesn't inoculate you against widowhood, illness, financial insecurity and divorce, or simply the depredations of advancing age. Indeed, in the wrong frame of mind you might feel depressed by the number of years that have passed; by crow's feet, corded necks and carefully tinted hair. But no one here seems anything but happy and energised, as we feast on *salade tricolore, jamon,* olives, French cheese and summer pudding, and our voices rise in pitch and volume the way they used to in the school dining room.

After a few minutes have passed, faces suddenly become familiar. Reflexively, decades after it might have been relevant, I classify everyone according to the House they boarded in, because to each other we're still Cranmers, Tyndales, Latimers or Ridleys and in some odd way always will be. I can see it on my gravestone: Here lies Julia Welch (R).

That R in brackets stands for Ridley, the stuccoed villa on the seafront in which Chrissie and I boarded. Our House mistress, Bretch, was a peculiar-looking woman – as well as her frizzy-hair, she had a severe case of strabismus. One eye went this way and the other eye went that way. It equipped her to spot miscreants at either end of the room simultaneously.

'Do you remember Bretch lining us up in the Middle Five commie?' says Gill, who is on a visit from Australia and still enviably leggy and boyish-looking. 'One big line, all fourteen of us in front of her. No idea what we'd done, but it must have been bad. And she fixed an eye on each end of the line and said, "And what have YOU got to say for yourself?" And Carrie, who was at one end, said ever so politely, "Please, Miss Cross, which one of us are you looking at?"'

'I remember Bretch discovering one of our first midnight feasts,' says Annie, who is tall and elegant with a mane of streaked brown hair. Who could imagine that she once wore bunches and had sticking-out teeth and was known as Rabbit, the naughtiest girl in Ridley? 'It was in Lower Four. We kept ourselves awake because it had to start at midnight, naturally. Goodness knows why, but we decided to go down to the junior common room and have it there. We were having a merry old time when the door opened and in walked Bretch. For some reason, we all stood up!'

'We had various ones in various dorms and later on we got quite brazen,' says Helen.

She seems barely to have changed, with her dramatic dark eyebrows and glorious, thick, honey-coloured curls. 'I spent the entire time twitchy with fear that we were going to be discovered. Bretch's shoes squeaked and we got frightfully good at hearing her. We'd wait, listening out for her walking away. But she was obviously quite crafty because sometimes she didn't actually walk away. We'd start again and then she'd fling the door open. "WHAT do you think you're doing?"'

'Do you remember when Alexa brought back the little camping stove after the holidays?' says Gill. 'With a saucepan and lots of packets of dried chicken noodle soup?'

'No!' we all chorus. 'What happened?'

'It was when we were in the five-dorm opposite the kitchen, and one of us would steal some bread, and the plate of butter from the fridge. Not long after Lights Out we'd get going on the routine of lighting up the camping stove on the floor by the washbasins in the former, and emptying the packet of soup into the saucepan and cooking it up. There was nothing instant about them in those days – they would take about ten minutes to get them to an edible consistency – but we couldn't wait that long. After a couple of minutes, if that, we'd be delighting in our crispy noodle soup drunk out of plastic tooth mugs.'

'How come Bretch didn't smell it?'

'No idea. Maybe it wasn't cooked long enough to release any aromas. But finally came the fateful night ... the door was flung open and the light turned on and there was Bretch, framed in the doorway. We'd already eaten and I was by the basins, washing out tooth mugs. But my bed was the one by the door, right beside Bretch. I dropped everything, she stood there staring, and I scrambled over Biddy's bed, landed my bare right foot squarely in the plate of butter and leapt nonchalantly into bed ... but I don't think she even saw it. There were no repercussions; she had no idea what we were up to – unbelievable! Maybe her eyesight was even worse than we thought.'

'You remember so many things but not that YOU nicked our House mistress's sausage!' declares someone else I haven't seen for fifty years, but whose tones I identify straight away. Lindy was our Ridley form-mate. She had been a lovely girl, determined, helpful, very into school life. Now she's in designer clothes (I recognise a skirt from Anthropologie that I coveted but couldn't afford) and has a hairdo like a gorgeous steel chrysanthemum.

'What? When? I can't have!' I reply. 'No, I certainly don't remember that.'

'From the fridge,' says Lindy inexorably, holding out a small, dog-eared Letts diary.

There it is. Monday 10 April 1965. 'Bretch v. cross etc.', is written in Lindy's schoolgirl handwriting.

'Oh dear,' I say weakly.

'I wish Jonah could see this book you're writing,' Lindy says. 'I'd love her to be able to hear you defending it all on the radio. If she looked over all her girls, she wouldn't have picked you to write about it, I'm sure of that. NOT part of the establishment.'

Della is a Ridley too. She is still fair and slim, and intelligence still shines out of her. 'Do you remember the term of bed-hopping?' I say, when we are out of earshot.

'I have a theory,' says Della, when I remind her, 'that if you segregate people, the sexuality still comes out but you don't have any choice who receives it.'

'Has the head of the table got all the right things?' says a lady who looks very county, tongue-in-cheek. It's Caroline, another Tyndale from my year. She had sung in the chapel choir, the silvery-grey robes and little ruff sweetly set off by her creamy skin and dark hair. 'Make sure the teacher's got everything. Never start eating before she does. That training's stayed with me.'

'Preparing for our coming out as debutantes!' exclaims someone. 'Walking down the main staircase in Cranmer. You had to put your hand on the banister and *glide* down.'

'I think of our mother as Mrs Bennet in *Pride and Prejudice*, with all these daughters to launch into society,' says Joanna, the oldest of three Tyndale sisters. 'Jonah said, "It's a college for young ladies," and that clinched it for Mummy. She

17

thought she was sending her daughters off to be finished, so we could all find suitable husbands. It was the social graces.'

That triggers off more reminiscences. The nightly strip-wash ('I could strip off in TK Maxx right now and it wouldn't bother me one bit!'). That time the Upper Fives put a scare-crow in Bretch's bed. Our first night in the dorm.

'Beth told me the facts of life,' says Chrissie. 'And a joke with "fuck" in it, and I didn't know what that meant.'

'It was shock horror for me,' says Caroline. 'I'd been dumped. I was eleven, couldn't really understand. It was hell. Absolute hell. The filthy supper beforehand. The smell. The horsehair mattress. I couldn't find anywhere to turn in the hollow. The bottom falling out of my stomach. Complete terror. Everyone ticking me off because I kept crying. I cried and cried.'

'I wasn't very sympathetic,' admits Di, her fellow Tyndale. 'I'd been at boarding school since I was four. I couldn't under-stand what the matter was.'

And then there was Jonah.

'Jonah,' sighs Cherry. 'Ruth Jones. Huge body, small eyes. Terrifying headmistress. She was powerful, full of masculine energy, she walked with a stride. Always on the job, never smiling.'

'She lived on site, imagine!' says Juno, marvelling. 'One term, we were in the eight-dorm next to her bedroom. Sleeping in a room next to your headmistress – how weird is that?'

'Yes, I think that was the only room in Cranmer I never managed to look into,' says Cherry. 'I was awfully nosy. I once walked into the matron's room without knocking. I felt so at home – she was rather like my mother. She had her dressing gown open. I saw her bush! Her face was frozen in horror and I dashed out. Nothing was ever the same again.'

'Oh God, do you remember being sent down?' says Juno.

If you talked in the dorm after Lights Out, your House mistress would make you get up and go downstairs to stand in the corridor for twenty minutes, trying not to giggle. It was the boarding school equivalent of being paraded as hostages.

'It struck me as a very odd punishment,' says Della. 'Keeping yourselves awake by talking after Lights, then they kept you up even later.'

'We used to have to wait for Jonah to walk past,' says Cherry. 'She would grunt disapprovingly to show she'd noticed. She was so big . . . do you think she ate cream cakes secretly? I think she did.'

'She always ate very fast,' says Lindy.

'She always moved very fast,' says Sukie, a merry, pretty Latimer wearing Roland Mouret. 'She led by her bosom. It swerved round corners before she did.'

'I'm sure she didn't wear a bra,' says Juno. 'If she did, it wasn't a boulder-upholder.'

'The Jonah Table!' someone shrieks.

The headmistress's table occupied a raised alcove in the school dining room. It was in a prime position, with a view over Cranmer's manicured, sweeping lawns and sunken rock garden. You had to sit at it once a year, moving up one place a day till the dreaded moment arrived when you were actually next to her and had to make conversation.

Joanna makes a face. 'That was so difficult. You were always worried the food was going to be something you didn't like.

The first time I had to sit next to her it was stew. Lumps of stringy beef. I was so nervous I couldn't swallow. I spat them out in my napkin and moved them to my tunic pocket. All the while continuing the conversation with a pocketful of half-mangled meat. It's taken me years to enjoy stew. For years I could only eat mince, not joined-up meat.'

'I picked up my knife and fork,' says Sukie, 'and a whole pile of peas shot out over her lap. "Oh, I'm so sorry, Miss Jones," I said, and she said, "Good shot, Susanne," and she picked them off her lap and put them on her plate.'

'Who remembers The Jonah List?' someone else asks.

There are groans of recollection.

'It was a slip of green A5 paper,' remembers Chrissie. 'I can see that typing now: "Girls to see Miss Jones". Her PA would pin it up on the noticeboard outside the Bilge lab on Thursdays and, if your name was on it, you knew you were in real trouble. You wouldn't see her till Friday, so you had twenty-four hours of dark foreboding. Like Christmas Eve in reverse.'

'And then you'd have to sit on the bench outside her study with all the others on her list,' says Joanna. 'Just waiting, waiting, then–' she shudders '–*your turn*. My sisters and I would fly out to Kenya in the Christmas holidays, where we would rub olive oil on our skin to get brown. The uniform covered every inch of your body because you were a Young Lady, but of course I wanted to show off my tan, so I wore it with my sleeves rolled up and the collar of my blouse open. "This is not a college for washerwomen!" Jonah barked. "This is despicable! The next thing I'll see is you with your hair in a scarf!"'

'That's nothing,' scoffs Lindy. 'What about the girl who got caught climbing back through the window after she'd spent the night with a boy? Jonah called a special meeting in the library and made her stand up in front of the whole school. Then she said, "Now take off every single item of clothing you took off in front of that boy.'"

The nicest part of the reunion takes place after lunch. Juno has assembled our items of memorabilia and arranged them in her garden room, and we have a mini-museum tour. Here's Sukie's boater, in the school colours of grey and red. With its faded straw and frayed ribbon, it seems as remote in time and exotic as a severed head brought back from the tropics. Lindy has produced every school magazine from 1960 to 1994. I skim through 'Events & Outings' for 1961–62. WIMBLEDON, because some of the parents were debenture holders. ALDEBURGH FESTIVAL, because our Head of Music had connections with Benjamin Britten. A LECTURE ON SKINCARE AND MAKE-UP BY LANCÔME, and A DAY AT HARRODS and THE LONDON FESTIVAL BALLET and goodness knows what else, all in one single year, all wangled by cunning old Jonah.

And the houses we boarded in! Practically Millionaires' Row! We Ridleys gaze at a black and white postcard-sized photo of our old house that Della has brought along. Its tower, which contained the very sought-after two-dorm (you could have secret sessions in there, trying out make-up), does rather resemble a sentry point from the outside. 'It looks wonderfully bleak, doesn't it?' says Della.

'It came on the market a few years ago,' says one of the younger Ridleys, looking over our shoulders. 'Some of us pretended we were potential buyers and went to have a look. The only thing that hadn't been changed around and done up was that cab on the first floor, the one with the frosted glass window in the door.' She turns to one of the sixth-form students. 'Cab was our name for the loo. You didn't go to *the* cab, you just went to cab.'

'With that awful hard paper,' says Juno. 'It was crisp and crackly, and the sheets either had IZAL printed on them or PROPERTY OF HER MAJESTY'S GOVERNMENT.'

The sight of a lacrosse stick brings forth a chorus of fluting cries as we mimic Coulo, the Games mistress. 'Shoooot! Bend . . . your . . . *kneeees!*'

'Do you remember one year there was that assistant Games mistress?' says Juno. 'She was actually young and pretty. Didn't last long. Jonah sacked her for having sex with her boyfriend on the beach, under an upturned boat.'

'How did Jonah find out?' says someone with wonder.

'Oh, Jonah had her spies everywhere.'

There are programmes from nativity plays and gym displays and the classical music concerts we had to attend at the Spa Pavilion on the seafront, which were thoroughly appreciated by the musical girls among us and a source of intense, life-depleting boredom for everyone else. Someone has brought along her girdle, the red one we tied around our tunics. A uniform list, four pages long, is next to my own rather nugatory contribution, some Cash's name-tapes bearing the legend JULIA WELCH (R). I found them not so long ago in my mother's dressing table, when I was clearing out her house after she died, and remembered her sitting by our living room fireplace before my first term, sewing them on to my new school clothes. It took her ages because there were so many things. It never occurred to me to help out.

The photos are wonderful: tennis and hockey teams, and girls swallow-diving from the high board at the inauguration ceremony for our swimming pool; a girl with a face rather like the horse she was sitting on at the school gymkhana; *Songs of Praise* when it was recorded in our chapel. The camera had focused on the staff in the front pew, and I feel about fourteen years old again, gazing at my favourite teachers – stylish Miss Sanford, nice, harmless Miss Wrinch, and peppery but caring Miss McNulty.

'There's Pollard and Williams!' someone whoops.

Miss Pollard and Miss Williams shared a bungalow in town, so their relationship was the subject of endless speculation.

A student looks at us as if we've unearthed dinosaur skeletons. 'Two of my daughter's staff in a same-sex relationship have just had a baby,' explains Juno. She turns to the student. 'And none of you batted an eyelid, did you?'

'We were so innocent,' says Caroline. 'Till I left school I used to think you took a pill and a baby came. I'd never seen a willy.'

'I remember going to the GP with a sore throat and a cough and it was, "Take your bra off",' hoots someone else. 'Touching up on the bazooka side of things. I had no idea that wasn't on! A few months later, I saw in the paper he'd been had up.'

'As our parents were in Kenya, we lived with our grandmother,' says Joanna, 'and when I was fourteen, Nana sat at the end of my bed and said she needed to talk to me about something. "This deed happens when you're married and it isn't very pleasant but it's a duty that has to be done. The man's private bit goes into your private bit and all you have to do is lie there and think of something else. And you don't want to think about it at all." I mean, I'd read about it in books and I thought it was meant to be quite nice.'

'Felixstowe College being by the sea led to interesting sex lessons,' says Gill. 'Alexa and I weren't the only people whose first experience of the real thing was coming across a couple on the beach directly in front of Cranmer one afternoon. God knows what we were doing going for a walk along the beach in Upper Four (it was my first term, I was twelve) but it was fascinating, and we watched for ages.'

We look more closely at the photo, at an immaculately groomed, slightly crone-like figure with impeccably 'done' hair.

'Oh my God, Cawley!' someone exclaims. "The future for girls is Science! We MUST have more Science!"'

'Miss Pipe!' one of the Latimers screeches. 'This girl has a box of TWENTY-FOUR Tampax!'

The sixth-form students giggle and look quizzical.

'Cawley taught Chemistry and she was also the Latimer House mistress,' we tell them. 'She was terrifying and mad.'

'She was obsessed with Tampax,' explains Sukie. 'Once, one of us came back from a long weekend with a large box of twenty-four. We were all having a go after Lights Out when we heard Miss Pipe, our matron, stomping along the corridor, so someone seized the evidence and threw it out of the window into the bushes. The next morning, the head gardener spotted us walking down to breakfast and said, "Them rhododendrons have grown some very funny blooms."'

Another Latimer chips in. 'Did you ever hear about that sixth-former who had to stay on an extra day at the end of summer term? Her parents were based abroad and that was the earliest she could get a flight out. Every house had to be cleared and cleaned out from top to bottom because Jonah rented them out to that Jewish summer school, so when the taxi arrived to take her to the station she had to leave behind a bag of used STs because there was nowhere to get rid of them. She was waiting for her train when suddenly Cawley flew at her and emptied the bag over her. On Felixstowe station platform.'

'It must have been some ten years ago when I spotted her death notice in the *Daily Telegraph*,' says Chrissie. 'I was amazed to find out she was only just eighty. She seemed nearly that age when she taught us.'

'Someone rang me up and said, "Are you going to the funeral?"' says Sukie. 'I said, if I do it'll only be to make sure she's really dead.'

Coffee is accompanied by a long session of whatever-happened-to ...? Some there is news of: the one who came out; the one who may actually have been a spy, though of course she couldn't talk about it; the mousey little thing who went blonde and became frightfully successful in business; the girl who became something big in hotels and ended up marrying her driver. Others have disappeared without trace. What of the one who went off to be an actress but ended up as some sort of mad stalker? The anorexic one who agreed to eat prawns, so everyone else wished they had anorexia too, in spite of the fact she'd started looking like a wire coat hanger? And she'd been such a gorgeous girl, too – all the juniors had pashes on her.

'What's a pash?' asks one of the students, pausing with the cafetière.

'It was a bit like the marriage market,' says Lindy. 'The

pecking order of your form against the pecking order of theirs. You had to remember her birthday, and give her a piece of your birthday cake on yours. Mine was a prefect. We were in Lower Four and everyone organised it so I was left alone in the cloakroom with her. I had to kiss her, otherwise the two of us wouldn't be properly pashed up.'

A Tyndale pipes up. 'The ultimate was to kiss them good-night. I didn't know whether to kiss mine on the mouth or the cheek.'

And there are sad stories as well. There's nothing more guaranteed to make you feel mortal than learning that people you remember so clearly as dear little Lower Fours or goddess-like Big Girls, so vividly, wonderfully alive, aren't here anymore – viciously snuffed out by cancer or a car crash. ('It wasn't even her fault. Another vehicle slammed into the back of hers and sent her into eternity!')

But for me this is all drama and tragedy at one remove. It's something else, not remotely sad, that sets off the emotion and makes my tears threaten to kick in, and that's when we Skype Wisty in the States.

Wisty was a Cranmer, so I didn't see much of her in term time, but she lived near me in Essex, and she became my 'hol-idays friend'. We spent whole days at each other's house. On some memory card in my head are images of the two of us in jodhpurs and hard hats, posing on the lawn with my horse, Applejack; of being fifteen and wearing wool polo-necks and those ski-pants with the stirrup things at the ankles; playing Roy Orbison 45s on Wisty's Dansette; of Saturday afternoons watching *Grandstand* on the television with my father. It was the only time in the week I got to spend with him. My mother would bring in a tray of tea and ham sandwiches. She was always happy to see Wisty. I think in some strange way she became a teenager herself, and sparky, adventurous Wisty was the teenager she would have liked to have been. My father, normally a distant, preoccupied figure, loved watching the wrestling on ITV (Giant Haystacks! Big Daddy! Mick McManus! Jackie 'Mr TV' Pallo!) and would get so carried away he would kneel in front of the set and bash his fist on the carpet, tomato-faced with laughter.

Wisty had a really mischievous grin. The sight of her on the iPad screen, with her lovely big Turkish nose and still-luxuriant dark hair, is what sets off the emotion. 'Wisty' I murmur, 'it's me.' (Well, of course it's me. This is Skype. She can see me. I'm a doddering fool.) We talk about her new grandchild, who is called Maja, after Wisty's half-Turkish mother.

'Your mum was a darling,' I say.

'I'm happy to have known both your dad and your mum,' she says. 'Spent some great weekends at your house.'

'I loved your dad too,' chimes in Chrissie. 'He always made me laugh.'

I clear my throat and hand her the iPad while suddenly needing to fetch something from my coat pocket in the hall. I love being reminded of my dad: the way he sent me the *Daily Telegraph* to read when he sensed I needed cheering up; how he could walk on his hands from breakwater to breakwater on summer holidays by the sea; the way he would bag my *Beano* to read after I'd finished with it. It was true; he did make us laugh. When you're a teenager, you just think how odd and embarrassing your parents are – and, believe me, there was something very odd about my family – but now I think of how well they did, with the grand house, the business empire; what a *go* they made of it.

And now it's time to end the reunion. Travelling back to London on the train, I still feel a bit emotional. What awesome women. And I'm astonished at the bond I feel with them, though perhaps I shouldn't be; we spent our formative years together, sharing the terror and hilarity. There's a whole language out there, like 'wapey' for wastepaper basket, and 'wigging' for hair washing, that nobody in the world ever uses now, and we don't either, but if we did we'd know exactly what each other meant. In some weird way they are my family more than my family was.

On the spur of the moment I type Ridley House into Google, and a photo comes up on the property website Zoopla. It's a different colour now, ice cream white. When I lived there the outside walls were coated in dismal grey pebbledash. But I'm still half-expecting to see Bretch waiting at the entrance, straight-backed and spindly in her trademark brown suit; the driveway full of cars at the beginning of term; an obstacle-course of suitcases and lax sticks in the hallway and, all along the corridors, girls bustling round the notice-board to see which dorm everyone's in, shouting about what they did in the hols and terrified they've forgotten to pack some vital piece of clothing. And my heart gives a strange jolt of excitement. I might have left boarding school but it never quite left me. A part of me still belongs there and wants to go back for the start of term.

# 2

# THE PROSPECTUS

The Felixstowe College prospectus was very smart indeed. It was bound in stiff, silvery-grey card with the school badge and motto on the cover, in red. A slip of cream paper fell out when you opened it. It wasn't ordinary paper, but thick and almost satin smooth. In embossed, italic font it read: *With the Head Mistress' compliments.* (I itched to change that to *Head Mistress's.*) Below were contact details. Postal address: Felixstowe, Suffolk. That was all it needed for the postman to find it. The telephone number was Felixstowe 269.

Inside were photos ('Gymnasium Block'; 'A Study Bedroom'; 'The School Library'). An aerial view in black and white ('Drawn by Leo Creak, 1949. Revised 1959.') showed all the school buildings and the grounds, which seemed to extend for acres. It was the size of a village.

There were tantalising details of all the extras girls had access to – four types of dance, swimming in the sea, riding lessons, 'two fully-trained hairdressers', badminton, fencing, lessons in public speaking and art history, 'first-class concerts in the town', drama, play-reading. You could learn Spanish and the harp, throw pots, order fresh fruit once a week, visit the tuck shop, have your deportment straightened and your flat feet corrected.

The college boasted seventeen tennis courts (hard, clay *and* grass), a music school and a wonderful art and dance studio. Not to mention a chapel, a domestic science building, a pottery studio, hairdressing salon, purpose-built geography room and an enormous gymnasium. As well as lax and hockey pitches, there was access to a golf course and squash courts and stabling for our ponies. Every year there was the school gymkhana to look forward to, not to mention the trip to London to attend Wimbledon. Girls in the Upper Sixth could take driving lessons. It was the first girls' school in the country to offer those. Beat that, Roedean. *Nyah nyah*, Cheltenham Ladies' College.

But where was Felixstowe exactly? I had visited a fair number of England's seaside resorts. Sheringham and Cromer, for instance, where we'd gone on bucket-and-spade holidays when I was very young, catching shrimps in rock pools and getting the landlady of our boarding house to boil them up for my tea. Folkestone and Dover, where my father went on business trips – a long, long crawl in the Standard Vanguard through the Blackwall Tunnel, and the inevitable braking to a halt by a convenient grass verge in order for me to be sick outside rather than inside the car, but we'd also stop at a toy shop on the way so I could add to my collection of model horses. My father's burgeoning business empire had taken us to Newcastle, from where my mother took me with my swimming costume and rubber ring to Whitley Bay and Tynemouth, with their gorgeous sweeping sands. We'd stayed in the Gower Peninsula for a holiday that passed into family folklore when a sweet shop caught fire and my father became a local hero, dashing into the burning building to save the jars of boiled sweets. Teignmouth in Devon, where the duty visit to two maiden aunts was quickly over and followed by diving off rafts and wild swimming in little rivers. And as we went up in the world, Cornwall was our destination – Bude and Widemouth Bay, and all the joy of surfing and riding ponies on cliff paths. So, for me, the seaside – the occasional roadside barf notwithstanding – meant sun and fun and family togetherness.

Felixstowe, though, was territory unknown. Just a railway poster that said COME TO SUNNY FELIXSTOWE – but no one I knew seemed to. In fact, you could chart not just the steady upward rise of our family's social status but also the decline of the British seaside resort simply through our holidays. By the start of the 1960s, the swanky thing was to go to the Costa Brava. That summer, the family next door, who were second-generation trade to our first-generation, and so slightly a cut above, announced they would be heading off there, too late for my mother to start booking flights. But it was our final summer holiday in Cornwall that resulted in the event that changed my destiny.

It was the end of August 1960, and on the very last day of that holiday I fell off a small bay pony called Prince. Spectacularly, at the gallop, head first, while descending a bank. I remember remounting and telling Mr Coutts, the riding master (an old soldier with a pink face and white hair, topped by a brown hard hat, like a living strawberry and vanilla ice with caramel topping), not to breathe *a word* to my mother because she would only make a fuss. In fact, I told Mr

Coutts this several times over, which should have made him aware I was not quite right in the head. I learned later that he *was* aware, but that Prince was the pony from which his own daughter had fallen and been killed, and he was so stricken by the prospect of history repeating itself that he couldn't trust himself to speak about it without letting the side down.

My sole subsequent memory of that day is of sitting in the back of our car being sick and complaining of a headache. I came round some time later to find myself in a cottage hospital in Launceston, with my terrified parents holding vigil in the dark, their holiday quite ruined. I was discharged after a week, and my parents kindly took me back to the riding school so I could give Prince a sugar lump. We drove home and then I just went back to school.

At the time, school was the City of London School for Girls, and I was expected to do well because I had a corporation scholarship. My older sister had been Head Girl and mainstay of the hockey team, and the old trout of a headmistress obviously thought she was getting a genetic repeat. More fool her. There were a lot of clever girls in my year and they all did much better than me. They all worked diligently, noses in their books from first bell to last, while I did my homework standing on the tube in the morning rush hour.

Over the next few months everything seemed to go haywire. I couldn't sleep, my concentration was in pieces, I was sent out of lessons and was finishing near the bottom of the class. Plus, my parents weren't getting on. Actually, things had been awkward, not quite right, since I was eight, but around this time, now I was twelve and perhaps more aware, they seemed particularly difficult and intense.

Now, I suppose I have to let you in on our family secret, which was that I had what amounted to three parents, because my mother and father shared their lives with a redheaded divorcee called Jane. She was big, posh and Scottish. Braw, cultivated and, unlike the cloud of frazzled rattiness that was my mother, composed. I adored her, she got on with us all but, not to put too fine a point on it, my mother was usurped – and indeed I was usurped – by this giant wondrous cuckoo in our nest.

Were she and my father having S.E.X.? Unimaginable. They were old. He had false teeth and she wore an all-in-one corset. But she was very definitely The One, and my father, the crafty thing, had sneaked her into the family structure by dint of making her a director of the business, along with my mother. At this point my father's companies were based in the northeast, but the head office was not only in London, it was in our house. In the room next to my bedroom, with desks and telephones and typewriters and a monstrous duplicating machine called a Gestetner. And there the three of them sat all day, the women typing invoices, my father rustling papers and making decisions.

She didn't go home at the end of the working day. She stayed for supper. They hung out together, playing Scrabble, going out for Chinese meals, attending functions, because my father was something important in the local Conservative Party. She was just there. *All the time.*

My mother and I had always been close. She was passionate and determined, but also a shy, proud woman who wouldn't have dreamed of sharing her problems with an outsider. Her only female friend was Jane, and how could she have aired her suspicions to the very person who was causing her anxiety?

33

My sister was nearly ten years older than me and, having graduated from university, now had her own London flat that she shared with her fiancé, a rather fast young businessman of whom my parents disapproved. So there was no one to share the load. Just me.

It was around then that I became not too keen on reality and developed a condition known in the family as 'cloud nine', immersing myself in a dreamworld of football heroes, great racehorses, fictional detectives, film and TV stars. In this I had been helped by the death of our old television, the faithful friend that had seen me through the *Watch with Mother* years to the 1960 Olympics. It had a pretend-walnut cabinet and tiny screen, and mysterious innards known only as 'the condenser'. If the condenser went bust it filled your living room with a terrible smell. It was your TV's death throes. Ours self-immolated in October 1960.

A new television arrived. It stood on four metal legs and had speakers either side covered in shiny fabric with a small badge that said ECKO. The screen was four times as big as our old one. Why worry about what was going on in the head office? I had more interesting things to concentrate on. A much-enlarged David Broome riding Sunsalve at the Horse of the Year Show. Michael Landon as Little Joe in *Bonanza*, so clear I could make out his lovely long eyelashes. Lester Piggott on *Grandstand*, bum in the air. The captain of Tottenham Hotspur, Danny Blanchflower, no less a hero for advertising Weetabix: 'Pass the hot milk, please'.

When I wasn't watching telly, I was reading. I read everything I could lay my hands on. The *Daily Telegraph*, front page to back, Micky Spillane crime thrillers, the entire

Sherlock Holmes oeuvre, *Mad* magazine, *Photoplay*, *The Register of Thoroughbred Stallions*, my old Angela Brazil school stories (I had regressed that far), because the actual walls of our house seemed to thrum with misery and tension and, whenever I returned to the everyday world, it was to be railed at by my mother because my father preferred another woman and I was a hopeless failure who was going to be stripped of my scholarship. I loved my family with all my heart but, one spring afternoon, sitting on my bedroom floor with *The Luckiest Girl in the School* on my lap, I thought, Why not escape? *Really* escape, back into a world of jolly japes and midnight feasts, and I said the fateful words, 'I think I would like to go to boarding school.'

After that, everything seemed to happen very quickly. Prospectuses appeared so promptly that I suspect they'd been in my mother's possession for some time and she had merely been waiting for an opportune moment. And, looking back, she had asked me in my Eleven Plus year what I thought about going. My two best friends, both a year older than me, had been packed off with their tuck boxes and lax sticks, and I'm positive my mother felt she had fallen behind socially by not doing the same with me.

I enjoy reading Fleet Street memoirs and, in a particularly entertaining one, *Goodbye Fleet Street* by Robert Edwards – an editor of the *Sunday Express* in its glory days of the 1960s – I found this:

*Sunday Express* readers ... had been skilfully led to believe that they were a cut above the others. John [Junor, the editor] said to me after one of us had written, under his careful direction, the usual warm, human editorial about children returning to boarding school after their summer holidays, 'In case you're wondering, I know perfectly well that many *Sunday Express* readers live in council houses and send their children to state schools. But they like to think they live in much grander houses and can afford school fees.

Of course, we didn't live in a council house – home was a six-bedroom Victorian pile overlooking Epping Forest, complete with duck pond, weeping willow, vegetable garden, separate double garage with gardener's quarters and a conservatory. But the family next door occupied an even bigger piece of real estate. They had a tennis court and a ballroom, a Labrador called Punch and a gnarled old retainer known as 'Clarkie'. At TV closedown, when the BBC played the national anthem, they stood up in their own living room. Why didn't we do that? We'd always done our shopping at D H Evans. They went to Harrods. Why couldn't we? They saw *My Fair Lady* when it opened in the West End; we didn't get there for another six months. The daughter of the house went to boarding school. Now I wanted to go too. My mother was thrilled. At last I'd done something to please.

I'm not being snarky. My parents *aspired*. They wanted to give me the best they could and, at the start of the 1960s, that meant the social graces that would guarantee me a step up the pecking order. Where my mother was concerned, there was a further issue. My father, silly old sausage, dreamed of my marrying a lord. My mother wanted me to go into the family firm. For that, she thought, I would benefit from the public school gloss.

Needless to say, I didn't want to go into the family firm. It specialised in plant hire. And I don't mean *plant* plants, begonias and bay trees and suchlike, which might have been all right, but lifting jacks and pushing jacks and pit-prop pullers and other greasy, weighty, smelly, clanking, *northern* pieces of machinery that were put to work in the bowels of the earth. Besides, when I was six, I'd had A Vision while lying on the living room carpet. With my exercise book and a pencil, inspired by a dream I'd had the previous night, I had started a novel called *The New Riding School*. It trailed off after two and a half pages, but I knew at that moment that when I grew up I was going to be a writer. There was bound to be trouble ahead.

My mother had narrowed down the choice of boarding schools to two. Felixstowe's entrance exam, which I took in a classroom at the City of London, was easy apart from the French paper, which was full of tenses we hadn't yet covered. The other prospect was Queen Anne's, Caversham ('renowned for academic excellence', according to its prospectus). This had two entrance exams. The first I had to complete at home. I did it at our kitchen table, with my father sitting beside me, which was nice. Then I had to go to the school and take the second exam, following on from which they turned me down because my Maths was 'lamentable'. So Felixstowe it was. With its mission statement, Felixstowe College style, it couldn't have filled the bill better:

The aim of the College is to give girls between the age of 11 and 18 a sound education on a religious basis and on modern lines, to stimulate wide interests and to develop individuality. Every attention is paid to the formation of character and the number of girls has been fixed with a firm belief in the importance of the personal interest of the Head Mistress in each individual child. Girls are encouraged amid their beautiful surroundings to cultivate a taste for the natural and unaffected rather than for the artificial and luxurious . . .

We had lived for the first five-and-a-half years of my life in a three-bedroom semi in a cul de sac. My parents married in 1937 and that was their first home. But in 1954 we went up in the world. My mother quickly dropped her embarrassing lower-middle-class rellies and reinvented her background, as befitted a house with a set of bells in the kitchen for the summoning of staff we did not have, apart from George the gardener who, legend had it, had been shell-shocked in the First World War but was quite, quite safe, even when he started chucking flowerpots over the fence into the road.

Anxious that our new neighbourhood might sense her previous house had only one loo, she hid her social insecurity under an increasingly grand manner on the principle that hoity-toitiness was the best defence. Hence, Felixstowe College, with its beautiful surroundings in which my taste for the natural and unaffected, rather than for the artificial and luxurious, would be cultivated, was going to be just the ticket. As well as keeping me safely locked away from teddy boys, juvenile delinquents, bottles of peroxide hair dye, coffee bars and rock 'n' roll, Felixstowe College was going to turn me into a Young Lady.

Of course, that didn't occur to me at the time. Neither did

I take any notice of all the dull stuff like 'sound religious education' and 'formation of character'. All I saw was midnight feasts, sleeping in a dorm, fun with my chums, scrapes and japes. Too marvellous for words!

And then the uniform list arrived.

# 3

# THE SMORGASBORD

*Felixstowe College*
*Felixstowe*
*Suffolk*
*1961*

*Trunks to be dispatched 2 or 3 days before travelling if sent by*
*rail or British Road Services. This list to be sent back on top*
*of trunk.*

*Everything must be marked by Cash's name-tapes and*
*returned to school in good repair. Shoes and regulation uniform*
*to be obtained from Harrods Ltd., Knightsbridge, London*
*SW1. SLOane 1234, Ext. 671 and 541*

*Parents are earnestly requested to place orders for uniforms*
*as early as possible so that every pupil arrives at School fully*
*equipped.*

My uniform list ran to four pages. I had never known you
needed so many clothes. Everything was required from gym
to hymn. The undies were multitudinous. Five vests, three
brassières and two suspender belts. Two white petticoats.

Three pairs of grey nylon crepe stockings – they concertinaed around your ankles and the wind from the North Sea always found the gap of bare flesh between their tops and your pants. On which subject, six pairs of white cotton linings and three pairs of grey gym knickers. These were known as 'grey bags', and you wore them over your white linings *at all times*. Two pairs of pants. And all those other wrappings. We were living games of pass-the-parcel.

The accessories took up a whole page. Two pairs of winter gloves – leather for Sundays, grey wool for the rest of the week. One linen bag, one brush and comb bag and contents, two face flannels, one sponge bag and toilet requisites. Six coat hangers, one school satchel, one music case ('if music taken'), one Bible ('Prayer & Hymn Book combined purchased at school'), one well-equipped work case for mending, one clothes brush. God knows how many hats, and squillions of shoes – you'd need to be a centipede to get proper wear out of them. But I was entranced. I was going to have *my own umbrella.*

There were things on that uniform list I would wear only once, or never: black wellies, a white sun hat, a grey flannel coat for Chapel in summer – and white cotton gloves to go with it. Not to mention stuff I thought only old ladies needed. One writing case and contents. A bed jacket.

Off we went in Mummy's Ford Anglia to Knightsbridge. My mother had passed her driving test five years previously and the Anglia was her second car, succeeding a green 'Baby' Austin. It was two-tone, its colours lemon and meringue, just like the pie. She loved driving, especially since Jane was still wearing L-plates, having failed her test once already.

We parked in Hans Crescent, behind the store. There were

no meters back then, and plenty of spaces. Harrods school uniform department was on the fourth floor. It occupied a huge space between childrenswear and the wonderland that was their pet department. You could order anything from the pet department back then – a monkey, a lion even – and right in the middle was a huge, lifelike stuffed horse, all tacked up and looking ready to go. We walked past a pen where a little group of blue Persian kittens played. I wanted to take them all home.

The uniform department was under the control of a Mrs du Cann. She was the mother of the Conservative MP, Edward du Cann, and had a very poised hairstyle. Her status was too elevated for her to appear on the shop floor, but she would traipse up to Felixstowe from Harrods every year to measure us up for the next tranche of uniform, because not only would we all have grown but something new was always being introduced. But even the bog-standard Harrods assistant was quellingly posh. Our accents went up a couple of registers, as she laid all the clothes on the counter like precious bounty.

Everything looked so expensive and felt so nice – wool, cotton, gabardine, Harris Tweed. My House tie was striped grey and red, patterned diagonally to brand me as a Ridley. I had a grey tunic and three cream blouses. I had a grey afternoon dress – to change into for dinner, like an aristocrat in a stately home. It was made of fine wool and was pleated from shoulder to waist. Girls with big busts opened them up like an accordion. Despite this, the effect (obviously intentional) was to make you look completely sexless. It featured a white Peter Pan collar that had to be attached by tiny buttons. You had to make sure every button the laundry removed was sewn back on. There was always somebody at supper with their collar hanging by a couple of buttons because all the rest had come off. The dress fastened at the side with hooks and eyes. These often fell off too, partly because Cawley (one of our House mistresses) would rip the dress open to check you were wearing a vest.

There was Sunday best, of course. It included a squishy felt hat and tweed coat, to be worn over the A-line dress of carmine red wool, which would turn out to be itchy and, on hot days, would dye your armpits pink. A mac, too. Grey, too. There were Games socks, a cardigan, a thick V-neck sweater. An overall for Art – ringing the changes by being a good plain green. Grey flappy shorts called 'divided skirts' for Games. One sanitary belt. Oh God, don't mention that.

For everyday wear there was a splendid cloak, grey with a scarlet flannel lining, and a hood. I tried it on and was completely shrouded, with my feet sticking out at the bottom.

'I look like someone hiding behind a pair of curtains,' I complained.

'We have to allow for growth, don't we, dear?' said the assistant.

'How does it do up?' I asked, after flapping the sides for a few moments. 'Where are the buttons? What happens when the weather gets cold?'

'I could sew a zip in,' offered my mother.

'Oh, you mustn't do that,' said the assistant. 'It's against the rules.'

Amazingly, in 1960, our uniform had been featured in *Tatler*, with photos and an article about 'The new English schoolgirl.'

'wears a uniform of which, happily, only the name survives to connect it with the drab institutional garments once prescribed by academic elders whose only concern was that everyone looked alike. For one thing, it eliminates jealousy and individual bad taste, discouraging teenage predilections for stiletto heels, winkle-picker toes and frilly petticoats'.

The article featured six schools, all fee-paying, naturally; the others were Sherborne, Riddlesworth Hall (which originated as an offshoot of Felixstowe), St Felix, St James, West Malvern and, lastly, St Vincents, Alverstoke, which was where my friend Lindsey was incarcerated. But they'd chosen us for the cover!

*Tatler* went on to say that, 'Felixstowe College has had a complete change of outfit since the war' and, golly, 'most of the uniform was designed by the art mistress'. That was Mrs Holditch, who might have been quite a girl in her day, but when we were there was old, stout and tetchy. She tottered around in baggy tops and skirts to hide all the pendulous bits. Who knew she was a secret Schiaparelli?

Our red dress was in the article, along with our winter Games kit, which included a rather natty cricket-type sweater: 'Long red socks provide a splash of colour. For swimming they can choose their own costumes (bikinis barred). Felixstowe is go-ahead and democratic [if, reading that, hollow, incredulous laughter sounds in your ears, that would be mine], senior girls receive make-up lessons from representatives of famous cosmetics firms and the school employs three permanent hairdressers'.

The star turn was a tussore dress. I gawped at it. Tussore

was silk, wasn't it? The kind of thing you dreamed of owning! Although perhaps not with quite so many tucks and frills and darts and flounces. Frightfully old-fashioned. Almost heritage. But was that really a surprise? Felixstowe College girls had worn tussores since 1929, when the school was founded. They figure in the 1930s section of *The Story of Felixstowe College*, accompanied by 'a matching tussore coat, very square and very, very expensive'. Junked, apparently, when one was returned by the laundry labelled: 'gentleman's large dressing gown'. Then, even worse, a matching dress and coat in black and white check. Unluckily these resembled what was on offer in that season's toiletries section at Woolworth's. As the girls took their Sunday stroll along the promenade, rude boys shouted, 'Washbags!' at them. It couldn't go on.

The tussore had been through the rise of Nazi Germany; it had seen the lights going out all over Europe, it celebrated VE Day, the Festival of Britain and the Coronation of HM Queen Elizabeth II ('with all its solemn pageantry rooted in an abiding tradition'). It was still on the uniform list when the Rolling Stones brought out their first single, in the summer of '63. The Stones wore gamy T-shirts and their trousers left nothing to the imagination. We were still stuck in our frilly, sashed tussores. Would they never go? At last they did – to be replaced by a grey-and-white-striped shirt-waister. Now we all looked like 1950s housewives. At least we were only ten years out of date.

Around the same time, the panama hats went too. Good riddance to those, too. Dreary in the extreme. At Ridley we danced on the lawn, snipping them to pieces. We cut holes in them and pulled our hair through the holes. Even the Head of House and Games captain joined in, jumping on them and casting them into the sea. Instead, we had boaters. They weren't nearly as comfortable to wear, but '*Il faut souffrir pour être belle*,' as Miss Sanford, who taught French and Spanish, advised us. Miss Sanford was very attractive, unlike most of our other teachers, who obviously hadn't suffered enough.

We loved our boaters. When you went on a coach trip you'd wait till you reached the first roundabout and then someone would shout, 'Hats off!' and everyone hurled them in the air. And they made our school very distinctive – no way could we have been mistaken for state school girls. Soon Jonah received a call from Mrs Oakley, the headmistress of St Felix, our big rival just along the coast, with a view to introducing them there.

'These boaters,' said Mrs Oakley. 'Are they any good?'

'No, no, complete waste of time,' barked Jonah. 'Keep having to send the boatman out to fetch them when they blow into the sea.'

So St Felix carried on with the dreary panamas. One up to Jonah.

Incidentally we were jolly lucky to have Jonah as our headmistress rather than Mrs Oakley. Mrs Oakley (Mr Oakley seemed to have been disposed of somewhere along the line) was said to be so terrifying that some Old Girls of St Felix refused to send their daughters there while she was in charge. I'm told she died while reading the *Daily Telegraph*. Her last words were, 'That's disgraceful'.

After the uniform had been tried on and paid for, my mother and I took the lift to the restaurant on the fourth floor. It was time for the main event, a smorgasbord in the Hans Buttery. Our first ever. Up until then, a mushroom omelette in the restaurant on the top floor of D H Evans had done us nicely. But the woman and her daughter next door had been swanking for sodding months about the Harrods smorgasbord, with tales of smoked eel, mortadella sausage, cold salmon (real, not tinned) and coronation chicken, with mayonnaise not salad cream. It was the hugest, laden–est buffet in existence. It was wonderful. I went for a second helping. And then another. And there was still pudding to come. I ended up so stuffed with food I could barely move. But my mother was happy, and therefore so was I. We were now on an equal footing with the house next door. And their daughter only went to Wycombe Abbey. Which hadn't been in *Tatler*.

# 4

# THE SCHOOL TRAIN

Mrs O'Sullivan took the twins to London. They taxied to Paddington Station, and looked for the St Clare train. There it was, drawn up at the platform, labelled St Clare. On the platform were scores of girls, talking excitedly to one another, saying goodbye to their parents, hailing mistresses and buying bars of chocolate at the shop.

ENID BLYTON, *The Twins at St Clare's*

Liverpool Street station reverberated with the rattle of porters' trolleys and smelt of diesel the way all London's termini did, but it was different as well because of the accompanying dead cod whiff, it being where trains from the eastern seaboard unloaded their cargoes.

The school train left from a platform at the far end. It was known as the boat train because it eventually ended up at Harwich, where you caught the ferry to the Hook of Holland. A famous railway poster of the time stated: HARWICH FOR THE CONTINENT, under which an even more famous piece of graffiti had been added: FRINTON FOR THE INCONTINENT. Finding the platform was easy because of the crowd of girls in grey gabardine macs over grey afternoon dresses, with grey felt hats and long grey socks or grey stockings, surrounded by suitcases and shrieking and jabbering, everybody so excited and full of news.

My father had dropped us at the front of the station while he went off to park the car, so while we waited for him to reappear I was allowed to go to the forecourt shop for some goodies to eat and drink on the journey. The shop was long and narrow, and what was going on behind the windows was obscured by magazines pegged on wires and strung across the glass. I bought some Penguins, a Tiffin and a tube of Spangles, then stopped by a machine to get my name printed on a narrow strip of aluminium. It wasn't something I'd ever have a use for, but feeling the raised imprint of the letters was very satisfactory.

My parental party was a threesome. My mother had roped in my father because it was a big event. I was going off to boarding school, the first in our family to be sent away. This gave him a reason to invite Jane along too. I rejoined them reluctantly. What must it look like to all those other girls and their families waiting on the platform? Could they sense this bizarre set-up in which I more or less had three parents? I wondered if I could pretend she was an auntie, but she wasn't auntie-like in any respect. At my last school my family hadn't seemed in any way peculiar. The mother and father of one friend were each having affairs (they were Hampstead people, both psychotherapists, so it was out there for all to know). Another of my mates lived in a commune.

Artists. Hampstead, too. They did that sort of thing there. But now, as I stood on that platform, I thought, If you had a conventional family, if you had a father who went to work every day and a mother who ran the house, the sort you read about in Ladybird books and *Malory Towers*, then everything would be OK. As it was, from the outside, I imagined we must have looked as weird as weird can be.

'Ridley! Any more Ridleys? Over here!' The speaker was a shapely girl with a helmet of blonde hair. She was so confident and in control that I thought she must be a prefect, though when I gravitated thankfully towards her little group it transpired she was in the same form as me.

'Are you Ridley? Lower Five? Are you sure?' She gave my guitar a dubious look. 'I say, I don't know if you'll be allowed to keep that.'

The guitar was cheap and flimsy, a birthday present. From time to time I would strum it inexpertly. I wasn't ever going to be Julian Bream and I'd only brought it with me to seem interesting. The thought flashed across my mind that the best thing would be to run back to my parents with it and ask them to take it home again, but when I looked around the station concourse they'd already gone, probably to have a Chinese meal followed by a threesome at Scrabble, and they were probably secretly relieved to have me off their hands, which was lowering.

So I just gave a weak smile and a shrug and, anyway, Bossy Helmet Girl was now performing the introductions. Her name was Erica, this one was Beth, that one was Marion, and there were Bobbie and Marlee, and Cath and Lindy would be getting on further up the line. Names, names, names. They were all nice and smiling but then they started gabbling away to each other again, so I went and stood beside another girl also standing on her own, looking solemn behind her spectacles. 'Hello. Are you on your own too?'

She told me her name was Chrissie and she'd come all the way from Guernsey.

'I didn't want to look babyish, so I told Mummy not to wait,' she said. 'But then when I got here everyone had their mothers with them.'

She seemed as forlorn as I felt, so I offered her one of my Penguins, because I do find that when you are a bit down there is nothing better than having someone to look after, and we soon cheered up, sharing our crisps and biscuits and talking about things that interested us.

At last the train was ready for us to board, so then came all the kerfuffle of finding a compartment and putting our suitcases on racks. I wedged the guitar under my case, which probably did it no good but at least it wouldn't fall on someone's head. Erica bagged the window seats for herself and Bobbie and, forgetting I was there, beckoned Chrissie to sit next to her, but Chrissie and I were already plonked down next to each other, by the door. The others filled the spaces in between, but we could see over them to the clutter of houses as the train chugged through suburbia. Then the landscape changed, becoming brown with woods and green with fields. They were Essex fields, impenetrable with maize, or empty but for one discoloured piece of abandoned machinery, or neat and trimmed with a few enticing show jumps set up in them, and a horse or two.

Chrissie and I played a game of 'spot the horse', and then

another of coming up with the silliest words and names we could think of.

'Gusset.'

'Lumbago.'

'Isle of Wight.'

'Dirndl skirt.'

By the time we got to 'peewit,' we collapsed in hysterics and got into one of those states when you think you might die because you're laughing too much to breathe, and it went on and on till Erica said imperiously, 'I'm glad you two have got such a wonderful friendship,' so we shut up.

At Colchester, the door of our compartment slid open to admit a girl with her hair worn in a thick brown plait. She had high, wide cheekbones, clear blue eyes with long lashes, and an interestingly sultry mouth. 'Back to school, worse luck,' she commented, heaving her suitcase on to the rack. 'Anyway, jolly good fun. Hello,' she said to Chrissie. 'You must be the new girl. I'm Lindy.' Then she turned to me. 'Who are YOU?'

I told her.

'Oh, you must have got Clare's place. She's gone to Australia. She was jolly nice.'

My heart sank. That must be like having a brother or sister who died before you were born. Someone you were never going to be able to live up to because they were now saints beyond reproach. After Colchester we had one more stop, at Manningtree, where we were joined by someone called Cath, who greeted Chrissie and me in a brusquely friendly way. She had freckles and vivid blue eyes and the most gorgeous coppery hair.

After Manningtree the landscape began to change. Goodbye to my Essex world of mudflats, hawthorn hedges, copses, ditches and dumpy medieval churches in the middle of nowhere. We were now in Suffolk. Instead of little clapboard houses were stud farms and gallops and rolling pastures, punctuated by villages of cottages with walls of dark, rich pink. Then busy roads and houses and factories began to appear. Ipswich. All change! We skittered along the platform and up and down steps, pushing and crowding on to a different sort of train, just two carriages with seats either side of an aisle. More girls got on. We made a Ridley corner, and Chrissie and I found seats next to each other again. Then, just before the train moved off, two girls came bursting into our carriage.

'I say, do you mind two Cranmer interlopers?'

This question was posed by a small girl with a playful smile and woolly fair curls sticking out from under her hat. The girl with her was gawky, with a tall person's stoop, a beaky nose and blonde hair in a boyish crest. There were cries of 'Cherry!' and 'Juno!' and we all squeezed up to make room.

'Did you have a good hols?'

'Oh, well, the bust exercises were a complete failure,' sighed Cherry. 'I still haven't got any bosoms.'

She and Juno plonked themselves down opposite us and then started bobbing up and down and twisting to say hello to Erica and Bobbie and Cath and Marion behind, and then they were all off, talking about tennis tournaments and weddings and gymkhanas, so Chrissie got out a book to read and moved it towards me so I could read it too, which made me feel a bit sick because the print jumped all over the page with the bumping of the train. But after another half-hour or so the countryside became roads and lampposts and bungalows, the train slowed and then halted at a station built of golden-yellow brick. Felixstowe Town. We were there.

# 5

## FIRST NIGHT IN THE DORM

Felixstowe College was not built for a school and so it has premises which combine the comforts of a home with the needs of a school. No two Houses and, in fact, no two dormitories in the whole school are alike.

*The Felixstowe College Prospectus*

As we spilled from the train we could hear loud revving and smell exhaust fumes, and there in the forecourt was a coach waiting to drop us all off at our various houses.

'Come on!' shouted mother hen Erica, pushing us through the chaotic throng of girls humping their suitcases into the boot and bagging seats. I couldn't find anywhere to sit, but Lindy ordered two small girls to budge up at the back, so we squashed in and off we went.

It wasn't what I was expecting. I still had a picture of Malory Towers in my head – a neat school, just one big building. But here we were, going all over town, and the coach journey took ages. First we went along the high road until we came to a halt outside a huge Edwardian house with creeper at the edges like a pair of mutton chop whiskers.

The two small girls jumped up and hurried off the coach.

Juno sat beside me. 'Poor little mites,' she said in a sepulchral voice. 'Back into the valley of the shadow of death.'

'What do you mean?'

'That's Latimer. They've got Cawley for a House mistress. She's quite, quite mad. There was this girl in Latimer who had two long plaits. One day she did something that incurred Cawley's wrath, and Cawley lashed out at her, then grabbed a plait and pulled as hard as she could. She almost scalped the poor girl – blood was flowing. Imagine six years with her!'

By this time the coach had moved on all of a hundred feet or so and stopped at another house, which looked almost the same as the other one but bigger. It had a driveway that went in and out round a lovely central treescape. Juno said it was Tyndale. 'There's a path at the back between the two houses, but it might as well be the Berlin Wall. No one's ever allowed to cross it into the other house. Ever. Maggie's the House mistress there. Miss Macartney. She's Cawley's chum. Not awful like Cawley but she had some sort of weird love life that went wrong, so she has her moods, let's put it that way.'

One more question. 'Why is it Cawley? Why not Miss Cawley?'

'Oh, just the way it is. If they don't have a nickname then behind their backs you just call them by their surname.'

'Except for Bretch,' said Cath quickly, squeezing in on the other side of us.

'Who's Bretch?'

'Our House mistress in Ridley. Her name's Miss Cross.'

'Why Bretch, then?

'It was her nickname when she was at school here herself, because her name was Bridget and she was a wretch. My father came to see me once and didn't realise, so he said, "Good afternoon, Miss Bretch." Do warn your parents.'

By now we were turning into a road called Maybush Lane, and I saw playing fields and tennis courts, and then came a beautiful, very ancient wall, the kind that encloses country estates. Some of its bricks were cracked, a bit crumbly, some dark pinkish-red, some silvery grey, and where it met the ground a few tendrils sprouted and trailed, so it was almost alive. What was behind it? Was all this ours too? Set into the wall was a pair of huge doors, and above them was a tower with a clock set in its centre that hung high above the whole building like a moon with hands.

A little further down the road the coach made its final stop. On either side, at the end of drives, were two houses, and between them I could see a promenade and a thin slice of sand and the sea and, in the muzzy late afternoon light, boats slid across the horizon.

'Good luck! Have fun!' said Juno, and she and Cherry fetched their cases and hurried off in a chattering crowd through two tall gateposts towards the very grand house on the left. 'Come on, this way,' said Cath, shepherding me towards the house on the other side. This was not quite as big, but its toes were almost in the sea, and I could see lawns all around it and an orchard full of knobbly apple trees behind. Cars were backed up in the drive, along with mothers in hats and pinstriped fathers, boot lids creaking open and being banged shut. Carried forward on the tide of girls, I lugged my suitcase and guitar across a big courtyard to a funny, greenhouse-like walkway, which Cath said was called the Covered Way. Inside, a shrieking crush had formed around a huge noticeboard: people trying to find which dorm they were in, hailing their friends, asking if their trunks had arrived yet, clattering up staircases.

'*Qu'est-ce que c'est que ça?*' said a well-modulated voice behind me. I turned round and there stood the most peculiar-looking woman I had ever seen. I couldn't tell who she was addressing, because each eye went in a different direction, but a pale, bony finger pointed at my guitar.

'I told her it wouldn't be allowed,' said Erica.

'We'll see,' said Bretch. 'Cath will put it in your common room for now.'

'Wait here, and then I'll take us up to the dorm,' said Cath, who had very kindly taken charge of me.

Each dorm had a number, though no one seemed to refer to them that way, but called them 'the nine-dorm' or 'the five-dorm opposite the kitchen', and so on. 'We're in the upstairs four-dorm with Erica and Bobbie,' said Cath.

It was at the side of the house, overlooking a big lawn and a long path that wound its way along a high wall in a shroud of trees and bushes. 'It's called the Ghost Walk,' said Cath. I turned from the window and studied the interior: four beds with bedsteads of black scuffed metal, a plain wooden chair beside each bed; four dressing tables, a wardrobe and two washbasins. Everything a bit jammed together.

The beds were already made up with one rough, thin blanket provided by the school, and the eiderdown, sheets and pillowcases that had been sent on before we arrived, so you couldn't choose which bed you were in. Sheet changing was once a week, when the top sheet was moved to the bottom and the new one put on top. 'You can give someone an apple pie bed,' said Cath. 'All part of the fun.'

My sheets and pillowcases had a pretty floral border, while everybody else's were white – so I clung on to this bit of individuality. My bed was beside the two washbasins, and Cath's was next to mine. Bobbie and Erica had the beds opposite. I put my flannelette pyjamas under the pillow and my slippers under the bed, and a torch and contraband Micky Spillane paperback, *Kiss Me Deadly*, under the mattress, then hung up my dressing gown with everyone else's. You were allowed to display three photos on your dressing table. Mine were of 1) my wire-haired fox terrier, Rebel 2) Mummy and Daddy on the patio of a Spanish villa, enjoying one of those married couple breakfasts where both parties stare silently into space, and 3) a rather wonky view of the back of our house.

Cath helped me unpack my suitcase and told me where everything went.

'Um, where's the lav?'

'You don't call it the lav,' she said. 'It's cab.' Cab boasted an old-fashioned, high-up cistern with a chain flush, hard toilet paper, and brown bags hanging from the door on strings for used STs. Beside the pedestal, in a pot, was a brush with spiky bristles and a long wooden handle. I studied the facilities thoughtfully, then followed Cath downstairs to our commie.

The junior commie was on the southeast corner of the house and had French doors and two sets of windows, so it was airy and light. A tiny TV was perched on a high shelf. The room contained four tables, one for Lower Four, one (bigger) for Upper Four, and the biggest for Lower Five. A further small table stood in the middle.

'That's for our tea things,' explained Cath, 'and Bretch comes in and puts our letter on it for us to open after lunch. You have to write to your parents every Sunday and Wednesday, by the way.'

'Twice a week! I'll never find enough to say!'

'Use big writing,' Cath advised, guiding me towards the lockers. These occupied all of one wall. Each was about a foot square and covered with a flimsy piece of curtain. I put my radio in there. It was a portable, although it wasn't very, being the size of a large biscuit tin, but it had a strap across the top for carrying. On the front was a dial that said Light Programme and Home Service, and a knob with a pointer that you twiddled towards the dial, and another knob that you used to turn it on and off, which was also the volume control. For a couple of hours every evening, a lot of fine twiddling could bring you Radio Luxembourg, the only source of pop music, and even that finished before bedtime with someone called Howard Bachelor, Keynsham – K.E.Y.N.S.H.A.M., who was advertising his football pools system. After that it was religious programmes.

What else needed to go in my locker? My Marmite, purse, well-equipped sewing case, copies of *Horse & Hound*, *Pony* and *Riding* and my photos of Danny Blanchflower and Lester Piggott. Lester Piggott was winning the Prix de l'Arc de Triomphe on a fine dapple-grey mare called Petite Etoile, and Danny Blanchflower, captain of the Tottenham Hotspur Double-winning side of 1960–61, was holding the FA Cup aloft. I finally found a place for my precious brown card-board file containing the novel I was currently working on, *The Horse From Hell*, along with several never-finished ones belonging to my crime thriller phase. These featured heroes with names like Corder Burns, because they sounded like Sexton Blake and Sherlock Holmes. I'd usually write a couple of chapters of those, then run out of steam because I was more interested in creating the character than any sort of plot. The same went for my westerns phase, which consisted mainly of pages and pages of descriptions of horses and sunsets.

The other Ridleys in my year were standing in a little group in front of the Lower Five table. We inspected each other Along with Erica, Bobbie, Marion, Lindy, Chrissie, Marlee, Beth and Cath, were two small, quiet girls, one fair, one dark. Della and Prue.

'You'll have to have a nickname,' Erica said to me. 'We've already got two Julias in our form.'

I said that at my last school I'd been known as Danny, and then of course I had to explain that it was in honour of Danny Blanchflower, and I showed them the two photos I had brought with me, the one of Danny and then the one of Lester Piggott.

'You're very original!' cried Erica, with a peal of very grown-up laughter, at which I felt rather an idiot.

But Danny I was to be, and I didn't really mind, as it reminded me of the person I'd been able to be before I came here. I knew I'd have to put that person aside for the moment, but she would be there waiting for me to come back to after I had finished being JULIA WELCH (R).

\*

My first night in a dorm! A strip-wash in front of three strangers! Everyone knew what to do except me, and I stood there trying not to look as they peeled their clothes off. They weren't quite starkers – you could keep your knickers on – but still. Embarrassing, embarrassing! And they all had more bosom than me. I faced the wall so no one could see I only merited a Rosebud starter bra, and removed my big pants and slightly less big pants under my dressing gown to prevent any flash of the lower department. Anyway, I got that over with. Then I jumped into bed. It was an unfamiliarly hard landing. And then came the exciting moment when Bretch took Lights, or switched the lights off, as the rest of the world would have put it.

'Settle down now. No talking.'

I was expecting all the fun of talking after Lights Out, as per Darrell in *First Term at Malory Towers* but, although everyone whispered for a bit, after a while came silence and then the sound of deep breathing. The old house creaked, the trees in the Ghost Walk sighed, the plumbing gurgled. I tried to get comfortable on the horsehair mattress. My demands weren't outrageous – I accepted there was no soft place – but could it not at least afford me somewhere level to place my body?

I said my prayers, putting my hands together under the bedclothes and muttering a quick request to look after Mummy, Daddy, Jane and Rebel. I was pretty sure my big sister was well able to look after herself, but I included her just to be on the safe side. After that I moved on to the main agenda, which was a request for seven horses, listed in order of colour preference: strawberry roan, blue roan, palomino, piebald, dun, red chestnut and a bay with a white mane and tail.

Sleep didn't come for ages. There was a deep hollow right in the centre of the mattress – was the last occupant of this bed a hippo? I folded the thin, mildewed pillow in half to make it more comfortable. I didn't feel a bit homesick but it was all strange: having to be careful what I said, not quite able to be myself, not sure how to go along yet, and having to go to sleep next to three people I didn't know. But I must have eventually dropped off because the next thing I heard was the clang-clang-clang of a handbell, a bring-out-your-dead noise. Ten to seven in the morning! It was the rising bell.

'Oh no,' groaned Cath. 'I'm here again.' And then we all scrambled out of bed and there was a race to get to the washbasins and cab and then into our cream blouses and red and grey ties and tunics and thick grey stockings, and it took me ages to fasten my red girdle and arrange it on my tunic the right way, with the knot at the back so it hung behind like a tail.

We congregated in the drive to go to Cranmer for breakfast. 'You have to walk in pairs,' said Erica. 'It's a rule.' Everybody seemed to be in couples already, crocodile-style. I looked round for Chrissie but she had gone on ahead with Beth and Cath, so I asked Erica and Bobbie if I could walk with them.

'You mustn't ask a couple if you can walk with them,' Erica said. 'You have to wait to be invited.'

'Oh! OK.'

'Here, Danny, walk with Prue and me,' said Della, and after that it was just another big whirl.

Cranmer's dining room was very big, long and narrow, and had several French windows opening on to a terrace and lawns and, beyond them, the sea, so it was very light. It had a beautiful parquet wooden floor and the most enormous Victorian fireplaces at either end, complete with Tudor folderols carved in the oak surrounds. One incorporated a mural in oils. It must have been at least seven feet long. I couldn't really decide what it depicted, but there seemed to be lots of sweeping garments and waving swords and back ends of horses. Of breakfast itself, the toast was cold, the cornflakes limp and the bacon greasy and accompanied by a huge blood clot of tomato, but it was set out very formally with toast racks and china plates, teacups and saucers, and our own table napkins.

After breakfast, another trek – this one to Morning Prayers, and a bit of a jolt that turned out to be, too, because at my last school we just had Assembly in the big hall that doubled as the gym, so we were surrounded by wall bars, the buck and the vaulting horse. Not exactly what you'd call numinous. We'd have one hymn, accompanied by the music teacher at the piano, Lord's Prayer, bish, bash, bosh, then back to our classrooms. Here we had our own church in the grounds and the service was really religious, with kneeling and praying and a hymn accompanied by a real organ, and a lesson. And we'd have to go back at the end of the day for more. And would do the same every day, with a proper service on Sunday – with more kneeling and praying and singing and *a sermon*. So this was what they meant by 'sound religious education'. I'd be at it hammer and tongs.

The whirl continued. We went back to Cranmer for 'Weighing', which was conducted on the top floor, in the San. Everyone seemed so skinny and I wasn't. I rued that smorgasbord and put my feet at the very edge of the scales, hoping that all that would be weighed would be the air between my legs. It didn't work. Eight stone 5 lbs. Almighty God!

I then fled back to Ridley for 'Unpacking of Trunks'. These were scattered all over the Covered Way, invading common rooms, spilling out into the drive. Up and down the stairs we went with armfuls of clothes, up and down, up and down. Walking past the Upper Five commie with another load, I heard hoots of laughter and a plump, pink-faced Ridley nicknamed Balloon bounced out. 'I say, is your name really Lester Piggott?'

'No,' I said, 'you've got the wrong man,' and hurried away. I was pleased with my wisecrack but I had to shut myself in cab for a little while to regroup. I longed for my best friend at day school, a lovely, demonstrative Jewish girl with a Helen Shapiro beehive hairdo. We would speak on the phone every night, pretending to be jockeys. She would be Lester Piggott and I would take the part of a less successful one called Johnny 'Kipper' Lynch or Scobie Breasley who, for some reason, we both regarded as a romantic hero, even though he looked like a walnut wearing a cap.

But I had to get a grip, because next on the schedule was a House meeting. As I belted towards the common room, something damp flicked against my calf. I felt behind me. My girdle was wet. I had gone to cab and forgotten to hitch it up. Panic, panic. I had weed on my girdle! What could I do?

You must rise above it, I told myself sternly. House meeting over, I was whirled away again for 'Timetabling of Extras'. Oh dear, oh dear. What a lot of whirling was involved. We went all around the school, up, down, along, over, through – we ran the gamut of prepositions so, by mid-afternoon, I had turned into an automaton, eating something, being told something, being pulled up for not doing one thing, and then being corrected because I was doing another, and I didn't come to until late in the day, when I found myself sitting in Lower Five A classroom.

It was in what was called the Modern Block. Huge cold windows filled it with that melancholy September light that lets you know you've come to the end of summer. The view through the windows was of half-a-dozen tennis courts with wet, sagging nets. Old desks, varnished dark brown, with a hole in the top right corner for the inkwell, were ranked across the room. Lines of strange girls dressed in grey. A partition painted sickly green, the sort of colour that milk turns after it's been on a windowsill in the sun for a very long time. It divided our classroom from the next one along and I could hear Maggie, House mistress of Tyndale, shouting from behind it. Apart from that, everything was very, very quiet.

My last school had been in the heart of the City, in Carmelite Street. It was narrow, Dickensian almost, sand-wiched between office buildings. There had been a mean little fireplace in one corner of our classroom. In winter the porter would shamble in and light a fire, which we threw our biros on. It was fun. The burning biros made a terrible smell that lingered during Geography. The porter was called Stringer, and he would place bets for you if you asked him. We were so high up that there wasn't much to see out of the windows except the top third of other buildings and a lot of sky, but you could hear exciting things, because we were so close to Fleet Street: the newspaper lorries with their screeching brakes, laden with huge rolls of paper for the presses, like Brobdingnagian loo rolls. The *Observer* had its offices nearby in Tudor Street. On the wall beside its front entrance was a display case with prints of that Sunday's photos pinned up inside. You could buy one for ten shillings. I would go there when school finished. That's where I bought the photos of Lester Piggott and Danny Blanchflower.

I came to, to hear our form mistress, Hewitt – who, possibly because she was married and lived out, was relatively sane – call out the register. Every surname was Anglo-Saxon, and a few were double-barrelled. I again thought back to my last school, and all the names there. Not just Maskell and Mackay and Wilkes, but Bhattacharya, Constantinides, Eastefield, Szamek, Wiener.

Suddenly I had this out-of-nowhere, waking-up-from a coma moment, as if I'd been whisked away by a tornado or washed up by shipwreck on an unknown shore. Where was I? How did I get here? I was on my own, and now I would have to survive.

# 6

## INSHALLAH

Luckily I wasn't able to spend much time feeling sorry for myself because, no sooner than all the rough books and textbooks and blotch and ink had been doled out and our timetables filled in, than we were all sent fleeing back to our Houses for tea. You'll see I've used a capital 'H' there. You hardly ever called it Ridley. Where we lived was referred to as 'House'. Furthermore, it was neither *a* house nor *the* house, it was just House. For example, after morning lessons and lunch, in order to change for Games (another capital there), you went back to House and then, if you hated Games, hid in a wardrobe (which was not capitalised).

Before I go any further, I must give you a Ridley guided tour, because it was the backdrop to my formative years and almost everything of fun and import that happened to me at school happened there. Now, this is all stuff I found out about years after I left. I didn't have a clue at the time what a fine, historic house it was, nor that it had once been the abode of a famous poet. Quite honestly, life was so absorbing and jolly (usually), that I cared not a whit about when it was built or who lived there but, now I am of mature years, I find it so interesting, of course.

It sat on the corner of Undercliffe Road and Maybush Lane and, before Cranmer sprang up and flaunted itself alongside, was said to be 'the grandest house in the place', with a carriage drive, orchard and, bang at the front where it got all the sea views, a tower room. By the time of our era, it had been turned into a two-dorm and was much sought-after because it was accessed by a set of creaky stairs and, if you were up to anything, you could hear Bretch coming and could get rid of the evidence before she burst in.

It was built in the nineteenth century by Sir Roger Harland, Bart., whose Italian wife was homesick for the shores of her native Mediterranean. It was her seaside retreat, and beautiful it was too, even in our day, surrounded as it was by flagstoned terraces, balustrades, urns and buttercup-strewn lawns, although, when the northeast wind blew and the winter fogs formed, it wasn't very Mediterranean.

In fact, that was the one downside of Ridley's being so close to the sea. Stationed three miles offshore at Cork Bank was a lightship. This looked a mild-mannered little vessel, with CORK in large letters stretching almost the length of its hull, and topped by a jaunty glass cylinder of a hat. The hat was actually the seat of its evil, because – especially in November, the month of peak lightship – it became an invisible monster, obscured by sea fog and intruding into our nights, its beam reaching into every dorm along the front and side of the house, feeling its way around the walls, accompanied by the plangent bleat of its horn every half-minute or so.

When first built, Ridley's name was Tamarisk Villa, though not for long. Under a later owner, Lady Login, one of those intrepid wives of Empire (her memoirs, *Court Life* and *Camp*

69

*Life*, can be perused online), Tamarisk became Vernon, her maiden name because, so she thought, Tamarisk was too exotic. Lady Login doesn't seem to have spent much time there herself, but used it as a holiday let. One tenant was the poet Edward Fitzgerald, who wrote the first and most famous English translation of *Rubaiyat of Omar Khayyam*:

> *A Book of Verses underneath the Bough,*
> *A Jug of Wine, a Loaf of Bread – and Thou*
> *Beside me singing in the Wilderness . . .*

Ridley's gardens were wonderful, not a wilderness but an absolute riot nonetheless. The Ghost Walk was its special secret place where we could go for midnight feasts. Secret, ha ha. Bretch knew all about it. Bretch knew everything there was to know about Ridley and Felixstowe College because, back in the mists of time, she had been a pupil there herself. In this Ghost Walk were huge dens, amazing elaborate things built by Annie and her chums. They would set up camp there, blagging cooking chocolate from the funny old boy who regularly hung around the perimeter fence. They'd only let you in if you said the password. Everyone knew it was *Inshallah*, but we didn't want to spoil it for them, so we kept away.

And you'd have little Lower Fours collecting ladybirds as pets and keeping them in their dressing table drawers. Or Gill and her best friend Alexa taking their pet grasshopper, Long John Hippity-Hoppity, for walks. They kept Long John Hippity-Hoppity in a matchbox in the commie – at least they did until the others decided it was cruel and let him out into the garden again.

Another piece of folklore about Felixstowe's gardens was that when you reached Upper Five you would play rounders on the front lawn, with the object of hitting the ball over the wall because then you would have to go outside and retrieve it and you might meet a member of the opposite sex. Boys and walls together were a terrible combination. Some came into the garden once, which sent Bretch sprinting round Ridley locking doors. What a fuss!

'You're not to go into the garden till further notice!' she ordered.

Just because three people spoke to boys. The girls ended up in Jonah's study at seven at night, with Jonah giving that basilisk stare over the top of her glasses. 'What would your mother think of such wanton behaviour?' And Helen – for on one occasion one of them was Helen, who grew up in a fabulously talented and eccentric family of musicians, who was told the facts of life aged nine by her mother while stirring food at the Aga – Helen thought, My mother probably wouldn't think very much about it at all.

Ridley, or Vernon Villa as it was in prehistory – and carried on being called until after the war – came into the school's hands in 1933. Our generation might have moaned about its lukewarm radiators and bleak cabs, but these earliest settlers, the 1930s girls, had to make do with one cab in the whole house and chamber pots under each bed. No washbasins, of course. Every morning, maids would heave jugs of hot water upstairs and into dorms for the strip-wash, although later – probably in a cost-cutting exercise, because at one point early on the school nearly went bust – the girls themselves had to take over the job.

According to *The Story of Felixstowe College*:

Watering-can monitors were appointed to each dormitory; a thankless task, one would have thought, since it involved getting up earlier than the rest and queuing in the corridor for enamel cans of warm water. These were carried into the dormitory and poured into china bowls on marble-topped washstands. If the monitor succumbed to the temptation to linger in bed, the water was cold before her dormitory was served and everyone screamed at her.

What amazed me, though, was back then your House wasn't your home for all the time you were there; you were peripatetic. It was almost like musical chairs. Lower Fours lived in Vernon Villa; Upper Fours and Lower Fives were in School House – which became Cranmer – and the rest of the girls pinged every term between another two school properties, Maybush and Highrow, with the overflow being accommodated in a rented pile called Happisburgh House. It wasn't until after the war, when the school bought Tyndale and Latimer, that Ridleys stayed in one place. And were proper Ridleys.

As you walked up the drive in September 1961, the first thing you saw was the front door. Trying to enter the house there would have been a mistake. The front door was locked and barred, a dead end. The vestibule it led onto, had it been a normal house, was turned into a library. You were supposed to have a book out of the House library all the time, but I didn't take out a single one. It was full of schoolboy adventure tales by Willard Price and really tedious serious books and sod all else. The only interesting titles were on the top shelf, like girlie mags at a newsagent's. These were the 'Angelique' books. They were banned till Upper Five, presumably because they might give us ideas. The Angelique series consisted (at the time) of seven adventure books set in seventeenth-century France. The eponymous protagonist was a provincial aristo-crat forced to live on her wits after her first husband (a count, *naturellement*) was executed by Louis VIV. The books featured the Paris underworld, the court of Versailles, war, rape, sex, childbirth, capture by pirates – everything, in short, that a thirteen-year-old banged up in a bear pit of old crones could wish for, so there was a huge trade in contraband copies.

On the right was Bretch's bedroom. Up until a couple of years before I was there, she hadn't had one. Not a proper one. Her sitting room had been a bedsit, so if you went in there to be given a row you'd see where she slept. This must have added an awkward element of intimacy to the occasion, because wouldn't you stand there imagining her in her pyjamas? This said, having her own bedsit was a step up from what went before, because the teachers at one point had to live on site, *in the same house.* Spinsters of indeterminate age all bitching away at each other – whoever thought that was a good wheeze?

Anyway, Bretch now had a boudoir of her own, if you could call it such, because it can't have been more than seven feet square. It was on the ground floor and must have been a butler's pantry or a housekeeper's sitting room back in the day – tiny and terrifically dark, because the window was high up, it was little more than a donjon. I'm amazed she could lie on her bed full-length. Her feet must have stuck out through the door, surely.

Between that, the posh staircase we weren't allowed to use, and an embarrassing area called the Other Cupboard, where the packs of STs were stored, was one of Ridley's four bathrooms. It was the biggest I'd ever seen, with high windows and exposed pipes and three baths lined up in a row, with cubicle curtains for preservation of modesty, not that you'd bother about that much once you'd been there a few weeks and got used to flashing everything in front of all comers. It was actually a friendly place, because if you were assigned to it on the bath rota you could lie there in the warm water chatting to your chums. But on Sunday mornings you would find it locked, and the following ditty would be ringing out around the house to the tune of 'Land of Hope and Glory':

> *Land of soap and water,*
> *Bretch is having a bath,*
> *Matron's looking through the keyhole,*
> *Having a jolly good laugh.*

Next, the other side of the corridor. That faced the sea and featured one of the most popular dorms in the house. Known as the downstairs six-dorm, its windows opened on to the patio, thus offering exciting possibilities for nocturnal escape. The windows still had their original shutters, with little planks behind them that you could ease out to hide the sweets you bought at the tuck shop for midnight feasts.

A few steps further along took you into Here Be Dragons Corner, where Bretch's sitting room and the Lower Six commie (warning: may contain prefects) were situated. A sharp right turn would take you to, on the left, the kitchen and the downstairs five-dorm. Midnight feasts went indoors for the winter, like tennis tournaments and athletics champion-ships, and this five-dorm was Ridley's top venue, its Wembley, its Centre Court, as it offered easy access to butter, bread and anything left over from Bretch's supper.

Between dorm and kitchen were stairs to more dorms. But if you kept going you would reach the Covered Way, the other commies, the cloakroom and another set of stairs, which led up to more dorms. The biggest in the place, the nine-dorm, was above the Covered Way and was so long it could be accessed by the staircases at either end. It was the dorm that was the most fun to be in because you could push the beds together in a line and somersault all the way along them.

I think this would be an opportune moment to tell you more about the girls I spent those formative years with, because I will be mentioning them a lot in the pages to come and it will be a help if you can tell one from the other: which ones were good sorts and which were wets; who was difficult to get along with; who went round with whom etc. etc.

Erica was our leader. She was physically perfect – a hooked nose excepted – with long legs, a pert bosom and a cocktail party laugh. How terrifyingly grown-up she was. I'd wake up in the morning thinking, Oh, please let Erica approve of me today, please let it be someone else's turn to be childish and silly.

She was going round with Bobbie, who had soft brown eyes and hair the colour of black coffee, and was funny and easy-going where Erica wasn't, but they do say opposites attract, of course.

The next most dominant character in our group was Beth. You'd have expected someone called that to be all doomed and sickly, like her namesake in *Little Women*, but not this Beth. Our Beth was the binary opposite. She had frizzy, sticky-out hair that never went the way she wanted and a tough face that was completely transformed by a lovely wicked smile. She was brainy and sarky – her jokes were the filthiest, her laugh the dirtiest, her pranks the most inventive, her put-downs the most quelling. Squish-squash-squish. Beth did not approve of show-offs, sneaks, rotters or wets. She made sure you knew when you were out of line. She didn't say much; hardly a word sometimes. Just smiled her evil smile. But you would know you had transgressed and, although I liked her, I found her a little bit frightening.

You might already have formed a good idea of Cath. She was the practical, helpful one, a good person to have around the place. She and Beth made a formidable couple so, after one or two unsuccessful attempts to boss them about at the start of every term, Erica mostly left them alone.

Della was easily the prettiest, though 'pretty' is rather a wet word, which Della The Blonde was not, as she was grave, somehow, as well as sexy. She wore her fair hair in one long plait down her back. Snake hair. When she had something important to say, she would signal it by giving a little sniff.

Prue, who Della went round with, was quiet and studious. The sort who you thought was a goody-goody because she just went calmly about her business, but if Beth had some sort of prank going she was always one of the first to volunteer. She never got into any trouble because, when it came to being lined up in the commie for the inquisition, Bretch would always say, 'Well, it can't possibly have been Prue!'

Lindy was what mothers in those days would have called a thoroughly nice girl, though with a deep-down core of steel. Jonah adored her.

Lindy went round with Marion, whose hair was a lovely mass of dark blonde curls and whose bust was the best in our year but, perhaps because she wasn't very happy at boarding school, always seemed to have some ailment or other. Each ailment was always of the kind grown-ups suffered. She had 'nerves'. Or her 'gall bladder'. Even housemaid's knee, once. It was never anything age-appropriate like mumps or verrucas.

Marlee wasn't really Marlee, of course – Jonah would never have accepted anyone with a name like that – her real name was Marilyn, which Erica, who was in charge of nicknames, thought was too like Marion, so it had been conflated with her surname.

She was small and inoffensive, the left-out girl, just one of those unfortunate people who seem to slip through the cracks. Poor thing, she just couldn't find a best friend. She never got the opening gambit right and didn't quite understand jokes, a sort of minor dislocation between her and the universe, summed up in the way she often did up the buttons of her mac in the wrong holes. I wasn't as kind to her as I should have been, perhaps because I was the left-out girl at home and saw something of myself in her plight.

Lastly Chrissie – my ally and co-conspirator, my fellow poet, the best girl in the world, my friend from the very first. Wasn't I lucky?

I will now tell you about the Davy. The Davy's full name

was the Abseil Davy Descender Automatic Fire Escape. I searched online for this contraption not long ago and was amazed to discover that you could still buy one, because I thought it would have gone the way of trolley buses and gramophones, but when I checked again, it was listed as discontinued. Your Davy was fitted next to the dorm window and consisted of two harnesses operated by a pulley arrangement. While you abseiled to the ground in one harness, a second empty harness passed you on its way up. You had to push yourself away from the wall with one hand so you didn't get skinned by Ridley's pebbledash, while your other hand tried to keep your skirt from riding up around your waist. It was great fun, although it took forever. I never thought everyone would make it out in the event of a real fire.

In my first year there was one prefect, Deirdre, who was an absolute rotter (and you'll find out why later). She was fat and I hoped her enormous bosom would be too big to fit into the harness and she would perish in the flames like Joanna at the end of *The Girls of Slender Means*.

And finally the cloakroom. You could only get to this by going through the Middle Five commie, and it was the site of strange happenings that took place in the first week of my first term, when the whole of Ridley seemed to have turned into a weird kind of dating agency.

The pashes were getting sorted out. Chrissie and I sat ignored in the junior commie after supper, pretending to read, listening to the whispers and the noises off. The activity seemed to be based on the conveyor belt principle. The blushing suitor of Lower Four, having declared herself to her Chosen One among the lax sticks and hockey boots by planting a tremulous kiss on her cheek, would clatter up the stairs to the waiting huddle of giggling dorm-mates. Della, being the prettiest in our year, had two Lower Fours fighting over her. Erica was annoyed because only one wanted to have a pash on her.

Curiously it was officially condoned. I suppose they thought it'd stop anything worse. You wrote to them in the holidays and let them carry your books. They'd cry in the corridor to make you give them some attention, because you were meant to be kind. And you had to kiss them goodnight, like Mummy. They'd cry if you didn't. They'd follow you down to school from a distance, like stalkers. I had no idea such a thing existed, and it all seemed absolutely ghastly, but it was obviously something that had to be done if you wanted to fit in, so I put myself on the market. All the attractive girls, the form captains and hockey heroines, were snapped up straight away but my dance card stayed unmarked till a rather quaint Lower Four started up an elliptical conversation by the lockers. But I lost my courage.

'Oh, you mustn't. Please don't,' I breathed.

We then simultaneously fled in opposite directions. The next thing I knew was that she had gone for a Middle Five called Lobster. We never spoke of it.

After pash night, the cloakroom reverted to its regular function, and Ridley returned to its normal calm, which involved everyone sitting in our commie playing card games and jacks, trying to find Radio Luxembourg and sewing and knitting misshapen objects to be sold at that term's Christmas Fair. This was going to be held at the Pier Pavilion, at the more louche end of town. The object of the exercise was to raise money for Jonah's Appeal Fund for a new, bigger chapel and a swimming pool.

'Nothing exciting ever seems to happen,' said Lindy, gloomily wielding her crochet hook.

# 7

# THE SEX MANIAC

No sooner had Lindy complained about the lack of exciting events than a sex maniac started roaming the school grounds. Apparently. 'It's not true,' said Lindy, and the rest of us dithered between taking Lindy's word for it and being absolutely terrified. We pressed our noses to the junior commie windows, searching for any action. What did a sex maniac look like? Marion let out a huge scream and cupped her cheeks in her hands because she saw a face, but it turned out to be Bobbie's, reflected in a pane.

The Cranmers were blasé about it, as they often passed the time after Lights by watching people having sex under blankets on the beach from the dorm window. Every House was on lockdown – Bretch and Miss Rayment, the matron, striding through the Ridley undergrowth; Poulson, the Tyndale matron, sprinting all over the house closing curtains, sliding bolts and pressing her back to the kitchen door. My bed was closest to the window and I stayed awake almost one whole night because I thought the sex maniac would climb up the drainpipe and get after me. The excitement lasted a couple of days and then everyone forgot about it because:

1) We had hockey House matches and Ridley 2nds beat Cranmer 2nds 10–0.

2) We were allowed to watch *Juke Box Jury* back at House instead of Saturday's film show in the gym because the projector had broken. Normally the prefects put a stop to that kind of thing. We were only allowed to watch *Danger Man* because they all fancied Patrick McGoohan and the TV was in our commie, so they couldn't very well turf us out.

3) Bretch gave us a row about the butter fight.

House Tea was the best part of the day. You'd eat it in your commie, ravenous and in high spirits after Games, with the radio on and all your friends around you. It was cosy and jolly except if you were in Cranmer, where they had to go to the cavernous dining room and help themselves from the table nearest the kitchen. Very, very depressing. On the other hand, Cranmer had all the nice things, so this was natural justice balancing the scales a bit.

Tea consisted of bread and butter, or margarine if you'd eaten all the butter. There was also a bowl of runny dark-red jam, like blood with pips in. The same stuff was served up at mealtimes, when we had semolina or tapioca. I couldn't believe anyone would want to spoil their food with it. You'd have to have no taste at all, just a sort of gollup-up-everything greed. I never saw any of us at Ridley put it on our bread, but there it was at tea, day after day, unwanted. It must have been years old.

The bread was delivered daily by a local bakery, Millars. It was against the rules to eat that which had arrived that day; only the day-old stuff was allowed. The excuse was that fresh bread caused indigestion, although really it was because when fresh it was so delicious that we'd scoff the lot and they'd have to order extra. But the deliveryman left the bread stacked in crates on the kitchen table and, if you were commie captain and had to help get the tea things, it was your solemn duty to swap the loaves so your table had the warm, soft ones baked only that morning.

So anyway, the butter fight. Lower Five vs. Upper Four. It was Sunday afternoon, when tea was accompanied by *Pick of the Pops*. This was greatly looked forward to, as it was one of the few pop music shows you could get on the BBC Light Programme, and the only one we could listen to from start to finish. Saturday meant *Saturday Club*, but that began at ten in the morning, when we were over at the school block in the middle of Prep. Prep ended at 11.30 a.m., and if you ran very fast you could catch the last ten minutes, but that wasn't very satisfactory. Then there was *Easy Beat*, which went out at 10.30 a.m. on Sundays, so unless we had Evening rather than Morning Chapel we would miss half of it. *Two Way Family Favourites*, created to link families at home in Britain with members of the armed forces serving overseas, followed immediately after that, but was much more square, playing the kind of music your parents liked.

I think I was probably a late developer when it came to pop, because I had only just started to enjoy songs such as John Leyton's 'Johnny Remember Me' and Billy Fury's 'Halfway to Paradise'. It was the era of the changeover from Bill Haley and the Comets, Alma Cogan, Lonnie Donegan and skiffle, and during my last year at the City of London I was regarded as quite square myself because I didn't like Helen Shapiro, who was only a little older than us when she made the charts with

'Don't Treat Me Like A Child', but already had that beehive hairdo and wore heels.

Cliff Richard had had a hit with a song called 'Dynamite', which contained the line, 'Let me feel your bosom when I hold you tight', which I listened to again and again to make sure, because I couldn't believe my ears. But by the time I did get interested in pop songs, and the boys who sang them, Cliff had cleaned up his image and now had the look of a young man who lived with his mother, who made him wear a vest. I much preferred that huge, snarling lump of testosterone, Elvis, and it was Elvis vs. Cliff that the butter fight was all about. I expect what triggered it off was that Elvis was ridin' high with 'Wild in the Country', while Cliff hadn't had a hit since 'I Love You', and there was a passionate debate about which was better. It escalated to the extent where people began throwing things, and the uproar brought Bretch into the commie.

What DID we think we were doing? What WAS this, the Wild West?

I adopted a saintly pose. I hadn't chucked any butter. I'd maybe flicked a bit of bread at Marion but really only a large sort of crumb and it missed, and bread was not the issue. But Erica, Beth and an Upper Four did flick some butter, and the Upper Four's missile got stuck on the TV screen, so a filthy row from Bretch ensued. They had to go to bed straight after supper. The rest of us had to clean up the mess because otherwise Rose and Burton would take one look at it and threaten to leave, as usual.

Rose and Burton were the cleaners. Rose was little and cherry-cheeked. She wore a flowered pinny, spoke with a lovely Suffolk burr, and shuffled around like Mrs

Tiggywinkle. Burton had glasses and dyed, bright-orange hair, and looked like Ronnie Barker in drag. They did all the horrid jobs, like cab cleaning and emptying the ST bins, while doubling as maids – they brought in our tea things, did the washing up, scrubbed floors. They were the House characters. 'The whole thing,' said Lindy, 'is to NOT upset Burton and Rose, WHATEVER HAPPENS, because they'll never get anyone else.'

Rows, rows, more rows. One about not closing the dorm window properly (we didn't take much notice). One about baths when it was Erica, Beth and Marion's turn on the rota to have their baths in the afternoon, all at once, in the big ground floor bathroom. One overflowed a little and Bretch went on the warpath and blamed it on Beth, who nobly took the rap, although Erica was the offender. She had to run round the Games pitches twice after Games, so she soaked Erica in revenge. Erica then hid Beth's pyjamas, so Beth got in a bate.

'ANOTHER row, worse luck,' commented Lindy.

All these offences were followed by a tariff of punishments. The mildest, for talking after Lights Out, was being sent down to stand in the Covered Way in our dressing gowns, where we would stand giggling and watching the hands of the clock move until the statutory twenty minutes was up. At Ridley there was absolutely no way we would not talk after Lights, or not start talking again after we'd been told to be quiet. It was a matter of pride. Even if you wanted to go to sleep. So, of course, we would be punished again, this time by having to get up twenty minutes early and report to the place of correction, otherwise known as the Lower Six commie.

Bretch would be waiting for us in there with a carrier bag,

from which she would fish out lots of knotted and tangled-up string, which we had to tease out and wind into neat balls. If that didn't do the trick, and we were caught talking after Lights again too soon after the second offence, we would have to put on our cloaks over our night things and walk over to Cranmer, to line up in front of Jonah in her study. Jonah would mutter 'Stupid', and send us back again, and on your House mistress's report at the end of term something would be written along the lines of 'Julia must learn to be more responsible'.

But really, everything we got up to was just harmless naughtiness, and Bretch and Jonah had seen it all before, and in between all the japes and pranks we behaved very well and tried hard to 'give back to our House', which was one of Bretch's favourite expressions. Really bad deeds were done by Big Girls, for whom the punishment was being 'asked to leave'. Quite early on in the term, one girl was caught behind the shed with the gardener's boy and was quarantined in the San, waiting for her parents to come and take her away.

'She's the one with a very large bosom and a terrible gap between her teeth,' said a Latimer, who seemed in the know. 'At tea she has jam and it comes through the gap.'

'She's a nymphomaniac,' Marion said knowledgeably.

I knew a nymphomaniac was a bad thing for a woman to be, and that it seemed to involve her doing it all the time, willy-nilly, with any Tom, Dick and old Harry, so somehow, although I was shocked in a thrilled sort of way, it wasn't surprising. The kind of person who ate that jam would not be fastidious.

# 8

# A MIDNIGHT FEAST

'I don't know why food tastes so much nicer in the middle of the night than in the daytime, but it does!'

ENID BLYTON, *The Twins at St Clare's*

We knew it was going to happen. There had been an undercurrent of excitement in the junior commie for nearly a fortnight. Towards the middle of October we had been gifted the opportunity for a midnight feast. An Old Girls' Sherry Night in London was going to lure Bretch from Ridley overnight, leaving us in the care of our matron, the kind-hearted, indulgent Miss Rayment. As the weather was still mild, and the autumn fogs not yet begun, the Ghost Walk was our chosen venue, leaving the Lower and Upper Fours to argue it out over who bagged the junior commie and who had theirs in the big downstairs bathroom.

Just because Bretch and her supersonic hearing would be absent, and we could slip outside without difficulty, it didn't mean we could dispense with proper military-style planning. That was part of the excitement. We moved food from our lockers, under cover of our cloaks, to the hiding place in the bushes. We'd been collecting it and stashing it away for a week. Della and Prue stole some bread from the kitchen, hiding it in their grey bags. We bought sweets and crisps from the tuck shop and solicited contributions from home. We had a Battenburg cake, ginger biscuits and bourbons, Wagon Wheels, Potato Puffs and lashings of orangeade. Prue's mother had contributed a tin of mandarin oranges, smuggled in via a parcel and wrapped in a pair of replacement pyjamas. My mother sent a box of Twiglets, some Dairylea cheese triangles and a packet of frankfurters. Erica's mother provided her noted homemade game pie. She would.

It had to start at midnight, on the dot. In the four-dorm we kept each other awake and, at ten to midnight, we crept downstairs in our pyjamas, dressing gowns and slippers and stole through the Middle Five commie to the cloakroom to fetch our cloaks. Then we met up with the others in the Covered Way and waited on tiptoe by the door for the clocks of Felixstowe to strike midnight.

We were all out at a sprint and across the drive to the front garden before the last 'bong' had sounded. The Ghost Walk was below and to the left was a little hollow behind the wall separating Ridley from the outside world. Its trees provided good cover from both Bretch's sitting room and the Lower Six commie. Along the patio we crept, down the wide stone steps, over the lawn. It was a clear night, with plenty of stars, and daisies sparkled and buttercups glowed in the moonlight. We stopped once or twice to make sure no one was left behind and that someone had brought the can opener and jug of water. Then we picked our way over the rockery and were able to disappear into the dip below the screen of tamarisks, where we retrieved the food from its hiding place in the bushes and took up our allotted places in a circle under the trees.

Erica, the boss, occupied the alpha position with Bobbie and Lindy either side of her like maids-in-waiting, and Marion was next to Lindy. Marion and Lindy might have been going round together, but Lindy really preferred Erica. They'd all been together since they were eleven years old and their friendships periodically formed into different patterns, like a shaken-up kaleidoscope. Bobbie, being kind, made room for Marlee, the left-out girl. The little married couples were Della and Prue, Beth and Cath, and Chrissie and me. As it was the first proper midnight feast Chrissie and I had attended, we let the others take the lead in serving the food.

Della and Prue cut the cake with a penknife that was part of a rather exciting multipurpose device belonging to Beth, who was given it by her older brothers when they upgraded to real Swiss Army knives. It came with a retractable can-opener, and they passed it to Beth to deal with the mandarin oranges. She divided them up, two per girl, and dropped them in our outstretched palms. The game pie was delicious, as well as grown-up, though should it have had all that runny stuff in the middle? I was the only one who seemed to know what the frankfurters were. They also looked as if they should have been stored in a fridge rather than in the back of my locker for a week. Never mind. Nobody else wanted one so I ate the whole pack myself. Scrummy!

Conditions were perfect. The Ghost Walk was dry-ish and the air had an autumnal nip but still smelt fresh and flowery. The sea, invisible behind the wall, made a faint sound like a brush on a snare drum. We drank out of the glasses we kept our toothbrushes in, so there was a hint of Colgate along with the orange squash. We talked in whispers, occasionally glancing back at Ridley, a ghost house in the moonlight, checking that no light came on in the six-dorm, where the some of the Lower Six were billeted. They surely wouldn't have been such rotters as to split on us, but you never knew.

I'd been living for this moment since I'd arrived at the school; since before that. I'd once had a French pen-friend to stay when I was ten, and I made her get up in the night to eat dried macaroni from a paper bag and drink milk diluted with water. That night in the Ghost Walk we were all schoolgirls everywhere, past, present and future, real and imagined. We were Darrell and her chums at Malory Towers; we were the O'Sullivan twins at St Clare's; we were the girls in their night rails consuming confits and sugarplums in a rose-strewn bower at the bottom of an eighteenth-century seminary garden. We were the real-life girls who had gone before us at Felixstowe: the Upper Sixth in their last ever night at school, celebrating with vodka, along with crisps and homemade cheese straws and sausages on cocktail sticks and four tins of cling peaches. We were Tyndales easing up a floorboard in their commie, hopping out the window and running across the lawn to the rose garden to eat Wagon Wheels in the moonlight while Maggie in her room overlooking the back lawn turned a blind eye. We were the poor Latimers who could only dream of midnight feasts because a real one would have had Cawley and their matron, Miss Pipe, at them. We were Cranmers whose middies featured tins of Roka biscuits and *pâté de foie gras* because one of them had a London dentist by whom she had special dispensation to be treated in term time, so every time she had a toothache the Cranmers said, 'Yippee!' because she would come back having dropped into Fortnum's. We were the Cranmer Middle Fives of 1953, creeping down to the kitchen in the middle of the night and picking the lock with a couple of Kirbigrips and plunging their hands into a big bowl of golden fruit – ooh, apricots! – but they were raw eggs waiting for breakfast.

Just utter bliss.

Around one o'clock we brought things to an end, not wanting to be seen falling asleep in class the next day. Crumbs had to be swept up and sweet wrappers pocketed prior to being discreetly buried at the bottom of a wapey, Beth first of all finishing up the flakes of Potato Puff left at the bottom of the bag with a wetted fingertip.

Our heads popped up above the dip. We scanned our surroundings. All appeared safe. One by one we scuttled back across the lawn but, just as we were turning the corner, a light went on in the kitchen. Everyone stood stock still, as though we were strung together on a washing line. Who was in there? Had someone woken up in the night feeling ill? Oh no, if Rayment had to be fetched to ring up Sister and get whoever it was admitted to the San, we were going to be stuck out there for ages!

*No one make a sound.*

Bobbie started to make little *herch-herch* noises in the back of her throat, trying to stifle a cough. This was potentially a disaster. Her cough was famed far and wide. It carried like a sea lion's bark. She grabbed the hem of her dressing gown, scrunched it up and stuffed it over her mouth.

The kitchen light went off. We waited, counting to ten, then ran, bent double under the window, back to the commie, in via the Covered Way, creep creep creep, to our dorms. We thought we'd never get to sleep after all that excitement, but we did.

> *A Book of Verses underneath the Bough,*
> *A Jug of Wine, a Loaf of Bread — and Thou*
> *Beside me singing in the Wilderness . . .*

I don't know if Edward Fitzgerald was inspired to write the *Rubaiyat* by Ridley gardens. If not, he jolly well should have been.

The next day Bobbie was sick three times in three hours, the last time just before lunch in one of the Cranmer cloak-room cabs, so Cath held her hair back from her forehead while it was all going on and then Erica took her up to the San. Some of the others felt a bit queasy too. Erica tried to blame it on the week-old frankfurters but, given the choice of admitting I was a greedy pig and being guilty of poisoning most of the form, I opted unhesitatingly for the former and confessed to eating the whole lot. So it must have been the runny gravy in the game pie, and Erica was awfully upset because she had swanked endlessly about that game pie, i.e., that it was a Closely Guarded Recipe handed down from great-grandmother to grandmother to mother etc. etc., so it was what I think Miss Williams, our English teacher, would have called 'hubris followed by nemesis'.

After supper, Bretch gave Chrissie and I the duty of taking Bobbie a change of pyjamas, her letters and my radio (as hers had conked out), which meant a trip to the San instead of going to a lecture in the library on 'The Pageant Commemorating the Signing of the Magna Carta' (what a shame!).

Cranmer was enormous – a Victorian mansion on a clifftop. You could see it from miles out to sea, as it dominated the skyline. It had been built in rip-roaring mock-Tudor style to house Felix Thorneley Cobbold, barrister, diplomat, brewer, banker, farmer, Liberal MP and public benefactor. It replaced a property owned by another family member, John Cobbold, whose son, John Chevalier Cobbold, the Member of Parliament for Harwich, had lived there.

The Cobbolds, along with the Tollemaches (another old family on the Suffolk superstratum), were behind the Tolly Cobbold brewery, a dynasty so important that they had not just a road on the seafront but a whole promontory named after them: Cobbold's Point. Cranmer was just called The Lodge in the old days, although anything less lodge-like it would be hard to think of. It was a fat, stuffed, stupendous house, flamboyant with mock-Elizabethan bells and whistles that made the facade look like a giant pincushion.

In the 1960s, two Cobbolds (wonderful Old Etonians known as Mr John and Mr Patrick) were the force behind Ipswich Town Football Club. They employed Alf Ramsey, who went on to manage the England team that won the 1966 World Cup.

It was special, the best and biggest, the holy of holies, because, when the school started, Cranmer was it – the entire school. Obviously Jonah lived there. She had her own room and sitting room, known as the Headmistress's Suite, although not an en-suite so, if you were a Cranmer, you'd sometimes catch her striding towards the bathroom with her kiss curls in butterfly clips.

Cranmer girls were also special, the elite, the Chosen Ones. Jonah wasn't really interested in the girls at interview. It was their parents who mattered, and she would cherry-pick the best prospects – titles, anyone related to titles, daughters of MPs and the upper ranks of clergy. Trade was fine if it was a blue chip company and Daddy could be tickled up to give money to the school. So if you were a Ridley or a Tyndale or a Latimer you'd failed to pass muster before you even started, and when you went in there you already felt a social inferior. For me it was like being back home all over again, with the house next door and their ballroom and tennis court.

The hall was a huge space, with dark wood panelling on the walls and a large polished table. It was open for two storeys, boasting a wide staircase with a beautiful blue carpet and carved banisters. All out of bounds, apart from when we had hair inspections and when we were training to be debutantes by gliding down the stairs. So Chrissie and I just poked our heads round the door to see what it was like, and then up we climbed to the San via the back stairs by the kitchen.

It was on the top floor and, along with the dining room and Jonah's study, one of the only places that we non-Cranmers were permitted to set foot in. It was completely unlike the rest of the school – all white paint and hush. There were two single rooms, a general ward with six beds in it, an enormous room that contained a bath and all manner of mysterious equipment, and a big consulting room with a desk and chairs and a map of Latvia on the wall, because that was Sister Berg's homeland.

Sister had come to us from St Monica's, Clacton, and was a bishop's daughter; her family had had to flee in the face of the Russian advance during the Second World War. Sister would point to a spot on the map, showing us where she had lived. She was tall, with long brown hair that she tucked under her cap – an attractive woman who was maternal enough to teach us how to do butterfly kisses, but who was also rather forbidding.

Bobbie had a room to herself, with a proper hospital bed and two whole pillows, and was already looking more cheerful and much less green. Luckily, owing perhaps to some premonition, two aunts, a granny and a godmother had all written and posted long epistles to her before the midnight feast and ingestion of the Game Pie of Doom had taken place, so she had heaps of letters to read. Chrissie had brought her pack of cards, and the three of us played Racing Demon and Spit, with the cards spread out on the bedclothes till Sister came in and shooed us out.

On our way along the scuff-walled and lino-floored corridor (Cranmer was only grand where visitors might see it), we heard, 'Psst,' and there were Juno and Cherry peeping round from behind a dorm door. They were both in their grey afternoon dresses, Cherry's very neat and clean and Juno's with an ink blob on one cuff and the white collar hanging on by a couple of buttons. They beckoned us inside.

'We didn't want to go to the lecture, so we hid in the wardrobe,' said Juno.

'You won't tell, will you?' said Cherry anxiously.

'Poor thing, she's a terribly obedient child,' said Juno. 'I regularly lead her astray.'

Their dorm was absolutely huge, with six beds on each side,

making twelve in all, and a dressing table at the foot of each. The dressing tables faced each other and the mirrors made reflection after reflection after reflection.

'You can climb along the top of the dressing tables and crash-land on the mattress,' said Cherry, sitting on the edge of her bed and bouncing up and down.

I looked at her photos and exclaimed admiringly at one of a huge Georgian house. 'Oh, we don't own it,' said Cherry. 'It's the rectory. Impossible to keep warm. *Brrrr!* My father's a canon. We haven't a bean, but clergy are allowed here on the cheap.'

Another photo was of a boy in a wheelchair, his limbs and head twisted awkwardly. I tried to look as though I hadn't seen it, but Cherry said, 'That's my brother. He's a spastic.'

So of course I then blushed bright pink, because it was one of those things you weren't supposed to mention, like cancer.

'He's a good brother,' Cherry said stoutly, and I was about to ask more about him, to show I wasn't sweeping it all under the carpet, when the door burst open and there stood a lantern-jawed prefect.

'What are you doing in here? Why aren't you at the lecture?'

'We've been visiting someone in the San,' Cherry said quickly. Innocent face.

The prefect glared at Chrissie and me. 'Well, you two get out and go back to House, and Cherry and Juno, stop hanging around your dorm and go to your common room.'

'Why aren't *you* at the lecture?' I should have said, I thought, as we clattered down the stairs (according to Miss Williams this was something called *esprit de l'escalier,* and meant a witty retort that came to mind after the opportunity to make it had passed).

Then we did something daring, which was to run from one side of Cranmer's grand entrance hall to the other, where the cloakrooms were, and then something even more daring, where Chrissie and I were concerned, because instead of going straight back to House we went to Cherry and Juno's commie, which was at the far end of the house next to the cloakroom. It was huge but looked a bit of a dark and friendless place, to be truthful, because it was wood-panelled and looked out on the overgrown part of Cranmer gardens, which were clogged with trees and bushes. But Cherry and Juno fetched their tuck boxes from their lockers, and brought out a bag of Murray Mints, some Ginger Nuts, a bar of Cadbury's Bournville, a bottle of orange squash and some plastic cups, so immediately everything seemed full of light and warmth, just because they were there and we were us and we were going to have a merry old time.

'Won't be a sec.' Juno darted into the cloakroom to fill the cups at the washbasins. 'We used to drink squash all the time at my last school,' she said, coming back with the cups balanced precariously in the crooks of her elbows. 'Then, halfway through one term, came this notice: "We'd like to announce the water is now suitable for drinking".'

'Tell her how your last school tried to kill you,' said Cherry. Golly!

'It was a convent,' said Juno, carefully setting down the cups, then taking a seat at the end of the table so she could stretch out her long legs. 'Ghastly place, an old house with lots of creaky staircases, on the point of falling down. A lot of the teachers were burnt-out nuns from the tropics, and when I left the only things I could do were Latin and Needlework. The dorms were all named after saints and were all in a long line, with fire escape hatches between them, so you could sneak in and out. We used to have amazing inter-dorm fights. Missiles of tissues soaked in toothpaste and shampoo, and sometimes wee. I was jolly good with a catapult. I could get my bomb right across from Perpetua to Bernadette.'

She unwrapped the Bournville, broke it into squares and shared them between us. 'Anyway, the food was even more disgusting than ours. They shut the kitchen down once when the Department of Health swept in. Baked beans once a day, every day, burnt on top. Dead baby's leg. Constipated bear – that was plate scrapings, which they formed into a sort of poo shape. Curried eggs consisted of curry powder and three sultanas, hard-boiled eggs floating in a sea of pus. And on Fridays they served fried potato and cabbage, which always made me sick, so I refused to eat it. Eventually the mother superior called me in and said, "You must eat it. You must learn to be like other girls."

'So the very next Friday I forced some down and was sick. By that time I'd started getting stomach pains, too, so I was sent to the Infirmary to be dosed with milk of magnesia and sent away again.'

Chrissie had made her empty sweet wrappers into a little mountain. Juno leant across and put the last of hers on top, like the fairy on the Christmas tree.

'Over a few days the pains got worse,' she said, 'but they thought I was swinging the lead, so more milk of magnesia, more stomach pains, till with very bad grace the Infirmary admitted me. It was only because a young assistant to the nursing nun looked at me late on and heard me groaning and got so worried that she called the doctor, who said my appendix was about to burst. It was about to turn into peritonitis.'

'Which is a medical emergency requiring immediate treatment, because if the infection spreads through the bloodstream to the major organs it can cause septic shock, leading to *death*,' said Cherry knowledgeably. 'Oh heavens!' Suddenly she jumped up, and her voice dropped to a whisper. 'Did you hear a noise? Prefect! Danny, Chrissie – hide!'

So we got under the table and cowered while Cherry crept to the door and opened it and looked up and down the corridor. 'No one there,' she said.

'It wasn't from the corridor,' giggled Juno, who was hanging out of the window. 'You can come out now.' She looked round. 'It's one of those water rats. Horrible great orangey things. They come up into the garden sometimes.'

So Chrissie and I crawled out from under the table and, of course, we were all in absolute fits, until Chrissie looked at her watch and said suddenly, 'Goodness, we'd better scram. The lecture must be nearly finished.' And we hurried back to Ridley in the dark, full of tuck and the feeling of having had a lovely time and liking Cherry and Juno so much.

No sooner had we sat down in the commie than everyone returned from the lecture, staggering with boredom and with stuff about the Magna Carta leaking out of their ears, and wanting to hear all about our visit to the San and whether Bobbie had finished being sick yet.

'Did you see the ghost?' asked Beth, giving me one of her more sadistic grins.

'What?'

'The San's got a ghost.'

'It's meant to be the original owner's disabled daughter,' said Della. 'She drowned in a sunken bath.'

'That's rubbish,' I objected. 'The San hasn't got a sunken bath.'

'Sunken baths can be removed. Ghosts can't.' Beth made *whoo-hoo* noises. 'She had long red hair. Now she patrols the corridors in her long white nightgown, her stick going tippety-tap, tippety-tap, like Blind Pugh.'

'People have heard her,' said Della. 'Tippety-tap, tippety-tap.'

Trust Cranmer to be haunted by a toff. But that settled it. Even if I were on death's door, I was never going to be in the San.

# 9

# FILTHY ROWS

Ailments too minor to qualify you for the San were dealt with at Sug, which was what we called Surgery. Sug opened for business just after the rising bell and was conducted in Ridley's kitchen, where Rayment kept all her medical supplies in the fridge, next to the milk and butter. Her dispensary was not extensive. It consisted of liquid paraffin for constab, all-purpose goo for chilblains and gnat bites, cough linctus for stinking colds and Anadin for everything else. I rarely had ailments. I was a very healthy specimen. But I did, from time to time, need . . . you know. At Sug, the more brazen girls would ask for the Other Cupboard *out loud*, when even whispering to Rayment in private seemed to me too daunting for words.

Mortifyingly, my first frightful row was Other Cupboard-related. Cath had clocked me sneaking my one sanitary belt into the dressing table during Unpacking of Trunks, and helpfully informed me that if I had the curse I could be off gym and off Games. There was a relevant piece of squared paper on the noticeboard in the Covered Way. All you had to do was put a cross against your name. You didn't have to say you couldn't do Games because . . . you know. What a relief! But I had not taken Bretch into account.

Now, Bretch seemed as much part of Ridley's fixtures and fittings as the bedsteads and washbasins, but hadn't actually been its House mistress that long, so I think when I was given the two filthiest rows I have ever been given, she was still finding her way into her style somewhat. I was a learning opportunity. Always pleased to help.

Bretch's predecessor, until 1957, was a lady called Miss Hoskin, or 'Hossy', as she was generally known. Hossy had been at Felixstowe since the beginning of time – before that, even, since she had been on the staff of the not-very-successful private school that begat Felixstowe College. Hossy taught Biology and was much loved. But then came the day of the huge drama, the morning that Jonah thumped into Chapel and made the sensational announcement that Hossy had died during the night. Everyone gasped with horror and sadness and then someone giggled, and the giggling spread from pew to pew while Jonah glared at them in majestic disapproval, though she never referred to this shocking breach afterwards, probably deciding it would just set everybody off in hysterics again.

At the time of Hossy's death, Bretch was assistant House mistress of Ridley. She taught Pitman's Shorthand & Book-keeping, and was very good at it – although cross-eyed she could spot a 'which' instead of a 'should' stroke from the other side of the room. Current Events was another of her subjects. This was usually the first lesson after break, which meant everyone would bolt down their milk and breaktime bun, then rush to the library to thumb through the *East Anglian*

*Daily Times* for some suitable talking point, such as the serial tractor arsonist in Norfolk. She ran the tuck shop, too. This had recently been set up in the garage belonging to Hooper, the Upper Sixth House. It was open on Saturday mornings, the day our pocket money was dished out. As well as sweets and crisps, the tuck shop sold stamps, pens, postcards, writing paper and envelopes. Bretch was also in charge of Careers Advice. For those not going to university, the options seemed to have boiled down to nursing or teaching, or to take a secretarial course. After all, she wasn't doing too badly out of it, because now, on top of everything else, Jonah made her Ridley's new House mistress.

She was an Old Girl, having gone through the school during wartime, leaving it briefly for a spell at secretarial college, then returning as a member of staff. That nickname, for instance: Bridget because her name's Bridget and the fact she's a wretch. Wouldn't you have got rid of it the moment you left? Bretch hung on to it. She was sardonic about it, amused almost. The school was her life. She hadn't had much experience of what it was like outside the walls. I mean, tall, stiff, fuzzy hair, bottle-thick glasses – no way was she ever going to get asked to dance. Though we obviously sniggered like mad about her supposed *tendresse* for Dan Dan The Boilerman. Dan Dan wore a flat cap and was short and old. He arrived at Ridley early every day in his three-wheeler van, parking it in front of the Covered Way before disappearing down the corner steps. What on earth did he do in there all day? We never saw him leave.

Bretch wasn't unlikeable. In fact, she was the best of the House mistresses, and we were all jolly glad we were in

Ridley, when the alternatives were Latimer's witchy Cawley or Tyndale's moody Maggie, or being in Cranmer where Jonah lived, overshadowing all like a giant meteorite. Cranmer did have a House mistress, but she was a pallid shape in comparison, a sop to convention who never stayed long. Every year came a new Mrs Thing whom no one remembered once she had scuttled off into the far yonder, except possibly for the one who wore flip-flops even in winter. And another because she was really big and her name was Mrs Bullock.

Yes, we liked Bretch, but naturally she was the enemy. She was famed for her eavesdropping. Her inadequate eyesight was compensated for by hearing that could pick up the love song of a bat, and she'd creep around and listen at doors. You'd get up to go to cab and – *aaaagh!* Bretch is outside! You could tell, even from a distance, when she was listening in – she would be standing very still, like a heron, on one leg. Fishing. If you were up to no good, the only warning that you were about to be rumbled was that her shoes creaked.

But in the year below ours were some of the naughtiest girls in the whole of Ridley. It was pranks, pranks, pranks all day and night where Annie and her chums were concerned: they followed up one midnight feast by sleeping in the baths; they shinned up the scaffolding that was the exoskeleton of the new music school that was going up behind the chapel; they stole Bretch's glasses *from her bedside table while she slept.* And one term they were in the seven-dorm, which was a very nice suite on the southeast corner of the house, with five beds in the main part and two more down a little step and overlooking the orchard. It always caught the sun. One of these naughty girls was wizard at Science and she put her studies to good purpose by designing the 'Bretch trap'. The girls made it out of two pieces of cardboard with silver paper on them and two wires, which they slid under the lino and threaded between the cracks in the floorboards, and on the end of each wire was a warning light that came on when Bretch was standing outside the door.

She lacked maternal instinct the way some people lack wisdom teeth, although there were attempts at being mumsily affectionate that didn't quite work out. Once she walked into the dorm where an unclad Gill was trying to scrub mud off herself after Games, and exclaimed, 'Gill, you are a dirty little girl!' which probably came out of knee-jerk embarrassment (Oh gosh! Girl! Naked!) but didn't go down well with a self-conscious thirteen-year-old. But she tried. Noticing that Marlee was always being left out of things, Bretch told Prue and Della they had to be friends with her. So they were a threesome sometimes, but Prue and Della didn't like it very much.

Nothing cosy about her, of course. No woman friends. At least Cawley and Maggie had each other. Bretch's chums were her prefects. At first I thought how sad that was. Thinking about it now, I'm not sure I'd reach the same conclusion. As mistress of Ridley, 'the grandest house in the place', she was in her element – top girl, leader of the pack – surrounded by the prefects who were her chosen subordinates. Together they made a very strong fighting unit, as I was soon to find out.

Our whole lives as juniors seemed like one big struggle against the prefects. We had a Head of House, a House Games captain, and two more girls who didn't have specific job titles but were sort of Prefects Without Portfolio, so I guess were just there to bawl, 'Will you stop making that disgusting noise!' when you were laughing. Della's big sister was in Lower Six. She was lovely, really nice, so of course she couldn't possibly be made a prefect. You could tell who the prefects were even without those little red badges they were permitted to wear. They looked prefect-y. Their hair was properly done, their sausage curls stayed circular and springy, and the collars of their grey afternoon dresses were never hanging off. And they licked their lips when they spotted a junior.

Shoe-cleaning. Friday after supper. What a chore! Indoor shoes, outdoor shoes, Sunday shoes, hockey boots, gym shoes, jodhpur boots. And when you finished you had to take them to one of these harpies to be passed, and you could have the teensiest speck on a toecap, almost invisible to the human eye, and she'd say, 'No! Take it back and do it again!' What beastly girls they were.

Chrissie's mouth turned down when she was trying desperately not to cry, because she was being told off so savagely. 'And don't sulk!' they'd snap. 'Stop sulking! Report to Bretch!' So then she'd have to go to Bretch, who'd tell her off for sulking, and her mouth would turn down again because she was trying not to cry. She just couldn't win.

The prospectus had misled us, you see. 'Under the prefect system,' it lied, 'the elder girls acquire self-reliance and responsibility, and a spirit of service, gentle courtesy and loyalty is inculcated in all.'

Twaddle, especially the gentle courtesy bit. You only had to meet Deirdre, the complete rotter to whom I alluded briefly when I was talking about the Davy. Deirdre had specs, spots, pudgy cheeks and a gigantic bust that jiggled when she thundered down the flank in hockey. You had to flatten yourself against the wall when she passed, partly because she was a goddess on Mount Olympus but also because you might get a sideswipe from that awful bosom. But it wasn't only Deirdre. They all seemed awfully grown-up and intimidating. They liked being in power, because they'd obviously been intimidated in previous years and were getting their own back. It was a case of 'girl hands on misery to girl'.

A week into my first term, I was swinging up the Covered Way in my grey afternoon dress when Bretch, with her phalanx of prefects behind her, manifested in the corridor.

'Why aren't you at Games?'

I was speechless. One never, ever, mentioned one's period. The nearest my mother could bring herself to refer to it was 'a little visitor'.

'I'm ... off Games,' I muttered.

'Why?'

Bretch was a woman who had gone through school looking like a human lavatory brush. It had put steel into her core and now it was payback time.

'I've ... started.' (You can take it from me this was said in the vocal equivalent of 6pt type.)

'So? That's no reason to put yourself off Games.'

'But Cath told me if you were, if you, you know, if ...' I wanted to die.

'Does Cath make the rules in this House?'

I've dropped Cath in it now. She may never speak to me again.

'Come into the kitchen.'

The kitchen doubled as Bretch's training quarters. It was where she coached her new batch of prefects in how to skewer juniors and make them cry. I trooped in there behind Bretch and her battalion, visibly vibrating with fear. Time has obliterated the memory of the row I got, but I do know I left shattered and sobbing.

The bigger row followed two weeks later. It was that damn guitar that started it. I took it from its resting place on top of the lockers and found the bridge had been detached and the strings hung loose. Someone had tampered with it, possibly to bring a halt to my renditions of 'Michael Row the Boat Ashore', which was the only thing I could play.

'I expect it was an accident,' Bretch said chillingly, probably because she couldn't be bothered to play 'hunt the guitar tamperer' on top of everything else she had to do.

Injustice! Injustice!

'Look! Look! Can't you see it's been deliberately done!'

'Go and wait outside my room,' she said, in a terrible voice.

'Danny, you mustn't be so rude,' cried Erica, after Bretch had sailed out.

What a shock! I thought everyone would applaud me for standing up to the old bat. Now the fallout was reverberating from both ends of the house, with me sobbing in the junior commie and Bretch venting to her prefects in the Sixth Form commie: 'She was SO rude!'

I trudged up the Covered Way and stood, knees going like castanets, outside Bretch's sitting room. I could hear all the prefects squawking in empathic indignation next door. Deirdre was fabricating a story about me shouting at my pony during Riding.

The pony, Huntsman, was an obstinate brown gelding who never got out of a trot. His favourite activity was to stop halfway through a ride and luxuriate in a long, noisy pee. You'd just have to sit there, trying to look ladylike, while the clouds of steam rose around you. Apparently I had shouted at Huntsman, who was refusing to move.

'Well, of course,' Deirdre declared complacently, 'I just said, "Go on, Huntsman," and he moved off immediately.' More injustice! I never! She never! This did not happen!

Bretch eventually emerged from this coven of young witches. I followed her into her sitting room and stared at the carpet, which was the colour of custard creams.

'P– p– please, Miss Cross, I'm sorry I was so rude.' Then I sobbed and sobbed and agreed that it was an accident (it wasn't! it wasn't!) and Bretch parped on at me for about 500 years while I thought about raising the issue of the prefect who had lied about my shouting at the pony, but decided I preferred to stay alive. Look what happened when you told the truth. It was far more important to shut up and obey the rules.

# 10

# WEIRD AND WONDERFUL RULES

There were so *many* rules. Life at Felixstowe College was regimented. I suspect this was deliberate, so you didn't have time to think. Because if you thought about it you would have to wonder why the school had so many weird and wonderful rules, and that would use up time better spent doing all the things you had to do because life was regimented. Sukie said she'd lie in her Latimer bed, on her mattress with a dip in it that probably hadn't been turned for year, just breathing. 'No one's going to tell me what to do till the bell goes in the morning.' Phew.

Oh God, those rules. Number one was that you weren't allowed to go to the college if you lived within ten miles of Ipswich. I've no idea why – perhaps there was deemed to be something especially plebeian about Ipswich. There was also a rule about what you could be called. Even if you hated your first name and had always been known by your middle name, it was your first name that had to be used. Jonah never bothered with given names at all. She just called us by our surnames. 'Welch! What are you doing?'

Another rule was about exeats. The dictionary definition

is 'permission from a college or boarding school for a temporary absence', and three times a term we were allowed to go out with our parents, or a friend's parents. On Saturdays, exeats were allowed after Morning Prep and on Sundays after Morning Service, and the rule was that you had to write to your parents (or your friend's parents) the next day to thank them, even though you had seen them only twenty-four hours previously. I can see that rule made sense, because it trained us to write thank-you letters, and I still do that because, as well as showing good manners, which gives you a feeling of self-satisfaction, they add a tiny amount to the happiness of the recipient, because who doesn't appreciate the fact that someone has taken the trouble to find a pen and paper and envelope and stamp?

But to have a rule about condiments? What was that all about? Why, if you wanted salt with your meal, could you not ask your neighbour to pass it to you? You'd have to say, 'Would you like salt?' and she was meant to reply, 'No, would you?' but often she forgot the 'would you?' bit of the exchange and you'd just have to go without. We were the Young Ladies of Felixstowe College, and correct etiquette was more important than food actually tasting of something.

There were rules about the number of baths you could take per week (three), and sitting on radiators. Not allowed because they caused piles. What were piles? Some juniors didn't know. They thought they were ridges on one's bottom. Washing your own hair wasn't allowed, either. Some tried, but there was more chance of escaping over the Berlin Wall. No one could hear you fill up the basin, but the water would take a suspiciously long while to drain away. Just before my time, there was a matron who had a lisp. At fire practice she would stand at the top of one of the two staircases in Tyndale, flapping a red cloth and crying, 'I'm the fire, I'm the fire, go down the other thtairth!' Anyway, Lispy Matron couldn't see very well but, as with Bretch, her hearing was compensatorily excellent. She would patrol the corridors, listening for the sound of running water, and pounce. The evidence couldn't be hidden. Wet hair. The girl and her wet hair would have to stand in the corner. 'You are vey, vey naughty. Thith uthed to be Felixstowe LADIETH College but that title went when LADIETH went.'

Our hair had to be washed for us in a ceremony called 'wigging', which happened once a fortnight, or weekly if you had greasy hair, but who wanted to admit to that? Wigging took place by the clock tower above the library, in three small attic rooms. They had once been the sleeping quarters of the Cobbold dynasty's grooms and stable lads, because in days of yore the library had been Cranmer's stable block, and stifling, airless rooms that had once ponged of horse and reverberated with stable lads' snores and farts now smelt of shampoo and lacquer and hummed with the sound of giant standing driers.

Those poor women who had to wash hair all day long! Their fingers were red and swollen, their eyes haunted, their own hair lank with steam. One of the women hurt more than the other. She would push your head forward, drench it with hot water, sometimes much too hot, then scour and scrub, then drag out the tangles. Next came the rollers. Drag, drag, drag again, yank, yank, painfully tight. Pins jabbing into your scalp. Then you'd be shoved under a boiling hot drier and left to bake. You would emerge a red and shiny-faced thing with sausage curls and have to walk through the library, the focus of everyone's stares, to get back to the classroom. It was known as The Walk of Shame.

Was there a book of rules? Where was it kept? To this day, I've no idea whether they were written down somewhere, whether there was an actual Felixstowe version of Magna Carta, in quill pen, on vellum, enshrined. My hunch is that they were all stored in some invisible filing cabinet, the one in Jonah's head, where they could be added to as and when, on an ad hoc basis. There's evidence. According to one Old Girl I spoke to, 'She told my mother she thought the rules were fairly foolproof but she'd had to fill in a few loopholes the girls had found.'

Even lovely House Tea had rules. These concerned spreads. Marmite and peanut butter were permitted, and Heinz Sandwich Spread, but not Bovril and Nutella. Nor were you allowed to share your spread with anyone else. Bretch did not leave it at that. She had something against marmalade. Marmalade with your tea was out of the question, because in Bretch's opinion, which was the one that counted, *it wasn't jam*. Della was outraged. She organised a petition and took it to Jonah, who said, 'Miss Cross is just being stupid. Of course marmalade is jam – orange jam.'

There were various other banned items and activities, of course. Plimsolls with black soles. Mules (they were sluttish). Babydoll pyjamas (*Lolita* connotations). All jewellery except crucifixes, and all crucifixes in the shape of the Celtic cross. Watching *That Was The Week That Was* (it was said to be provocative). And in the 1930s, when the school was under the control of a dragon called Miss Clarke, no sweets were allowed. Nor were cakes, except at birthdays, and birthday cakes – 'which may be sent or provided locally' – were subject to a subset of rules. Even when Miss Clarke was long gone, a cake meant a cake. Meringues did not qualify. Janet Copland, an utterly wonderful Old Girl who joined Felixstowe in 1951, once ordered half-a-dozen meringues. On her end of term report, Jonah wrote: 'I consider her behaviour at her birthday party was disgraceful.' Janet's father sent back the report, with the comment, 'I don't consider her behaviour disgraceful. Disgraceful is having strange men in your room. Half a dozen meringues isn't disgraceful.' The report came back with 'disgraceful' changed to 'unfortunate'.

This is one of my favourite stories about Jonah and her rules, along with one told to me by another super Old Girl, Alison Ferry, who went to Felixstowe in the late 1950s – we overlapped by a year or so. Alison was in Tyndale, where Maggie always vetted the letters received and checked those sent. When Alison and her friend Hermione were about thirteen or fourteen, they were crazy about Elvis and, on seeing an advertisement for his fan club, decided to join. On receipt of a self-addressed stamped envelope, the fan club would return signed photos and information about the club. What a good idea, thought Alison and Hermione, and no one would know who the letter was from if they sent the envelope themselves. How wrong they were. The letter arrived with a rubber stamp all over it saying 'Elvis Presley Fan Club'.

Maggie was furious and called them both into her study for a dressing down. 'I'm sending the letter to Miss Jones and she'll be seeing you in due course.' Sure enough, the summons came and Alison and Hermione trooped into Jonah's study in Cranmer.

'Why did you do this?'

Contrite mumbling.

'Young ladies don't do that sort of thing.' Blah blah blah. Jonah took the letter off the desk and opened it in front of them. Out fell two signed photos. She picked them up and very slowly and carefully tore them both into shreds in front of them. 'That's the end of the matter.'

While the school banned some things, they made others compulsory. At least twice a year, each of us had to attend a celebrity concert. Celebrity concerts were held at the Spa Pavilion on the seafront and known as 'celebs'. The arrangement worked two ways. Our presence bulked out what would otherwise have been a rather meagre audience, and our parents could reassure themselves that we were exposed to a regular dose of culture. Not that most of us appreciated it at the time. Parents were charged £2 per ticket and certainly in my case it wasn't money well spent.

The notice went up on Ridley noticeboard: 'Who wants to go?' Only Helen. She went to every single one. It was such an antidote to being incarcerated, she said – a mental, physical and emotional escape. But Helen was truly musical; her sister was the best keyboardist in the history of the school, and her mother was a pianist ('I play fistfuls of wrong notes but I make them all sound nice.'). The family DNA was made up of breves and minims and demi-semiquavers joined together in a cadenza. My parents' idea of a concert was *The Black and White Minstrel Show.*

Having to sit passively through any kind of performance is

something I still find difficult and it would have been better all round, would have engaged me much more usefully, had I been given the job of describing the experience, making it real for people who weren't there, painting a word picture: walking along the seafront in the rain and dark while the waves slurped and hissed; the way the Spa Pavilion's entrance doors were at forty-five degrees, as though it were talking to the promenade out of the side of its mouth; how one of the madrigal quartet seemed to be suffering from a stomach upset and kept running off stage, trilling to the very last; how the Lower Fours would have aniseed ball races, rolling them down the auditorium floor. How we fled to cab in the intervals to eat sweets, and slept through Peter Pears singing French folk songs. Four bloody encores. How my bottom got so stiff that I rested my feet against the back of the seat in front. Then walking back to House, in the rain and dark again, with the Upper Fives lagging behind talking about various methods of smooching and the Lower Six shouting at us to hurry, and Erica telling Bretch I'd put my feet on the back of the seat, so that was another ticking off.

I think now of what we were exposed to. How privileged we were to hear the likes of Julian Bream, Gervase de Peyer, John Ogdon and all those other musicians at the beginning of their careers, who would go on to become fabled names. Instead, celebs were occasions of boredom and discomfort at the end of which would be a row. It was ages before I learned to love classical music. Shame on me.

What I find strange, now more than I did then, was the rule about books in the school library. Ours was wonderful, the most beautiful building in the school. As it had once been a stable yard, it was huge and roomy, with a parquet floor laid over the cobbles, and well-spaced tables and chairs made of pale wood and, instead of a ceiling, there was a glass dome, so above you was the firmament, filling the place with glorious light. Never was there a better place to engage a child in the joy of reading. You would have thought.

Gill was not particularly happy at home. She was the youngest of three, her father was a busy, much-loved local GP and her mother absorbed in building up her own life. What a nuisance Gill was, and Mummy wasn't nice to her at all. She was sarcastic, she put Gill down, and passed up no opportunity to tell Gill that of all her children she liked her the least.

Gill's sister was already at the school. This was no advantage. Elizabeth had already warned her about all the scary things and mad teachers before she arrived. She'd heard about petrifying Miss Cawley, and how you were made to play Games whatever the weather, and the rule about how you had to stand up in front of everybody in Chapel and read the lesson once a year. Whereas for other girls these ordeals would have come as an unexpected surprise, for Gill the full terror was already in place. What with that, and the nastiness from her mother, books were her means of escape. In her first week at Felixstowe she was getting stuck into a huge, bound Walter Scott when she was nabbed by a prefect.

'Upper Fours aren't allowed to touch books in the main school library.'

How could that ever be a good thing? It made no sense at all. It was one rule too many for Gill, and books were what kept her afloat. So she just ignored the prefects and doggedly went on, developing not only an enduring love for the works of Walter Scott but the skills essential to not being caught.

On the subject of getting caught, everybody said that the worst thing the powers that be could do to you was send you to Jonah, but this was an absolute misapprehension because Joanna actually received the cane once.

Joanna was already quite a personality when she first arrived at Felixstowe. She was the oldest of three sisters, and something of a proxy mum to them, because their parents had moved to Kenya, where their father had been offered the plum job of commanding the national air force. It was an opportunity not to be missed, but their mother was concerned that life there might be dangerous and the schools inadequate, so the girls were enrolled at Felixstowe College. It was expensive for three, and the RAF would only pay to fly the girls out to Kenya once a year, but at least the college was close to the Suffolk village in which their grandmother lived, and they could stay with her in the hols. But Nana was more interested in bridge than grandchildren, so the three girls were very close and Joanna was their leader and protector. She had to organise their uniforms, packing and exeats, and it was to her the two younger girls went when they had to choose their O Level subjects.

But one time, Mummy was going to be home, in Suffolk, and Joanna thought how nice it would be to speak to her. Tyndale, like all the other Houses, was equipped with a pay phone, above which was the rota. Calls could be made only between 6.00 p.m. and 10.00 p.m. on Sunday evenings, so Joanna wrote down her name and the time she wanted to make the call. She was very excited.

When it was her turn to use the phone, she rang the local exchange and asked for a reverse charge call, and the operator dialled her mother's number. And her mother picked up and said, 'Hello, hello?' and the operator said, 'Your daughter is calling from Felixstowe, will you accept the charge?' And Mummy said, 'No, sorry, tell her to ring later, I'm having a party.'

'That's mummies for you,' Joanna said philosophically, but there were also floods of tears.

Joanna was very bossy even before she arrived. Their brother was born when she was eleven and, as Mummy had to spend six months in hospital during the pregnancy, Joanna ran the household. She began to feel a bit above her station and thought the restrictions at school unjust. It was like being in prison.

Joanna's younger sisters were goody-goodies because they didn't want to get into the terrible scrapes that Joanna got herself into. She was rude to teachers. She skipped classes. She got the worst ever percentage in the school's history – two per cent in a Latin exam. She was threatened with expulsion once, when she was in Middle Five, because she talked to the gardener's boy. In the holidays, while Nana was playing bridge, Joanna and her sisters mixed with the village boys, so she was used to them and felt she could talk to any class of person. She never did anything but talk to him, on the walk to Cranmer from Tyndale. It was innocent. Of no import at all. But Jonah had her spies; she knew everything that went on.

She was caned in the gym once. On the bottom. She had to pull down her pants. Coulo the Games mistress did it. Coming out of the gym, all Joanna's friends were there, and they all gathered round her. She was shocked at the whole thing. It did hurt. But Joanna was thrilled as well as hurting because she was now a hero – all those hugs and *poor yous*! – because the braver you were, the more friends you had, and who wouldn't have wanted to be Joanna's friend? She was bold and capable and stout-hearted and optimistic. Everyone adored her, even Maggie. Especially Maggie, who made Joanna her Head of House when the time came.

She was a very conscientious Head of House. When her sister Rosie brought her shoes to be inspected after shoe-cleaning, they were deemed not up to scratch.

'But . . . but . . . but they're really clean!' protested Rosie.

'No! Go back! Do them again!'

It was a long time before Rosie forgave her, but the last thing Joanna wanted to do was show favouritism.

And Joanna went on to be a senior prefect. Jonah adored her too. She was made of the right stuff.

# 11

## MAD TEACHERS

Tampax was forbidden fruit. We had to wear sanitary towels, hitched on to those awful pink sanitary belts. The brand used by the school was Dr White's. They came in Size 1 and Size 2. You wouldn't want to be Size 2, would you? It was dismal enough to be clomping around with a horrid Size 1 squished under your white linings and grey bags, worried that it stuck out at the back, worried that everyone could see that you had the curse, that you'd got the gravy, that you were on the blob, unclean.

But *Honey* magazine regularly featured a small adver tisement for Tampax, with a photo of a motherly looking woman, Nurse Anne. Nurse Anne offered a dream of salva tion, because she invited you to send off for a free sample. I was volunteered by my fellow Ridleys and, when the sample arrived, I was marched to the first-floor bathroom to have a go while everybody stood behind the door asking how I was getting on. Not a success. We sent off for another sample. This time, Della stepped up to the plate.

'How are you getting on?' we asked from the corridor side of the bathroom door.

'It's interesting,' she said.

None of this was possible in Latimer. If Bretch knew what we were up to, and she knew most things, she would have turned one of her blind eyes, because Bretch was no control freak; she wasn't a woman who stopped you doing things just because she could. But Latimer's anti-Tampax laws were rigid. Miss Pipe, the matron, kept a register of STs to keep track of how many one used.

The sporty girls in particular hated wearing Dr White's because of those ridiculous, uncomfortable shorts that showed everything. But the mother of one girl was a nurse, very progressive, and her daughter was the only one of them who knew the facts of life. She brought Tampax back for her fellow Latimers to try. But Pipe, rootling around, found the cardboard applicators in the wapey and scurried away to tell Cawley. Who went ballistic.

She ordered the Tampax Seven into the common room, shut the door, turned the television off, and screeched and screeched and screeched about the health hazards of tampons. They were to use them under no circumstances! Didn't they realise they could wreck their virginity? And if one got stuck inside they'd have to have major surgery to have it removed!

Mad. But when you're in your teens most of your teachers seem mad. Well, they did in our day. We drove them that way. How easily would any woman deal with rows of beady-eyed girls who almost without exception despise you for your wispy hair, deplorable dress sense and absence of sex life and/ or putative lesbianism, every day for what seems like eternity, while delivering the same lesson on William Pitt the Younger or seeds and plants that you gave last year, last decade, and would give every subsequent year until you retired, the sum total of your life's work a *valete* in the school mag? Not surprising if some of them went a bit round the bend. Most of us were too young to realise their humanity. And I've ended up torn between letting rip and not having the heart to make them figures of fun.

On the other hand, mad teachers are so, so funny, and I'm afraid my Dark Side has prevailed. A weird kind of loyalty stops me from expounding on the slightly batty nervous mannerisms exhibited by several of our teachers, but I think it was Boris Johnson who, on the topic of cake, said he was in favour of having it and eating it. A quick straw poll among friends who attended similar schools in the same era as I did produced gems.

Miss Bang. Dandruff the size of sixpences. She chomped.

Miss Milner, a rather eccentric Latin teacher who wore purple clothes. She broke her leg roller-skating and slipped under the great high desk and everyone stood around watching her struggling to get out. It was a long time before anyone said, 'We'd better help her.'

Miss Dawes. Her pupils spent a long time trying to destroy her. She had a breakdown in the class – screaming, ranting, raving, blubbing, carrying on.

Miss Bickersteth, known as Beak. More than a little odd, especially about sex. Every Sunday night she would read her girls Elizabeth Goudge and pass over a few pages: 'I don't think we'll read that.' Sex just didn't exist. She had a dog, Misty, and she used to take it for a walk round the boundaries, hunting for sweet wrappers like truffles. If she found one, all the girls would be kept inside, while she'd tell them all about the walk. 'Ooh, I saw two rabbits this morning, they were doing some silly things together.'

Mrs C had diabolical halitosis and, when demonstrating the sentence, '*La gomme est dans la bouche*,' would take some poor girl's rubber and put it in her mouth, then hand it back covered in foul-smelling saliva. She hated girls rocking in their chairs and would make them stand with hands on heads reciting French verbs.

A cookery teacher who lasted for about a month before the powers that be realised she was totally bonkers. They didn't cook anything. Every class she gave, she had everyone scrubbing ovens, floors, walls, absolutely everything. The school only realised she was nuts when she had the girls sat out on the second-floor windowsills scrubbing the glass and bricks outside with bleach.

Mad Murgatroyd, a Head of Latin, who was one of those rather sad maiden ladies who wandered around talking to herself.

A French teacher, M'mselle B, who lived with the Geography teacher Miss D and who used to throw chalk or even the blackboard cleaner.

Also on the staff was a Maths teacher who had a first from Cambridge but couldn't teach to save her life. She had appalling B.O. and was mercilessly tortured and teased. She never really recovered from the time the swimming pool was pouring smoke, as it was on fire (really), and she told the girls not to be ridiculous when they pointed this out and couldn't they tell the difference between smoke and steam? She disappeared soon afterwards with a nervous breakdown.

Even so, in a competition for mad teachers, there could be only one winner. Cawley was a different class of bonkers. Seriously. Absolutely stark staring. We thought so, anyway. The Chemmy lab was in a separate building next to the Bilge lab, and though it looked harmless enough from the outside it should have had a warning whiff of sulphur emanating from it, because this was Cawley's lair, her cave.

She kept that lab immaculate. Spotless benches, gas taps, Bunsen burners, sinks, fume cupboard, an enormous copy of the periodic table. Everything labelled, in the correct position, and laid out specifically. Racks of clean test tubes. Clean lab coats, white, hanging on the coat rack. Then she'd have some kind of brainstorm and lay waste to it, throwing test tubes and Bunsen burners all over the place, and send you scurrying out of the lab with equipment flying after you and crashing on the ground. Glass splinters everywhere.

It wouldn't have been so bad had she confined herself to the lab, because then you could have easily avoided her, but she was ubiquitous. She prowled, holding her books close. Very determined, slightly hunched. Smart clothes, a groomed hair-style – white hair, impeccably 'done'. A frightening woman with cutting words and looks, poking her nose in, giving us the death stare. She caught us talking in cab at break once and made Cherry write down everyone's names. Another time she was haunting our form room after French for some reason and wouldn't let me get my wigging towel. What business was it of hers? As for being a Latimer, well.

*The girls in this House have been told repeatedly that they must not have evening baths, unless they are down on the list, without special permission. The girl who took a bath without permission this evening will not be allowed to have any more evening baths this term.*

What makes it all the more peculiar is that she doesn't seem to have always been like that. Not quite as awful, anyway. Her first manifestation, when she arrived to teach towards the end of the war, was more Joyce Grenfell than Wicked Witch of the West. A little while ago, I met a charming Old Girl of that era, Penny Grossett, who remembers how the newly employed Cawley announced herself with a notice pinned up on the board: Who wants to go blackberrying?

Penny got on with her. Other girls were terrified but she was kind to Penny. Once, Penny came back from the San, still weepy, so Cawley sent her to bed and lent her a book, *Her Good Grace* by Elizabeth Goudge; Penny loved Goudge's books after that. In Penny's last term, when she was taking Oxbridge entrance, Cawley gave up her bedroom to her and bedded down in her sitting room. Though it must be added that when Penny thanked her, Cawley said gruffly, 'Jonah told me to do it.' Heaven forbid that anyone mistake her for someone nice.

It sounds as though she was reasonably normal back then, though. Normal for Felixstowe, anyway. I was riveted by a school photo that had been taken on Cranmer lawn in 1949, only a couple of years after the school had returned from its exile in Norfolk during the war. There, next to Miss Pipe, is a strikingly attractive young woman in a clingy jersey dress, her confident expression and pugnaciously squared jaw softened by thick, wavy, shoulder-length hair. This was someone who knew how to dress, even in Austerity Britain. Was that Cawley? Really?

Somewhere along the line, things must have gone a bit wonky. In those early years, she liked to play the piano. The girls would be in the dorm, lying in bed, and the Warsaw Concerto would start up. It was noisy but jolly good. Before the war, Cawley had been out there. She was obviously letting herself go. Speculation did the rounds. She had supposedly 'lost her fiancé in the war'. We conjectured. Just how had she lost him? Had he been killed? Had she, you know, *given* herself to him, and the chap then scarpered?

But poor Latimers. People in different Houses didn't know their luck. All the other House mistresses were tame in comparison. She was the most unsuitable woman you could possibly imagine to be in charge of between forty and fifty impressionable teenagers. Liz Bruce, a Latimer in Joanna's year, emailed me from Australia.

'Not a good choice for a House mistress. She really had everyone extremely anxious and nerve-ridden at all times. She was unpredictable – vicious at times and then delightful at others. One moment she would be putting her arm round you and the next she would be giving you a rather vicious pinch. She had some stomach problem. We were told part of her stomach had been removed and she couldn't eat seeds. Hence we weren't allowed to give her raspberries as a present. Not that I had any intention of giving the old bat a present anyway.

'She also had her favourites – poor Georgie was one. She became House captain, which we all knew about from even the beginning of school. I don't think Georgie revelled in her popularity with Cawley at all. Anyone who was vaguely intelligent was almost forced into doing Chemistry – out of the ten of us Latimers in Lower Six I would say more than half took it at A Level.' Liz was one of them. And she hated Chemistry.

Also, Cawley was High Church. According to the tradition laid down by the school's founders, the place was Low Church, so this must have been bloody-mindedness and a way of making herself conspicuous. In Chapel, the choir would look down from the choir stalls and wait during the Creed for 'In the name of the Father, Son and Holy Ghost', which was the cue for Cawley and Maggie – who would never have done such a daring thing on her own, but who was in Cawley's thrall – to cross themselves. We'd never seen that before. And on one occasion Liz got called into her room and berated, as her parents had taken her on exeat to St Andrews, Felixstowe. 'St Andrews is fundamentalist!' screeched Cawley.

Another Latimer who responded to my round-robin appeal for informants was Sue Robinson, who was in the same year as Liz. Sue was a lovely looking and serious-minded girl who joined in Middle Five, when she was fourteen. Her parents were based in Aden, where her father was in Air Sea Rescue. A cherished only child who was used to her own room and her own space, she was now having to sleep on a squeaky bed with a concave mattress. She was very tearful at first, cried at the drop of a hat. Hugely unhappy. Somebody noticed she ate left-handed. She was made to sit in one place, wear a bib, and forced to eat right-handed. The humiliation was astonishing. All around, people laughing at the fact she was pebbledashing herself with food.

The only upside was that Cawley was so nasty it made everyone kind to each other. They all vowed they were never going to treat young people that way, ever, when they grew up. Or old people, either. She bullied Pipe horribly. Squawked at her. It got some girls crying, just listening to Cawley absolutely going for her matron. She was *foul*. And that poor woman would just look cowed and scuttle off to her room next to the Other Cupboard.

She lurked round corners. She snooped. Both women, she and Pipe, kept cats, black ones with white paws. Chut'n and Pickles were believed to join in the snooping, like witches' familiars. Everything was peered into or under – cupboards, pillows, drawers, mattresses. She opened post, opened parcels, made random decisions about phone calls to girls from outside. Her room, to the right of the front door, was a homage to chintz. On a magnanimous day, she would invite people in and chat, but it was almost always chemists. These, her favourites, were allowed to take more calls than everyone else. They'd get the screech down the corridor as a summons. 'Come 'ere!' And then Cawley would sit there and listen in.

Why did she have to be like that? It wasn't as if they ever did anything naughty. Well, hardly ever. She had a rota of girls who ran errands for her. Fagging, basically. Going to and fro with the tea tray, feeding the cats, having to get up early to make her breakfast. She was exacting. She had mustard with her sausages and it had to be freshly made from powder. One term the girls who were on breakfast duty mixed the mustard powder with spit instead of water. They also had to make Cawley's birthday cake that year. One girl cut her toenails into the mix and then the others all spat in it in turn.

The rest of us felt very sorry for the Latimers. What a madhouse it all sounded. Thank heavens we didn't have to live in it. But there was one thing none of us were able to escape – The Cawley Table.

# 12

## SCHOOL DINNERS

One thing I must say before I start is that school dinners were never called that. In fact, dinner as such didn't exist. We had breakfast, lunch, tea and supper. When we Ridleys reached Middle Five, we were joined by a very nice new girl, Gwen. Gwen had previously attended a state school where such distinctions did not hold, and on her very first day she made the mistake of asking Bretch, 'What time's dinner?' which shocked Bretch so much her hair would have stood on end if it hadn't been standing on end already. 'You don't say dinner, you say lunch,' Bretch explained, after she had recovered from her swoon.

My first meal at school was supper, and jolly good fun it was too, because it was the first night of term and we were allowed to sit anywhere we wanted, and there was only one thing I had to secretly drop on the floor because it was so disgusting. But the next day was different. It was a Monday, and Monday was the day of table picking.

What happened at table picking was after morning lessons you would walk over to the dining room. At the door would be two prefects, one armed with a sheaf of cardboard squares, on which

131

a letter and number had been inked, and the other to act as an enforcer. The enforcer was necessary because the letter denoted the member of staff at whose table you were to eat that week, and the number would tell you your placement, and what sort of week you were going to have, because every day you moved along a place until you sat next to the teacher at head of the table.

The M card wasn't great. It meant you were on the table headed by Miss Maggie Macartney. But N, the next table along, was the dreaded one, The Table of Death, the ruination of your entire week, because N meant Cawley, and you had to make conversation with her. Because if you didn't she would stand up when the meal was finished and address the whole dining room: 'This girl on my right has not uttered a single word this lunchtime.'

One week Helen was on The Cawley Table and, when it was her turn to sit next to the mad old bag, she asked her, 'Do you prepare *all* your lessons, Miss Cawley?'

'What?' Cawley screeched. 'Miss Macartney, did you hear what this girl said?'

And Lindy was on The Cawley Table when her salad had a caterpillar in it, huge and green with a red stripe and still alive, trampolining across the lettuce. Lindy was doubly terrified. A caterpillar *and* Miss Cawley! She managed to get the caterpillar on to the table and then on to the floor, and then spent the rest of lunch holding her feet up. And the worst thing of all was if your cardboard square said N1 or N13, because that was the place either side of her, and you would have to *talk to her twice*, once at the start of the week and again at the end. Every Monday girls were running among their friends saying, 'Please, please will you swap?' And the cold, dead eyes of the enforcer prefect would alight on them, and make sure they submitted to their fate.

In 1963, Gill, the Walter Scott enthusiast, was halfway through her first term in Lower Five when the school was told that the Oxford Board of Examiners was thinking of bringing O Levels forward. Girls were going to have to decide their O Level subjects then and there, rather than at the end of the school year. It so happened that only a few days previously Gill had been sitting on the steps outside the Chemmy lab and Cawley, enraged at this act of trespass, hit her with the lab doors by throwing them open on to her back. So that clinched it for Gill: Chemmy to be dropped at the earliest opportunity. Then, the very next day, the Lower Fives were told they had to choose their O Level subjects early, and Gill nixed Chemmy, but she had to sit next to Cawley at lunch.

Cawley started the conversation straight after Jonah had finished saying Grace. 'I'm going to get two scientists out of Ridley Middle Five.'

'Yes, Miss Cawley.'

'Don't you want to know who they are?'

'Yes, Miss Cawley.'

'You and Rosemary.'

Cawley had no idea. Gill never spoke up. God no. Would you have done?

I used to pretend that school dinners were vile, Cawley or no Cawley, but I didn't really mean it. Well, some of it was quite edible and, considering she was having to feed 300 people three meals a day, seven days a week, Mrs Kahn did us well. The prospectus called her 'the nutritionist', but she was much more involved that that. The school kitchens were large and had a hatch where the food would be passed on to trolleys, which would then be wheeled into the dining room. If you looked in you'd see bustling women and steam, and hear clatter, and Mrs Kahn would always be in the thick of it.

She was small and old, with dyed yellow hair and yellow, nicotined fingers. Very, very witchy, always with a fag in her mouth, and she muttered and limped, and had a twisted leg. Out at the back, next to the kitchens, were some store rooms and the room where she lived. There was a covered walkway, like half a courtyard, leading to these rooms, and then a gate to the drive. It was where the deliveries came and where the fire escape began. She was often seen pacing from her room to the kitchen and back, or to the stores, dressed in her white overalls, with a bunch of keys clanking at her side. The rumour was she had been the cook in a concentration camp. We would say the most terrible things about some of the bits and bobs we found in her stews and rissoles. One of her signature dishes was jugged hare, which always yielded an above average supply of teeth and hairy stuff for comment

You were allowed to be 'off' three things, and these had to be in writing. A lot of people avoided the so-called scrambled egg, which was actually reconstituted out of powder and sat in a brick in a puddle. Or the fluorescent haddock, which was so dyed and overcooked it flopped on your plate like a single Marigold glove. Della was off liver, roes on toast (very tasty, in my opinion) and milk. But one day she was caught by surprise in the form of Eggs Florentine – a new departure for Mrs Kahn. It had been in the oven for hours. The spinach was black and the eggs were like jelly on top, with crispy bits. Everyone had to eat it because we weren't off it, because we didn't know Eggs Florentine was a thing. Della threw up afterwards. Probably out of sheer willpower.

But Mrs Kahn's homemade sausages were delicious, and so were her puddings, especially the apple crumble and the steamed chocolate sponge with chocolate sauce. Sometimes we got chocolate sauce to pour over our ice cream, too, and that was just heaven. The liver would occasionally have pipes sticking out of it, but it came with lovely oniony gravy, and we had proper chips and real kippers, and sometimes roast chicken . . . if it *was* chicken. The pieces were awfully big. And chewy. We spotted Mrs Kahn once when we were out riding, and she was moving very purposefully, in her outsize ortho-paedic shoes, along the clifftop, armed with a giant carrier bag. What was she doing out there? Was she clubbing seagulls?

Nobody liked the spam fritters, and you had to be very greedy to eat them. Karen was very greedy. She was Ridley's assistant matron, though not for long. She was young. She had long, tangled dark hair, and wore hairy black jerseys and baggy cotton skirts. Where did she spring from? How could the school have employed someone as exciting as her? Matrons weren't like that. They were either kind, motherly types, like our Miss Rayment, or gorgons like Miss Poulson of Tyndale.

Poulson was squat and squinty, humpbacked and stoopy, and she smelt of Algipan. Her cure for everything was a double Anadin. She went round all the dorms at night, making sure the curtains were closed, because if girls were prancing around people could see. She used to shout at them from the other end of the corridor. She popped up in the bathroom once when Joanna was in the bath. 'I don't believe it! It's you again! It's not your turn to be in the bath!' and tried to haul Joanna out. And she wouldn't let anybody go to cab after Lights Out. She would wait in the corridor, in darkness, to catch you out. It got so bad that the greatest dare was to go in the washbasin. One night, Joanna's sister Rosie bravely tiptoed into the corridor, at which came a scary, nasal voice: 'Who's that? What are you doing?' So embarrassing. Now the whole House knew that Rosie was going to cab.

But here in Ridley we suddenly had this amazing Karen creature who, instead of taking Lights, would sit on the ends of our beds, telling us about her boyfriend Derek and the Ban the Bomb marches she went on, and how she was an atheist, and what French kissing was, and how she sometimes went around with no knickers on. I thought she was brilliant, the most exciting thing ever to happen in Ridley. But Karen was greedy because she was eating for two and, one night, spam fritters were on the menu at supper and she ate the lot and then rushed out into Cranmer gardens and threw up over the tamarisks, so that was Karen sacked.

Even more thrilling than Karen barfing over the tamarisks was the day Rosie found The Body On The Beach. Rosie was very self-effacing. She once nearly choked on a sausage skin at lunch and nobody noticed because she was such a quiet little thing. Rosie had arrived for breakfast early and, as no one else was around, she decided to walk in Cranmer garden. She looked at the beach and there it was. A woman who had drowned herself, it transpired. Rosie never got any credit for spotting the woman. As soon as she saw her she ran back into Cranmer and told another girl, and the other girl hogged all the limelight.

# 13

# LESSONS

I discovered the school part of school wasn't too bad – most of the time, anyway. There was, however, one 35-minute spell of gibbering fear every week, which was Chemmy with Cawley, and Scripture could be nerve-wracking if Maggie was in one of her moods. But I liked being able to walk to class without having to spend an hour on the tube first, and we must have all made a splendid picture, hurrying from breakfast to Morning Prayers and then our classrooms, hugging the sides of our zip-free cloaks together against the northeast wind, like people in a costume drama.

The school day was different to what I'd been used to as a Day Girl. In the morning were six lessons, four before break and two after, and then we went to Cranmer for lunch. Then, instead of more lessons, we had Games. One's brains did yawn and go phew by the afternoon, so this was not as ghastly as it sounds. *Ru-uuun! Shoooo-oot!* Blow those cobwebs away! Fortified by the rites of House Tea, we would return to the intellectual fray for four more lessons, and then round things off by belting out a hymn at Vespers.

And however dreary the morning lessons were, there were

always the breaktime buns to look forward to. They were staggering. They came from Millars, the local bakery that supplied our bread, and we would have a different kind each day, laid out on three shallow trays in the playground next to the little bottles of milk with the tops already punctured and speared with straws.

Monday was a jammy doughnut. It was all soft and sugary on the outside, and then you bit into the lovely pale-yellow springy interior and burst it so the jam splattered all over your chin. Tuesday was a currant bun, which may sound dull in comparison, but the currant-to-bun ratio was spectacularly generous. Wednesday brought forth a Danish pastry, though that was my least favourite, as the lemon curd in the centre looked like phlegm. Thursday's was an elongated iced bun. A sticky willy. No further elucidation necessary. Friday saw a repeat of the jammy doughnut. There was always someone on a diet, so if you hung around the playground long enough you could have two.

As for lessons themselves, my desk in Lower Five A was in the third row and Chrissie bagged the one next to mine, so I had someone to pass notes to when things flagged. We were in note-passing range of Della and Beth, too. Plus you could usually rely on Beth for a few pranks. At one stage we had a supply teacher who wore her hair done up. We had to take our exercise books to her desk for marking, and Beth took a magnet and made all her hairpins fall out. And by the time our year started doing Physics, the school had appointed some poor little wet-behind-the-ears 22-year-old youth, and all the girls ran rings round him, even Cherry who was normally so well-behaved. He always wore red socks, so we would hold our noses when he came in: 'Poo!' He resigned after a term. What fun!

And we put chalk on Miss Evans's chair, so she would get it on the back of her gown. Miss Evans took us for English Literature and was a dreadfully boring teacher but kind, like a granny. She had a great head of fluffy white hair, and you could see the tops of her woolly stockings when she sat down. She gave us stuff to read while she did the *Daily Mail* crossword or surreptitiously knitted. We were meant to be doing *Pride and Prejudice* but you could read anything. You could even walk out of the classroom and go and talk in cab. She never noticed. She looked very old, even older than Cowley, who was Methuselah, but neither of them was as ancient as nice Miss Wrinch, who taught Geography. Miss Wrinch was so serenely old that I thought she had been granted eternal life.

Wrinch had one unfortunate nervous mannerism – after finishing a sentence she would draw back her lips and suck air between her teeth. *Shluuuurp*. She was lean and virginal, wore her hair in wings, walked on tippy-toe and said Him-*ah*-layas instead of Hima-*lay*-as. We had to go to the Geography room for her lessons. It was a special building tacked on one side of the gym. *The Story of Felixstowe College* rhapsodised about its 'delightful view over the lawns to the sea'. The room was light and airy and contained a massive black globe, which you could write on with chalk. This was a gift from 'Jonah's Jews' – a summer school from North London that rented the college buildings. At the end of summer term we had to clean out every dressing table and locker, every scrap of our day-to-day detritus, everything that made us who we were, because 'the Jews' were coming. One summer they held a beach party and chopped up some of our furniture to make a fire. They gave us the globe as reparation.

Wrinch was tall, and so was her desk. Perched on a high stool, she tootled on about volcanoes and how they worked, and meandering rivers, and populations in valleys, and where crops were grown. And fjords. She loved going on about the fjords. She started with the fjords and never got off the fjords, it sometimes seemed, and you whiled away the time staring at her scraggy neck and the stick-like body under her gown. Oh dear, she was such a kind, safe teacher, doling out glucose tablets to everyone before exams. She never shouted or threw chalk, and she certainly never put rubbers in her mouth. But *so boring*. I'd have to write down everything she said otherwise I'd forget it straightaway. Nothing stuck. Not one single fjord. When it came to exams, I had to memorise entire essays in cab overnight beforehand. 'Wales is a very mountainous country, with some peaks over up to 3,000ft high.' A few days after one exam, I was on The Wrinch Table at lunch and boasted about my feat of memory. 'Yes,' she said drily, 'it rather read that way.'

I was fascinated by her Christian name, Lois, which should have belonged to a jazz singer, not someone who was a living history of our school. I hesitate to say 'BJ' because those initials stand for something altogether rather rude these days, but Miss Wrinch had been there BJ – Before Jonah. She had been a day pupil when it wasn't even yet Felixstowe College, but an obscure private school called Uplands.

Uplands had occupied a site called Bulls Cliff, 200 yards from the sea, and Lois Wrinch was there to witness the drama when Bulls Cliff went up in flames in the summer hols of 1927, and the speedy reopening on new premises, Cranmer.

She was living at the time on the High Road, near Tyndale and Latimer, in a house designed by her father, and Wrinch *père* was the architect who transformed Cranmer's stable block into our beautiful library. She was there in the autumn term of 1928, on the morning of the Great Announcement, when (I quote *The Story of Felixstowe College*), '... the Head Mistress gave the pupils the exciting news that, as from January 1929, Uplands School would be no more for it was to become Felixstowe Ladies' College, a Public School for Girls'.

I've been able to find only one school photo from the time when it was Uplands. Lois Wrinch is standing in the back row – an attractive girl, tall, chin up, with long, wavy brown hair, good bones and a slightly stubborn set to the mouth. This was Wrinch as a teenager, not scraggy and wrinkled as we knew her, but tingling with hormones, worrying about spots and bras and periods, trying on clothes, swotting for exams, getting letters from boys (there must have been some, she was so lovely), making plans about university. Off she went to King's College, London, where she was a star and won prizes for the best female Science student. When the Second World War broke out, she joined the WRENS and became something mysterious in the Met Office. Lois the weather girl, gesturing at cloud formations and storms over the White Cliffs of Dover and Normandy Beach. Anyway, after the war she came back to Felixstowe and that's where she stayed.

So, as I've said, Miss Wrinch practically had heritage status by the time she taught us. She was knocking on a bit, all that girly lusciousness long gone, and it turned out she wasn't very well. One lunchtime she was doling out rice pudding at the head of The Wrinch Table, and she fainted into it. Was it a prank? Had someone put knockout drops in the rice pudding? But no, this was real.

The very decent Tyndale Head of House, who was passing by, put an end to the paralysis that had descended on the dining room by lifting Wrinch's head out of the green enamel tray, and tenderly wiping clean her face and straggly hair. Awful for her. A shock for us, too. She was also real; not a Geography machine. Teachers were human. I should really not be horrible to them.

Miss Wrinch wasn't the only nice teacher. French and Spanish were taught by a poised, very attractive woman, Miss Sanford, who treated us like people and won our hearts with a risqué joke: 'Madrid is nine months *vierno* (winter) and three months *infierno* (hell).' You'd remember your seasons in Spanish easily after that, wouldn't you? Sanford was half-Spanish herself, with black hair and flashing eyes, and she rolled her Rs. When, later, we were studying Lorca as one of our set books for A Level, and the word 'castrated' cropped up, Della, all butter-wouldn't-melt, stuck up her hand and said, 'Please, what does castrated mean?'

'*Strrrripped* of his manhood,' replied Sanford cheerfully.

Della knew perfectly well what castrated meant, having been brought up on a farm where there was a lot of castrating.

Sanford lived in the town, keeping house for her widowed father. Big bust, slim hips, a bit of a Barbie doll. Wonderful. Not the slightest bit mad, even though she'd obviously had a stricken love, because why else would she be single? A soldier who died, perhaps. Or she wasn't allowed to marry him because she was a Catholic and he was of another religious persuasion. Actually, it turned out she had a lover in Spain and used to pop over to be with him in the school holidays. No wonder she was so sane and cheerful.

Sanford's main chum in the school was Miss McNulty, one of the Maths teachers. She was nice, too, if fierce. Sanford and McNulty went to the same Catholic church and the same hairdresser. Both wore their jackdaw-black hair in the same wavy bob, McNulty's the more wild and vigorous, especially when she was annoyed. You couldn't get away with a thing in her lessons. She would threaten to push you into a peat bog. She was one of the school stalwarts, a fiery Irishwoman, tall and angular, with a strong accent and a real Irish face, like a beaky female version of Father Ted. Wore just the most awful clothes, of course. But she liked young people and would talk about where she grew up, where she learned. A bit before the end of the lesson she would disappear to get a book from the library, to talk about Pythagoras, but really to have a cigarette followed by a strong mint. She was magnificent.

Bilge (that's Biology) was taught by young, freckle-faced Miss Beynon, who was one of the few teachers who had a modern bust, i.e. she wore a pointy bra, not a boulder-upholder, under her crisp flowered blouse, along with a light floral perfume that we thought was probably Coty's *L'Aimant*. Miss Beynon was engaged, which was most likely why she was fun and not a bit neurotic. She let me keep the dead shrew I found on the Games pitches and, while it awaited dissection by me, kindly allowed it to be stored in formalin next to The Foetus. We were very proud of our Foetus. When we played home matches against visiting schools, we would have to amuse them after tea and once it was a Catholic school, so they were taken to see it. They left horrified.

Everybody should have at least one memorable teacher who encourages your enthusiasm for what you want to do later on and, in my case, it was Miss Laycock, who taught Elocution. She seemed different from the other staff. Tall, humorous, affectionate, long-legged and, to look at, a cross between the novelist Elizabeth Jane Howard and the principle boy in panto. I think she might have trained for the stage – she had a deep, deep voice that came from somewhere located between her bosoms. Perhaps she had ended up with us because the work in rep had dried up now she had reached a certain age. But I had the impression she had lived a life and she was someone who could be talked to about everything. I was not going to be able to act, because on stage I froze, knowing everyone was looking at me, but she gave me confidence in my reading voice, brought out my love of dialogue and the rhythms of sentences, and encouraged me to say what I wanted to say. Far more than ploughing through set books with Miss Evans and Miss Williams in English, this was real learning for someone who wanted to be a writer.

As for the difficult teachers, it was just school, wasn't it? The kind and nice outweighed the mad and nasty, and that was the important thing. So lesson time wasn't bad, and most days there was something to look forward to – French, Art, Gym, Bilge, Elo, Current Events. The only day of dread was Thursday, not just because that was Chemmy morning. It was also the day of The Jonah List.

## 14

## MORAL WORTH

'Attendance at one of the Chapel services is an inspiration and a touch of refreshing grace in so wonderful a company of future womanhood and potential mothers of a new England.'

From a *Suffolk Fair* magazine article
on Felixstowe College

Miss Beynon's Bilge lab might have been a happy place, but the wall outside was sometimes not, because on it was a noticeboard, and on Thursday at breaktime a little knot of girls would be crowded round, anxiously checking the green slip of paper that had just been pinned up.

Girls To See Miss Jones
J. Welch

Jonah had a beautiful study. It was on the top floor of Cranmer – large, high-ceilinged, and with an oriel window that looked out over the sea. There were comfortable chairs for parents to sit in, and a drinks cabinet to give them drinks from, and Persian rugs for them to admire. Over the mantelshelf, behind an enormous desk, hung Annigoni's portrait of the Queen. And at the enormous desk sat enormous Jonah. Jonah was just a nickname, of course, a matey version of Miss Jones that she'd been known as since time immemorial. Mentally I associated it with Jonah and the Whale, and whale-wise she certainly had the build.

The wait outside, sitting on a bench, was petrifying; miles worse than having to wait at the dentist. But I couldn't think of anything I'd done wrong. The work was easy-peasy and I had sailed to the top of the class. That was it! She was going to tell me how clever I was. I stood smiling at her complacently.

'People are saying you're conceited,' she barked.

Wham! It was like being punched on the nose. So this must be what that prospectus meant by the close personal attention of the headmistress. I didn't like it one bit. I went red and looked down at my feet, the alternative being Jonah's eyes fixed beadily on me over the top of her glasses. Oh vanity, thy name is JULIA WELCH (R).

But what people were saying I was conceited? Jonah hadn't seen me in action, so how did she know? Which teachers had given me the raspberry? Was this Bretch's revenge for the guitar? Had I been self-important in Geography, pompous in History, smug in English? Had I been altogether too pleased with myself in Scripture or a show-off in Latin? Much too full of myself in Maths? Probably. I was so awfully pleased to have my brains back, you see, having made such a hash of things at my previous school.

'W-w-well, I don't *think* I'm conceited,' I muttered, because right at that moment I wasn't at all, I was a balloon someone had stamped on. Absolutely crestfallen. Oh dear. I began to realise that this school was not just about midnight feasts and learning how to play lax. I was going to have all my moral failings pointed out, too. I was a girl, so I'd have to develop dreary virtues like modesty, and being useful, and darning.

*Boom, boom, boom.* Jonah was rattling on at the speed of sound. Mainly I nodded. She wasn't really cross now she'd got her point over, which was that people wouldn't like me if I was conceited. How did she *know* I so badly wanted to be liked? Was she some kind of mage?

With a final 'Yes, Miss Jones,' I staggered out of the door and took a rather wobbly walk back to House because my knees were still knocking. This was obviously how life was going to be from now on. Would I have to pray? Claim that I earnestly repented and was heartily sorry for my misdoings, and that the remembrance of them was grievous unto me and the burden of them was intolerable? Wouldn't God be able to tell I was lying? I didn't find my misdoings intolerable at all. If I was going to pray for anything, it was that I wouldn't get any more filthy rows as long as I lived. Though as God had still not come through with the horses in seven colours that I'd asked for, I didn't hold out much hope that He'd be all that bothered.

Even so, Chapel, week in, week out, without let up, got you in its grip. It was God, God, God, all over the place. One continuous sermon. The school chaplain was a plump red-faced reverend whose nickname was Elly-J. In Chapel he droned through the service, blah blah drone ... sin ... heavenly host ... while we shifted from buttock to buttock and passed the time by counting the number of times he said 'Bible'. The only fun was arranging beforehand which one of us was going to faint. Two of you could escape that way, as one had to carry the other out.

The hymns part was lovely. Three hundred young virgins (and two dozen menopausal ones) singing their hearts out: 'Love Unknown'; 'For All the Saints' (tune: 'St Patrick's Breastplate'); 'Lift Up Your Hearts'. But then you had to sit through everything else. Or stand. Or kneel. The Psalm was always embarrassing, because the lines didn't scan and nobody knew the tune. Up we went when we should have gone down. Most people chucked it in as hopeless after a few bars, and Miss Parfitt, the piano teacher, who looked like a large, mild sheep, would have to parp away on the organ unaccompanied. And sometimes during the hymns she would strike a wrong note, which was as embarrassing as the Psalm rigmarole. I'd go hot and cold all over for her. But it wasn't half as embarrassing as when one of the verses had a rude word in it like 'womb', which no one would sing out loud, so there was this one beat of silence, as loud as a gunshot.

And once a year you'd have to read the Lesson. However frightened you were, it was compulsory. No exceptions. Even the girl with learning difficulties had to do it, and the girl with the Yorkshire accent that got everyone in hysterics. Now, I didn't mind, because although it gave me a few butterflies beforehand I had a good reading voice – see what Jonah meant about me being conceited? – and there were few things I liked better than showing it off in front of a captive audience. But some found it the most awful thing they had to do in the entirety of school, to be dreaded more than being on The Jonah List or having to sit next to Cawley at lunch.

It would hang over them for weeks. The prospect once made Gill physically sick. All she had ever done in public before that was appear as a jester in her primary school play. She'd had to walk across the stage on her hands but no speaking had been required. If only she could have mutely walked up the aisle of the chapel on her hands and left it at that. But no. The instruction was to leave your pew two lines before the end of the hymn to give you enough time to get to the front, and Gill would have nightmares about it – that she'd got the timing wrong and had to run all the way. Or that she'd got up there and find out it wasn't her turn to read. And she couldn't say her Rs properly yet, they came out as Ws, and once she had to read, 'Thou rulest the raging of the sea'.

And what if something went wrong and the Bible hadn't been left open at the passage you were meant to read? One poor girl spent the whole Lesson hunting among the Habbakuks and Jehosephats for the right place, turning over page after page in complete silence, apart from the flop each heavy page made, and then the despairing thump at the end as she gave it up as a bad job and finally closed the Good Book.

It wasn't even as if our chapel was a proper church. It was built of tan-coloured brick, as plain and unremarkable as a pencil box, and the business end inside was plain and simple too. No altar, no cross, just a table covered with a blue cloth. That was the way it had to be. When the school changed its name from Uplands to Felixstowe College, it was because it had been taken over by an organisation called the Martyrs' Memorial Trust, which belonged to the hair shirt wing of the

Church of England. It was a militant army in the Protestant cause. They laid down the rules. No fancy rituals, no paraphernalia filched from Rome. Old Ridley and Cranmer and Tyndale and Latimer had died for that cause. How could we be so ungrateful as to put up decorations?

I'll tell you a bit more about this Trust, because it has much to do with how our school was run and why they wanted to churn you out as, well, the kind of person the prospectus promised they'd churn you out as. In the 1920s its dominant figure was the Reverend Percy Warrington, a Derbyshire farmer's son. Squat, sleek and completely humourless, with boot-button eyes and a hairdo that you might call 'accidental monk' – he went bald in his twenties, leaving him with a tonsure that most times he concealed under a big black hat. The rest of his outfit featured a black coat, complete with a flower in the buttonhole, and a clerical collar so uncomfortably wide it must have been a small act of martyrdom to carry on wearing it.

Despite his off-putting appearance, he was very good at persuading wealthy widows to chip in to the Trust's coffers and sourcing weak-willed members of the great and good to serve as trustees and school governors, which he recruited in droves. At one point he seemed unable to learn of a stately home coming up for sale without snapping it up and converting it into a school. Over the course of ten years between the wars he founded fourteen public schools, all designed to propagate his own brand of hardcore evangelism. As his fame grew, he came to be known as 'the financier in the cassock', though the pupils at the first school he founded, Wrekin College in Shropshire, were more inclined to refer to him as 'Pompous Percy', and those of his next venture, Stowe, as 'Prancing Percy', because of the way he walked.

He liked to portray himself as 'a simple country parson', although if he was it was one who swanned around in a Daimler. There was nothing simple about his financial arrangements, either. The man responsible for Felixstowe College favoured an accounting system so shady and labyrinthine that it was described by one churchman tasked in due course with untangling it as 'like living in a Dickens novel'. Warrington bought Wrekin on a loan, and every other purchase was based on a mortgage, guaranteed at first by Wrekin and then by each successive school until, eventually, the Trust was in a colossal amount of debt, at which point came the Depression. In 1932, the Reverent Percy's empire was headed for ruin, and Felixstowe College along with it.

An organisation called Allied Schools was formed to salvage what it could. Nearly half of Warrington's schools were closed down but Felixstowe was one of seven to avoid the chop. Off went Warrington to spend the rest of his days in obscurity and paranoia, fulminating against those he claimed had given him his marching orders. The nature of our school didn't change, though. The 1930s prospectus promised 'a high moral tone', and Miss Clarke, the headmistress appointed by Warrington, was high moral tone in person.

'Miss Clarke was known as MC,' says Mary Large, a delightful Old Girl who joined Felixstowe in 1937, and who is the aunt of my Tyndale friend, Di. 'She looked a bit like Queen Victoria. Very dignified, just like a grandmother. The classroom doors had windows, and old Clarkey could go round the hall peeping in. Quite honestly, she was God, really.'

God had iron-hard hair and a penchant for plain but voluminous black dresses. She was said to have been an early member of the Women's Cricket Association. It's rather hard to imagine her striding to the crease, but an entry in the Schools Directory of 1933 lists cricket, along with tennis, as the summer sports played. It wasn't on the curriculum during our time. I was told, 'They used to play it but it got dropped because someone got hit in the bust,' but that might just have been one of those myths that did the rounds, like the girl with learning difficulties owing her condition to having been dropped in a coal scuttle as a baby. More likely is that, by the 1960s, it was impossible to find another girls' school in the area that played it, and with whom fixtures could be organised.

So anyway, Miss Clarke taught Scripture and Classics and was said to be superhuman, formidable, imperious and terrifying. To be fair, that was the way all headmistresses rolled in those days, though Miss Clarke took it to outstanding lengths. She instigated a trophy called the Moral Worth, made the girls do their mending every Saturday in total silence and, on Sundays, when no pastimes were allowed except knitting, had them sit on the library floor and listen to her grimmest of grim evening sermons. From deep in Miss Clarke's subconscious would come the image of a giant Christmas tree. 'Thousands of babies ... THOUSANDS ... sucking milk from bottles attached to the tree by red and grey ribbons and EACH ONE TAKING FROM THE SCHOOL AND GIVING NOTHING IN RETURN.' Desired result: the more girls crying their eyes out with tears of remorse, the better.

This was the era that forged Bretch and Maggie, when

anyone who broke the rules would be handed a black counter, like a tiddlywink in mourning. Each evening the House captain would stand underneath the House noticeboard and the shelf of House cups. Evildoers would form a queue to hand her the counters they had accrued that day. Later on the counters were junked in favour of the notorious Black Book that had to be signed in the Red Hall, which was the entrance to our library. No one thought that was anywhere near as terrifying as the ritual of the counters.

According to Mary Large, 'You didn't really talk to her.' Instead, she talked to you. Or at you. 'Certainly,' states *The Story of Felixstowe College*, 'her presence was all over the school and many ex-pupils still remember the ideas and ideals which she propounded in her Sunday evening talks.'

Miss Clarke seems to have been a bit of a tub-thumper, the scourge of all slovenliness, untidiness and secret sweet-eating. That was certainly the way she seemed to treat her pupils, as brands to be rescued from the burning. And she had a thing about initials. The initials of train lines, to be precise. She brought them into her evening sermons. L.N.E.R. stood for Let Nothing Evil Remain. L.M.S. meant Love My School. The Great Western Railway transmogrified into Grousing Without Reason. I would have been in fits, but Miss Clarke demanded, and got, total respect from her pupils: 'We were brought up that way,' says Mary.

Being a junior, Mary boarded in Ridley, or Vernon Villa, as it was then known. The House mistress was called Mrs Welsh and she was middle-aged and kindly. Mary had trouble with her teeth and Mrs Welsh always accompanied her to the dentist. Miss Marstand was the matron. 'After our bedtime she always used to play The Donkey Serenade on the piano in the common room.' Bretch was in the year below her. 'She was no beauty,' observed Mary. 'Brown frizzy hair and cross-eyed, poor girl.'

Mary rapidly became best friends with a girl called Pat, with whom she's still in touch. She gave me, to keep, the loveliest snapshot of the pair of them, side by side, close together, holding their lax sticks, dressed in their Games outfits. These were called *djibbahs*, boxy tunics made of heavy, silver-grey linen and far, far nicer than the ghastly divided skirts and Aertexes we had to wear. The photo is more than eighty years old, but happiness – that magical happiness of having a friend, someone you've chosen for yourself, not just because you were the last two left – still absolutely shines from it.

'I grew up on a farm in the fens,' Mary says. 'I'd been stuck in the middle of nowhere with no friends. I thoroughly enjoyed my schooldays.'

She enjoyed them even when, in September 1939, the Young Ladies of Felixstowe College went back for the start of term, only to discover it was going to be a very truncated one. Britain at war with Germany! Parental consternation ensued. Felixstowe was on the east coast – why, Hitler might pop over any day. Cranmer's beach was cordoned off and strewn with tank traps. The sea was mined. The waves broke on rolls of barbed wire. When sentries were posted on approach roads and entry passes demanded, parents cracked. They took their daughters away. The autumn term was over almost before it started, and the following term Mary didn't go to school at all. Hardly anyone did. So, faced with the prospect of a school so empty that it went out of business, Felixstowe College moved its operations to Norfolk, re-opening for the 1940 summer term in a stately home.

Riddlesworth Hall was off the main Diss to Thetford road and came complete with its own village. Pummelled into shape by the dynamic young Maths mistress, Miss Jones, it became a functioning school. Bedrooms and dressing rooms turned into dorms. The Cricketers' Wing became the San, the nursery was the staff room and the butler's pantry a Chemmy lab. They put up blackout curtains on what seemed like the largest windows in England. The billiard room transmogrified into a classroom. Behind it was a little cloakroom that the girls used as an illegal hideout for midnight feasts and sessions with an Ouija board. Mr Cooper, the tennis coach, made a mud court in the piggery yard.

Mary remembers her Riddlesworth days with affection. 'It was very much a makeshift school but they did very well, to be quite honest,' she said. 'All the ablutions and things were very old-fashioned and there were really no extra-curricular things, but the food was all right. It was wartime, after all. They looked after us very well. We had lots of picnics and things. I would think basically it was a happy school.'

Another spiffing Old Girl, a little younger than Mary, is Diana Platts, who joined in 1941 as a nine-year-old, and so went straight to Riddlesworth. Diana was two years below Bretch, and described her as 'very straitlaced'. Diana's big sister, Yvonne, was already a pupil and actually had the same birth date as Bretch, 18 June 1928. 'So they were identical! Though,' she added hastily, 'not in looks.'

With Riddlesworth Hall now popping at the seams, Diana boarded at first in Garboldisham Rectory, the annexe the school had commandeered for the little ones and immediately christened 'Garb'.

'I was there entirely, for lessons and sleeping,' she said. 'Then, when we were old enough for Riddlesworth, there wasn't enough room, so we Tyndales were pushed out to Market Weston Old Rectory, and it was bleak. We had to go there in a bus, after supper. It was over the bridge, on the Suffolk border, three or four miles away. I was the one who carried the jug of milk for the cocoa. Every room was a dorm except for the House mistress's bedsit. One bathroom. Forty-odd people wanting the loo first thing in the morning. Then we'd go back to Riddlesworth by bus for breakfast. We accepted it; who knows why?'

It was bitterly cold there. During the winter the water in the washbasins froze overnight and face flannels were frozen stiff every morning. The snow came up to the top of the telegraph poles. They never played Games all one term, they had no coal, and they had cold baths over at Riddlesworth, in the sunken bath. The glass had been blown out of the dorm window and replaced by meat-safe wire.

'Tiny Greenlaw slept next to the window,' said Diana, 'and in the morning snow was all over her bed. I used to wear three vests at a time. I took off the bottom one to wash and the clean one went on top.

'We had the most awful pudding. It was meant to be steamed pudding but it was just sog. Pumpkin pie, watery. Liver on Fridays, tough as old boots. Puddings – sago, tapioca, bread and butter pudding. I hate them now. In our spare time we always knitted for the services. We knitted like anything: sweaters, balaclavas, sea-boot socks, ordinary socks, scarves.

Ridley always won the cup for the most done because Hossie, their House mistress, made them sit and do it.'

Tyndale's House mistress was a Miss Burrow, who taught Geography and History and was known as Lady B. Diana remembers her as a lovely woman, round-faced and enormous, with dark hair. 'The only harmless great thing', as John Donne described the elephant.

'She was there all the time I was there,' said Diana. 'I was ever so fond of her. Huge woman – you'd hear her thundering down the passage.' Their matron was Miss Fletcher. 'A bit vicious but quite nice. Well, it's how you treat people, isn't it?'

The girls were taught how to put out incendiary bombs and had gas mask practice, and the war was close enough for air raids often to occur twice in a night. Bombs fell on Norwich, which was only thirty miles away. People seriously thought that Hitler might invade through the Wash, that giant square estuary that divides Norfolk from Lincolnshire, putting Riddlesworth right in the battle area. After four years of it, the strain told on Miss Clarke. Something snapped. *The Story of Felixstowe College* tells of the school being 'shattered' by the news. She was stepping down. God was leaving the stage.

There was no need to advertise the job vacancy. All along, there had been only one candidate.

# 15

# JONAH

Jonah used to slide down the banisters at Cranmer. Well, that story could easily be apocryphal but I've heard it from so many sources, and it's such a delightful image, that where's the harm in putting it out there?

Jonah – Miss Ruth M. Jones – was born in 1906, and grew up on a farm in Llandindrod Wells, where she helped with the calving. She went to the local grammar school and from there to the University of Wales, where she gained a first-class mathematics degree. It was an era when hardly any girls went to university, let alone did degrees in Maths. She'd also had her arm up a cow's bottom, so you can see she was unfazed by life's challenges. She was special, a legend, a complete one-off. Any girl at Felixstowe whose surname was Jones had to become double-barrelled, i.e. Something-Jones, because there was only one Jones at Felixstowe College.

The first time I clapped eyes on her was at an Open Day in 1961, the summer before I joined the college. We prospective pupils were given tea in the giant L-shaped classroom to the side of the library, and I can see her now, surveying us with her back to the windows, lit by a shaft of June sunlight. The head at my previous school had been a forbidding old trout known as Coalhole. Coalhole had a deep, well-modulated voice, all the better to rumble, 'Julia, I am accustomed to people being alert in my lessons,' in her Scripture class. Jonah, in contrast, looked sort of ho-ho jolly. That may have been a trick of the light.

She had very fine, greying fair hair styled in a sort of pudding bowl 'do, but with a kiss curl held in place by a sur-prisingly girlish slide. She had always been on the roly-poly side and, by the time I joined the school in 1961, she was absolutely monumental, but I swear she possessed a super-power. She could teleport herself. One minute I'd have my head over my exercise book, writing a scurrilous satire about various staff members, complete with cartoons, and the next the offending object would be tucked between her arm and considerable bosom and I'd have days of that sudden-sinking-of-the-stomach, sweat-trickling-down-my-armpits wait for my name to appear on The Jonah List.

I've told you what her study in Cranmer was like, with that oriel window. It offered the most breathtaking, panoramic view of the sea. Huge container ships would inch past, so close you wanted to wave at the people inside, but as I was usually in there to be given a row that would have just meant more trouble.

Jonah joined the school in 1931, to teach Maths; it was her third teaching post. By this time, in need of extra accommo-dation for junior girls, the school had bought Maybush House, up the road from Cranmer. The house came with an exciting backstory; it was said to have been an inn at one point, and the haunt of smugglers. Some of the staff were plonked in

Maybush, too, including Jonah. Her room was in the attic, and a wooden slide was constructed outside her window as a fire exit. To fully appreciate the image of Jonah using a slide at fire practice, you need to have seen her in the flesh, but I can understand how the banisters story gained traction.

She was powerful and energetic. Intimidating. A big character in all senses. There was a public Jonah and a private one, and in that way she was kind of two-faced, and you were never quite sure which Jonah you were going to get. The public Jonah wore a poker face. The private one had a mischievous sense of humour and the ridiculous. Was Bretch giving us a hard time? 'Takes things too seriously,' she'd grunt. 'You ought to give her some gin.'

Her voice was deep and she spoke, as she did everything else, from eating to thinking, very fast. She enjoyed sport, particularly golf – or 'goff', as she insisted it was pronounced – and had been a formidable hockey player in her time. I often thought of her charging down the flank when she entered the dining room, whipping past all the tables at race-walking pace to get to The Jonah Table at lunch. She would start saying Grace before she got to her chair, and galloped through it so rapidly some thought she was saying it in Latin. Her *bête noir* was the word 'surely', as in, 'But surely, Miss Jones . . .'

'Surely isn't a fact!' she would bellow, rat-tat-tat.

I must have been hauled up to Felixstowe to be interviewed by her at some point before I joined but, strangely, I don't remember that at all, although I bet she terrified the life out of my parents. I hope she didn't write 'L.O.' beside their names in her files. Because she did that, you know – made notes about prospective parents. A group of Cranmers once sneaked into her study, opened the drawers and pulled out the files. Among the gems they discovered were: 'father has limp handshake' and 'mother's hat too big'. L.O. stood for Lower Orders. 'Jonah,' said one Old Girl I talked to, 'was a delightful snob.'

She was not flawless. She taught Maths to the Lower Fours, to find out who they were, and would stride into their first lesson and draw a perfect circle on the blackboard. *Just so you know.* What a show-off. She could be mischievously mean, too. One girl, a Tyndale, lost her bra. It was such a small bra that it was more a token effort than anything else. 32A. Who wants to be 32A? The girl turned Tyndale upside down in the hunt for it, but it wasn't to be found, and at the next school meeting, Jonah said, 'Is there any lost property?'

Silence.

Jonah pointed to the girl. 'I think you lost something.'

More silence.

'I think you lost a bra. What size is it?' and that poor girl had to broadcast her tiddly titties shame in front of the whole school.

As for some of her attitudes, well, let's just say they were of the age into which she was born. One year Tyndale had a Head of House called Daphne. Her family lived in Esher and her father was in banking. After Upper Six she went on to the LSE, and met a fellow student who was studying Law. He was from Somalia. They became engaged and, at that time, mixed marriages were frowned upon. But they were determined to marry, and the news made the *Daily Mail*, the *Daily Express* and the *Daily Telegraph*, where various people were quoted, including 'Daphne's former headmistress, Ruth Jones'. Asked what she thought of Daphne getting married and going to live in a village in Somalia, Jonah replied that she didn't approve, and added that her children 'would look like streaky bacon'. Oh, Jonah, how could you?

But in the face of her otherwise wondrousness, the imperfections count for little. You can ask any one of us for our Jonah memories and they'll be there as though they happened last week; they exist at the very core of everyone's brain, tattooed on the hippocampus. That curl bouncing as she walked into the dining room while we all stood, almost bowing. Did you catch that naughty little flicker of a smile on her face? The billowing gown as she strode past us, while we stood up straight, like soldiers, *bang, bang, bang*, backs against the wall. In that musty-smelling gown, she looked *inflated*. Under it would generally be some businesslike suit, with the jacket flapping in time to her walk, though one Speech Day she broke out and packed her large, manly frame into a beautiful, brightly coloured silk dress. What should happen but the school's most stunning mother turned up wearing exactly the same one.

One very nice, very *good* girl in our year was Jan, who was in Tyndale. As was quite a naughty girl called Marjorie, who one Saturday invited Jan out with her on exeat. Marjorie's father took them to Thorpeness Meare, where they rented out a rowing boat. They spent rather a long time on the water and, by the time they set off back to Felixstowe, Jan was worried because she had a choir rehearsal. 'I'm going to be late,' she said.

'Oh,' said Marjorie airily, 'we'll just pretend we had a puncture.'

All this was being said while Marjorie's father was in the

driver's seat, so he must have heard every word, but when they arrived back at Tyndale an absolutely livid Maggie greeted her with, 'Where have you been all this time?'

'We had a puncture,' Jan blurted out.

Maggie turned to the father for confirmation.

'What puncture?' said the rotter. And of course poor Jan was petrified, especially when a prefect marched up to her and said, 'I'm very disappointed in you,' because very soon after that her parents were going to see Jonah for a chat about what Jan's future subjects might be, and she thought she was going to be expelled. But Jonah said to her father, 'You wouldn't have done that, would you? You'd have stuck up for them.'

One of the loveliest things about writing this book was meeting women who had known Jonah at the very beginning of her time as headmistress, who could put flesh on the bones (not that more flesh was something she necessarily needed) of her early years, and give insights and perspectives about a younger Jonah.

When the war ended, she could not take back the school straight away. Its buildings had been taken over by the army and, although they moved out quickly, the premises were not derequisitioned until the end of August 1945. You can imagine the state the place had been left in. There were air raid shelters and the cookhouse to be demolished, the overgrown Games pitches to be re-turfed and the drives re-laid. Furniture had to be dragged out of classrooms and labs, where it had been dumped, and plywood torn off all the staircases and panelling and fireplaces on to which it had been nailed to protect them. The place was a mess.

There were long, long negotiations about compensation

with the War Department. All this and more was overseen by Jonah, travelling to and fro between Norfolk and Suffolk because, far from losing pupils in its exile, Felixstowe College had plenty of extra ones and, now they were about to return to the coast, they had to find somewhere to put them all.

In Cranmer, the walls of Miss Clarke's sitting room came down and the whole of the back of the house was remodelled to provide the vast dining room overlooking the sea. More tennis courts were added, central heating was installed, and the school layout re-planned, which meant Jonah spent a lot of time with Mr Creak, the school architect.

'He was an absolute whopper,' said Diana Platts. 'I always thought there was something going on between the two of them.' What a picture that makes.

Felixstowe College returned home in time for summer term, 1946, leaving behind a little bit of itself. The junior department at Garboldisham Rectory became Riddlesworth Hall School, which, unlike its begetter, still operates today. Diana's daughters, Philipa and Juliet, went there before joining Felixstowe College. Another pupil was Lady Diana Spencer; she and Juliet were in the same year. Their guinea pigs lived next to each other. Lady Di didn't go on to attend Felixstowe; she was turned down by Elizabeth Manners, Jonah's successor, as not being bright enough. Jonah, of course, would have had none of that. An earl's daughter? She would have taken her in a heartbeat.

As soon as the school went back to Felixstowe, Jonahville started taking shape. She bought Tyndale from the widow of Sharp's Toffees, managing to bag a supply of free sweets in the process. Latimer next door was concurrently on sale, so she grabbed that too, because Jonah did not believe in hanging about, wavering. In those days, Speech Day was held on Cranmer lawn, and Diana Platts told me about the one when proceedings were persistently disturbed by a raucous bird, high up in a tree. Jonah conferred briefly with a father. He went to his car, fetched a rifle from the boot and shot it forthwith. 'Forthwith' was Jonah's default state.

Sheelin Cuthbert went to Felixstowe in 1949, the first daughter of an Old Girl to thus be enrolled. Her association with the school lasted to the very end, as she became what was known as an Old Girl Governor: that is, the board of governors always had a member of the Old Girls' Association among their number. At this point, though, she was ten years old, the place was still painted yellow from the army occupation, and rationing was on. They ate lots of spam fritters. Sometimes the drinking glasses would blow up, because they were cheap. You would pick them up and then, *bang!* All over the floor.

Sheelin was in Cranmer, and she quickly got to know Jonah's very distinctive tread. You always knew it was her. She strode on her heels, but up and downstairs she went on her toes. One night, Sheelin and her chums broke into the kitchen and were helping themselves to ice cream and golden syrup when they heard the tread, and they were caught red-handed.

'Up to my study and bring all that with you,' said Jonah. They had to sit on the carpet and eat it all up in front of her.

'What was that like?' I asked Sheelin.

'Sickly.'

That was the year Sheelin was in Lower Five, when she was also caught in Prep writing out who should be in the hockey team. Back to Jonah's study she was despatched.

'I pay someone to decide who's in the team,' Jonah told her. 'You get on with work.' Because, as Sheelin said, Jonah didn't use too many words but they all meant something.

Janet Copland, who also went on to become an Old Girl Governor, was almost Sheelin's contemporary, being younger by three years, and she too was in Cranmer.

'She was the reason my parents chose Felixstowe for me,' Janet said. 'They wrote off for a prospectus and she wrote back saying, "We are delighted you want to send Janet here." She had actually read the letter, not just chucked it at a secretary to deal with. Other schools just sent pro forma replies but she had the personal touch.

'She knew *everything*. And she was very sensible. Before A Levels I had two invitations to go to twenty-firsts, one after the other, Friday and Saturday night. My parents said, "No, you mustn't accept," so I appealed to Jonah, who said, "Well, if you don't go, you'll just sit here and be cross, so you'd better go and when you get back you'll work harder."

'And there's another thing she did, which shows you how shrewd she was about people. There was one child in Cranmer – my father knew hers – whose mother had died. Jonah rang the father to say she had noticed the girl never had letters. She told my father later that she knew his handwriting and she'd quoted him as an example: "Janet always seems to have a letter in her father's handwriting in her hand."

'She wasn't afraid of naming names, though. I swallowed a safety pin once. A girl told matron and I was whisked off to hospital. Jonah called a school meeting, specially to talk about this stupid child who had swallowed a safety pin.'

But another Old Girl, Anita, reminded me that Jonah had

her humane side. The House mistress of Hooper was called Mrs Parker.

'She was a widow, not one of those awful spinsters,' said Anita.

Her husband, a retired surgeon, had been one of Jonah's friends in town and, when he died, Mrs Parker was totally distraught. So Jonah persuaded her to be Hooper House mistress, looking after ten near-adults. These Upper Sixth girls loved her company – if she went out at night, Anita would put a hot water bottle in her bed for her to come back to – and Mrs Parker liked to say Jonah saved her life.

But women, on the whole, she just tolerated. She liked men better, particularly the fathers, because she knew which side the bread was buttered. And of course we speculated. She was too together, too confident with men, not to have had *something* going on at some stage. Thinking of Jonah doing the deed was a bit like imagining your parents having sex – you just couldn't. But as per my earlier observation that she grew up on a farm, it's obvious that she knew what went where. Joanna met a boy called Ross one hols. His family were very advanced. He called his parents by their Christian names. They were both having affairs. Ross wrote Joanna passionate letters, very open and explicit. Maggie passed them on to Jonah.

'Your mother's abroad – who's this chap?' Jonah said. She was quite nice about it, started to talk a bit about boys. She'd picked all this up in the letters. Very maternally, she said, 'I really don't think this is a good idea.'

What a relief, as Joanna didn't like Ross much. He was a bit of a pest and she wasn't strong enough to deal with the situation on her own. Mummy wasn't there; she was fourteen hours away. Nana was absorbed in her bridge. Joanna felt protected: 'Jonah's going to solve this.' Jonah was her security.

She whizzed around in a racing-green Jaguar XK140. The Head Girl was the only one apart from her allowed to drive it. Short-sighted, Jonah screwed up her eyes quite a lot, which made them even piggier, and was probably why she misjudged the gateposts at the entrance to Cranmer and inflicted so many scratches on the Jaguar. That and the fact that if she went into town in the evening to mingle with Felixstowe's great and good, she'd roar back having had a few. She drove terribly fast anyway. One yarn about her passed into school folklore. It concerns a time she was barrelling through town with a sixth-former in the passenger seat when the nearside wing mirror caught the handle of a female pedestrian's shopping bag. Jonah roared on regardless, arriving back with the shopping bag hanging off her wing mirror.

I'd heard this so often I began to wonder whether, like the banisters story, it was apocryphal, because everyone who recounted it gave the name of a different girl in the passenger seat, so when I started writing I decided to see if I could put a name to that girl. Then Diana Platts confirmed that it was indeed true, because the sixth-former involved was her older sister, Bretch's time-twin, Yvonne.

Then there were the races with Cawley. No speed cameras then. The police used to say they couldn't catch them because their cars couldn't keep up. Jonah and Cawley would try to cap each other. Cawley would say, 'I've driven from Ipswich to Felixstowe at so-and-so miles an hour,' and Jonah would go, 'That's nothing.'

She came from the Gower Peninsula and would go back there every hols to visit her family. In those days, the approach to Felixstowe was through Trimley, so she was obviously very familiar with the journey, as she'd done it countless times for more than thirty years. On one particular occasion, a policeman stopped her for speeding. Beside her on the passenger seat were strewn maps galore, and the policeman said, 'Oh, I see you are a stranger, Madam,' and Jonah replied, quick as a flash, 'Yes, yes, I am! Where am I?' and she was allowed to get away with it.

She was a brilliant organiser, which went without saying. Oodles of committees were sat on. At one stage she was President of the Association of Headmistresses of Boarding Schools, to which end off she sped to their annual conference. She had a prang on the way, and was still quite shaken up by the time she arrived. 'All I wanted was a stiff gin,' she said later, 'and all they gave me was a cup of tea.'

Two fathers were once overheard discussing her at Speech Day. Both war veterans, they had been naval officers. 'Do you know,' one said, 'she's someone I'd like to see in charge of a destroyer.'

'Hmm,' observed the other. 'Give her a good navigating officer and I'd make it an aircraft carrier.'

He wasn't far wrong. She must be the most impressive woman I have ever known. Surely. And that *is* a fact.

# 16

## COME TO SUNNY FELIXSTOWE

> Felixstowe, although on the East Coast, faces south
> and enjoys the bracing properties of breezes from the
> North Sea. Statistics prove that it has one of the lowest
> rainfalls and one of the highest sunshine records of
> any seaside resort in the British Isles.
>
> *The Felixstowe College Prospectus*

In 1962, Felixstowe College opened a special boarding house
for the Lower Fours, from which they would emerge like
hatchlings to join the main houses in Upper Four. It was called
Wycliffe, after a Protestant martyr who, in spite of popping
up like a bad penny to denounce the official line on this and
that, managed to stay alive long enough to die of a stroke,
though he needn't think he'd got away with it. The Papists
declared him a heretic, removed his corpse from consecrated
ground and burnt it before casting the ashes into the River
Swift. That was him told.

The Lower Four house he gave his name to was a riot – cosy
and cuddly, not nearly as strict as the rest of the school. The

House mistress was Miss Jackson – very jowly, lots of extra chins, lots of make-up, but not scary. The dorms were four interlinked rooms along the top, in the attic.

Gay, Joanna's sister, spent her first year there in 1964, and told me: 'Once we were up there they used to forget all about us. We had amazing games, such as The Bra Shop. Buying each other's bras. I don't know what with because we didn't have any money. People had brought dolls, and we pretended we were giving birth to dolls.'

So Wycliffe was a happy house; so happy, in fact, that lots of girls cried when they had to go home for Christmas but, in the years before, for some, it had been a place of angst and trepidation. Before the college unveiled its purpose-built music school next to the chapel, Wycliffe had been known by another name, Highrow. The music school was in there back then, and the Head of Music was a tall, *maquillée*, good-looking woman of great talent, perhaps too great to be condemned to a life of teaching piano to the sausage-fingered and tin-eared.

It is my bounden duty, before I say anything else, to emphasise that Miss Cornford was a huge force for good in our musical lives. Three of my friends, Helen, Gay and Caroline, have nothing but praise for her. Through her connections we were introduced to some of the most prominent musical names of the era including Imogen Holst and Benjamin Britten in Aldeburgh, which was how we were able to hear a performance of Britten's 'War Requiem' in Ely Cathedral in 1965, and how we got to go to Orford Church for *Noye's Fludde*.

Our school was wonderful for music; second to none. I took piano and clarinet and was lucky enough to sing in the choir and play in the orchestra (third clarinet – there was rather a glut of those, whereas there were few takers for the trombone). My timetable was loaded with music. Theory once a week with Miss Cornford, singing with Miss Cornford, choir practice with Miss Cornford, piano lessons (with Miss Cornford), orchestra practice (conductor, Miss Cornford), clarinet lessons. I loved my clarinet lessons. They were with Mr Hailes, who had a comb-over like Bobby Charlton's and shared my interest in horse racing, but there was a bit too much Miss Cornford for one's peace of mind. The reason why Highrow could at times be a place of misery was that she took offence very easily, and could be a bit of a tartar. A whole thirty-five minutes with that scary woman was in some ways worse than Chemmy, because at least with Cawley you had safety in numbers whereas with Cornford you were on your own. Sometimes she was very batey indeed.

'Cornbags said I was dim,' said Lindy indignantly. Miss Cornford had just pushed her off the piano stool for being unable to do her scales. 'I hate her with all my heart.' Lindy was going to go to Jonah and ask about dropping her in favour of mild-mannered Miss Parfitt.

Others sought more immediate relief. The way into the school dining room led through the cloakrooms. On one side were cabs, and on the other a row of washbasins. One morning, on the way to breakfast, I came across two Tyndales, Jan and Chel, hunched over the basins. Jan was holding Chel's wrist.

'Go on!' urged Chel. 'Hit it!'

Jan, who wouldn't have hurt a fly, looked aghast and tapped it rather gingerly against the edge of the porcelain.

'Hit it harder!' urged Chel. So Jan tried again, a bit harder this time, and then Chel, teeth gritted, took over herself.

'She's got piano with Cornbags this morning,' Jan explained.

Chel was trying to damage her hand so badly that she wouldn't be able to go to her lesson. It ended up so red-raw and inflamed that she had no difficulty getting Sister to sign her off piano. When I saw Chel later that day, her wrist was bandaged and in a sling.

'But Cornbags didn't come in to take my lesson,' she said. 'She was off sick.'

What performances she got us to put on, though. This was where she was really in her element, with her wavy blonde hair and her twin set and tweed skirt, always neat and tidy, waving her conductor's baton, readying the choir. We loved it, and were all ready to bounce off as the first note struck. And at the end, when the sopranos hit the top notes, she would beam and put her hands together and say, 'Thank you.' When she wasn't in a bate, it was great; she made you want to perform. The nativity play at the end of my first term is one of my loveliest memories.

It couldn't be just any old nativity play, of course. This was The Nativity of Our Lord Jesus Christ, and it was to be held at the Spa Pavilion, as our chapel was too small to accommodate the slaves, citizens, angels, candle-bearers, boys and choral speaking group, along with the usual suspects, to say nothing of the parents. The aisle of our chapel wouldn't have been long enough for the opening procession, complete with twinkling lights and expectant hush, which was partly down to the solemnity of the occasion but also because we knew that after it was over there would be HOME. A comfortable bed, Rebel the terrier, my shelf of model horses and my books, and putting up the tree and making paper chains, hunting for mistletoe in the forest that was right opposite our house, choosing the most berried sprigs from the holly bushes in our garden, and wrapping presents; and with luck my mother wouldn't whinge because the present Jane had given her was cheaper than the one she'd given Jane.

Caroline and Jan trilled away in the sopranos while I was lower down the register in the altos, and Helen's big sister, Lydia, sang a solo. Lydia was the music school's special one, la-la-la-ing all the way to Girton College, Cambridge. I've no idea what the solo was. All I remember of it now is a few bars, the moment that voice, young, silver, true, rang out in the dark silence.

The solo was Lydia's swansong. I'd never hear her sing again, as that was her last term. But I didn't need to. The sound has never gone away. Transcendence, in just a few bars of a song.

Summer brought our next big production. We were going to perform 'Hiawatha's Wedding Feast', a choral work by Samuel Coleridge-Taylor, who had been so inspired by Henry Longfellow's epic poem, *The Song of Hiawatha*, that not only did he set it to music but he also gave the name to his son. Hiawatha Coleridge-Taylor. Poor little chap.

It was the climax to a term of unfettered bliss (for the most part – there was still Chemmy to be endured). But all the things I enjoyed were in the summer term. We swam in the sea (gorgeous), changing into our swimming things on Cranmer lawn, then picking our way down to the water over the steps – huge stones, really – in hideous rubbery bathing caps and regulation cozzies. The bathing sessions took place in a rough square from breakwater to breakwater. Coulo, the Games mistress, would supervise from a boat, eyes travelling from one of us to another in turn, rowing automatically as if – were her attention to lapse for a moment – some calamity would ensue, as we splashed around, trying not to swallow salt water or meet a jellyfish. What fun! But not for Coulo.

We had the school gymkhana, and Erica won the showing event on her own pony. I rode Huntsman in the show jumping. We were disqualified for three refusals, but at least he didn't stop to pee. The seniors had their annual trip to Wimbledon, and we all celebrated Bretch's birthday, when her present was made by Ridley, and had to be bigger and better than the previous year's offering, and she would give us a treat in return – ice cream with our tea, strawberries, toffee apples.

It was the midnight feast season, too, because in June came Old Girls' Weekend, when by tradition Lower Fives gave up their beds, so former inmates could have the excitement of sleeping in dorms once again. In return we were allowed to camp out on the floor of the junior commie – more fun! The French doors opened directly on to the garden, which meant another exodus at the stroke of twelve, and this time a banquet that included tinned pears and asparagus (not together), granny smith apples, Penguins, Ginger Nuts, Oxo crisps, chocolate cake and, best of all, a pomegranate. We were allowed to order fruit once a week from the greengrocer, and this was the surprise that Della had sprung on us. We had never had pomegranate before. She shared it out – one seed each – and we savoured them.

And going on all through the term were rehearsals for this monumental Speech Day production of 'Hiawatha's Wedding Feast'. And not just on Speech Day – we were going to do it three times, floodlit on Highrow's lawn, to raise money for Jonah's Appeal Fund for the new, bigger chapel and a swimming pool. On Wednesday and Friday the performance would follow a barbecue on the Games pitches, and on Speech Day it would close a fête that included a dog show (prizes for 'Most Attractive Dog' and 'Dog with the Waggliest Tail'). The choir would sing, the orchestra would play, and 117 girls dressed as leaves and Indians would mime the action. I was to be in the choir, and was looking forward to it awfully. But I had not reckoned on Beth.

It so happened that to pay her back for cracking an egg over my head I had very recently given Beth an apple pie bed, incorporating her hairbrush and two spam fritters. She had accepted it without comment and even good grace, which should have alerted me, because Beth was very much an eye-for-an-eye girl and firmly in the dish-best-eaten-cold camp. But the days passed without retributive action and I suppose I was lulled into a sense of false security.

We were on our way to Singing. The walk to Highrow was a long one but lovely in the summer, with the sky an old-fashioned postcard blue, the gardens a riot of colour, the Games pitches spruce and all-over bright green, and the grass courts echoing to the thwack of tennis balls and shouts of 'Played!' and 'Shot!' Highrow's trees were in full leaf, and from the shrubbery came the intoxicating smell of lavender.

'What's Beth doing?' Chrissie said suddenly.

She was kneeling by the herbaceous border, the skirt of her

red-checked summer dress tucked over her knees. She seemed
to be rummaging around the soil and now she was scooping
something into a matchbox. Then she straightened up, slipped
the matchbox into her pocket and brushed earth off her dress
before gazing at us with that evil smile of hers.

'This bodes no good,' I said to Chrissie.

We were starting on the second verse of 'The Ash Grove' (as
arranged by Benjamin Britten), when I felt a tickling around
the back of my neck. It moved to my shoulder and then down a
bit and, when I looked, a bug of some description was crawling
along my arm. I jerked my elbow out to dislodge it, catching
Cherry right between her non-growing bosoms, and she let
out an involuntary shriek. There was a rattle of the baton on
the music stand. Miss Cornford's eyes bored in on me.

'Go outside. Miss Jones will be told how you misbehaved in
Singing. See her after supper.'

I walked slowly out, head bowed, trying not to cry. Then
I sat and waited for Chrissie to come out, and when I saw
her I just burst into tears. 'That's done for me now,' I sobbed.
'Cornbags will throw me out of the choir and I won't be in
Hiawatha!'

I wanted to murder Beth, but she was keeping out of my
way. At tennis she made up a four with the Tyndales, and
at tea she sat at the other end of the table and grinned at me
evilly. Everybody seemed to think what a great joke it was.
How mean of them. It wasn't as if I'd made a big thing about
being in the choir. Well, I might have trilled a bit. But I
hadn't swanked. I hadn't lain in bed softly humming 'Onaway
Awake, Beloved' while everybody else had to spend hours
scrubbing greasepaint off their arms and legs and faces because

they were only leaves or Indians. I endured the rest of the day as best I could and, after supper, I trudged up to the top floor of Cranmer and Jonah.

'Apparently you misbehaved in Singing.'

'Yes, Miss Jones. Sorry, Miss Jones.'

'What happened?'

'I jogged the arm of the person next to me and made her sing the wrong note.'

'Why did you do that?'

'I don't know.'

'Did something happen?'

'Not really.'

'That's not true, is it? A girl did something that made you do it.'

'Well . . .'

I can't tell on Beth. It's dishonourable to sneak. I was enjoying the feeling of being virtuous, although a small voice told me it was really because Beth would despise me if I told on her.

'Miss Cornford knows you weren't to blame. Off you go.'

Chrissie was waiting for me when I got out. 'How did it go?'

'Oh, she was jolly decent. She knew it wasn't my fault. Someone must have told on Beth.'

'No. Cath's just told me. Beth owned up and apologised.'

Well, bugger Beth, to be honest. By then I was looking forward to being hailed as a hero and a martyr. She had stolen my thunder. She had owned up and apologised, and taken her punishment, which was a letter to her parents and having to run twice round the Games pitches before breakfast. She was the hero now. But at least it meant I was still in the choir.

Whenever I thought about it in later years — and it was always one of my favourite school memories — 'Hiawatha's Wedding Feast' was bathed in sunshine. Highrow's lawn was stippled with daisies and dappled with shadows. Miss Cornford waved her conductor's baton against a background of gaily painted wigwams and a tree transformed into a totem pole. Bees hovered above the lavender hedge. There were butterflies.

The school had hired a professional singer called Grace Something to sing the lead but, because she was a contralto, with one of those rich, vibrato voices like quivering treacle, she dropped an octave every time she had to sing the top note. Each time it happened I felt a kind of existential jolt, as if all the rivers in the world had suddenly started flowing backwards. It must have been the dress rehearsal I was thinking of as so idyllic because what actually happened was the opposite — as inverted and topsy-turvy as Grace Something's solo. It poured with rain. All week. It didn't rain all the time; deviously, it would stop long enough for the skies to clear and the roads to dry, and the parents to set off to enjoy the Wednesday and Friday night barbecues, and the dog show and raffle and darts and stalls on Saturday.

Once everything was set out, the face paint applied, the cars turning in to the temporary parking on the Games pitches, it would start to rain again. The Right Reverend, the Lord Bishop of St Edmundsbury and Ipswich, opened the fête hanging on to an umbrella. The choir and orchestra had to go inside and sing and play with the French doors open. The French windows were opened and the parents, probably driven by Jonah with a pitchfork, had to sit outside and listen. How could I have forgotten that?

In fact, my recall of 'Hiawatha's Wedding Feast' was completely unlike what really happened in all respects except one. Grace Something was still singing 'Onaway Awake Beloved' upside-down. But the fact I remember everything as being bathed in sun proves how much I loved it. Though it would be some time before I forgave Beth for the bug.

# 17

# THE PHANTOM CLOTHES STREWER

Something had happened when we came back after the summer hols of 1962. Our orchard wasn't there. Instead we had a building. The Art and Dance studio had sprung up next to Ridley. Chrissie and I signed up for Modern Dance. Life in Middle Five was leotards and leggings, the soundtrack 'Slaughter on Tenth Avenue', 'Rhapsody in Blue' and 'Je Ne Regrette Rien'.

Our new commie was spacious. We didn't have to share it with the juniors. We danced in there too, in the space between the tables. We bopped to Bobby Vee and 'The Night Has a Thousand Eyes', and Mark Wynter's 'Venus in Blue Jeans', and 'Sherry Baby' by the Four Seasons. We held twist competitions to the sound of Chubby Checker. *Let's twist again, like we did last summer* . . . and we did, again and again, knees wiggling, heels jiggling, arms swinging. The Middle Five commie was jam-packed with undulating hips. We heard the Beatles for the first time, a muffled and crackly 'Love Me Do' on Radio Luxembourg. Why did I like it so much? 'The Night Has a Thousand Eyes' had more of a tune but 'Love Me Do' gave me the strangest feeling. It was a kind of snapping of a rope. I was separate from my parents. I was entering a world they couldn't share.

Middle Five meant perks. We were allowed to have a boiled egg with our tea. We could put our names down on a list for Rose the maid to cook, specifying whether we wanted hard-boiled or soft. We ironed the bread. The end product was damp, but it was warm, and butter melted on it deliciously. We could put up posters. Of matadors, mainly – gorgeous young men in tight trousers and spangled jackets, flapping cloths at huge creatures mad with pain. Who cared about the moral rep-rehensibility of a spectator sport that featured the torture and killing of an animal? It was the matadors' buttocks that inter-ested us. Anyway, we were used to all those images of Christ on the cross. Blood, gore and suffering were our wallpaper.

The best perk of all was choosing our O Level subjects. Lindy fought to give up Maths. 'You don't need Maths O Level to do a job,' she said. 'Anyway, women don't have to work. You give up when you get married. We don't go anywhere, so, come to that, what's the point of Geography and Languages? It's all just very, very hard work. And boring. Why do it?'

But nobody gave up Maths. It was something you just had to do, like Chapel and Games, whatever the weather. You might as well say you were going to put a halt to the sun rising tomorrow. But in and out of Jonah's study Lindy went, stating her case. She had found something called RSA Arithmetic. What on earth was that? She explained. RSA stood for Royal Society of Arts or, to give it its full name, The Royal Society for the Encouragement of Arts, Manufactures and Commerce. It was a major examining body concentrating on vocational and non-academic subjects, mainly in commercial and office skills and Languages. One of the exams offered was Arithmetic. It was considered to be more useful to office staff and shopkeepers than Algebra and Geometry.

'Shopkeepers and office staff,' I said. 'Jonah won't like that.'

'How many tins of paint do you need for a sitting room if you have a ceiling height of fourteen feet?' asked Lindy rhetorically. 'How much weedkiller do you need for half an acre of lawn? Knowing about an isosceles triangle isn't going to solve any of THAT.'

I was astonished by Lindy's fixity of purpose. It was a battle Jonah was never going to win. No more Maths for Lindy. And for me, no more Chemmy. My O Levels would be English Lang., English Lit., French, Spanish, Latin, Maths, Bilge, History and Geography. Never again would I have to enter Cawley's shard-strewn lair.

## Girls to see Miss Jones
### J. Welch

'Your mother's written to me asking why you've dropped Chemistry. She wants you to keep taking it because she thinks you'll need it when you go into the family firm.'

Oh, of course. Now my sister was going to marry the fast businessman, whom my father flatly refused to employ, my mother had designated me in her dynastic fantasy as the one who would take over the business.

That was the trouble with adults; they couldn't just let you get on with it. They were always trying to make you into something you didn't want to be, and either what you did want to be was something they didn't approve of, or they told you it wasn't possible because you were a girl, and girls just couldn't do that. Because even if I'd wanted to take over the family firm, my father wouldn't have let me in a million years, not even if I'd been all the most brilliant business brains in the world rolled into one, because I was a GIRL.

And so my mother then blamed me because I wasn't a boy, because if I'd been a boy all this wouldn't have happened; bloody Jane wouldn't have been made a director of the company and everything would be wonderful and skippety-doodah. Etc. etc.

So it was all my fault, but as I would never be anything but a girl there was nothing much I could do about it. And never, never, would I go back to Chemmy and sit in that lab while Cawley squawked and threw test tubes. The woman was deranged.

'I don't want to go into the family firm. I'm going to be a writer.'

'Hmph?'

You could always tell when Jonah was really interested, rather than being about to deliver a ticking-off, because she would put her head on one side and look at you straight through her glasses, rather than glare at you over the top of them. 'What are you going to write about?'

Everything. Heroes and gangsters and glory. Horses. My friends. Having adventures. Everything about being alive. I want to make people laugh. And cry now and again. Writing's everything to me. It's all I've ever wanted to do, it's what I've known I was going to be, it's the only thing I'm really good at. I want to write the whole world.

'Um . . . not sure yet,' I mumbled.

'I'll write to your mother and explain that English is your strong subject and you need to be doing Languages,' said Jonah firmly.

So no more Chemmy for me because Jonah was on my side. She had protected me. Her word was the last word. Even my mother knew that. All was well with the world again.

Except it wasn't. In fact, it was about to end. October 1962 was the month of the Cuban missile crisis. The USA vs. the Soviet Union. JFK vs. Mr Khrushchev. It was something to do with the deployment of nuclear missiles. I didn't really understand all that stuff. I just knew that I was I was about to be vaporised out of existence before I'd barely begun.

We huddled in the commie with the prefect who'd come in to tell us to go to our baths. She sat down with us instead and discussed how long it would take for the fallout of a bomb dropped on Russia to reach Suffolk. That was even more frightening because she was a Big Girl and if Big Girls were taking it seriously we really were doomed. What would we do when the four-minute warning came? Ridley didn't have a nuclear bunker. The only place we could think of was Dan Dan the Boilerman's cellar. And what would Jonah do, hide under her desk?

But of course all that cowering would be pointless because Felixstowe College would just go up in clouds of smoke and steam and dust like everywhere else. And if it didn't, it would still be The End. Eventually. I had read Neville Shute's *On the Beach* and remembered how the hero didn't get blown to smithereens, or die of radiation sickness along with his friends and loved ones first time round. He got it and recovered. But he knew the sickness would come back, so he sat in his car, the solitary survivor, and took a kill pill. Perhaps Rayment would supply something similar to us at Sug when the time came.

I didn't want to die. Except for going to Heaven, there wasn't much to recommend it. Even Heaven might turn out to be not all it was cracked up to be. What would we all do up there? Would it be lovely, like summer term, swimming in the sparkling sea and playing tennis and having midnight feasts all over the place? Or more like Sunday afternoons in winter when *Pick of the Pops* had finished and it was too wet and cold to go outside, and we had to sit around mending stuff and Erica would start picking on someone because she was bored, and then we would have to go to Evening Chapel for all eternity, with nothing to do to pass the time but count how many times Elly-J said 'and'.

And what if you were punished for past sins? I'd probably be dragged along to see Grandma and Grandpa Welch, like I'd had to when we were all alive, and I'd had to sit still and be quiet amidst the gloomy Victorian furniture (one room was filled entirely with glass cases of stuffed owls); Grandma with arthritic fingers at an angle of thirty-five degrees, so she couldn't even knit any more, and Grandpa empty-eyed from glaucoma, and thus empty of everything in life that had amused him, like reading books and riding bicycles and walking on his hands. We had to see them every Wednesday, and one day my big sister told me to fake a sickie, and then we wouldn't have to. So that's what I did, and two days after that Grandma was found dead on the floor of her kitchen. It was a judgement. I might as well have clubbed her over the head myself.

And I'd go there without having written any of the books I was going to write. Or having got married and had lots of children, which was my next ambition after being a writer. Would Jane be there with my parents, leaving me to play gooseberry till the end of time? And apparently animals weren't admitted, so what would happen to Rebel? Would he be left out in the cold? And Chrissie would probably have to be billeted with her family, so I wouldn't even have her. No one to get into absolute hysterics with, or save me a place on coach trips, or write stories and draw cartoons or imitate Bretch and Wrinch with; no one to put their arm round me if I cried. I would be so lonely. Forever.

This could not go on. It was all getting very silly. Miss McNulty restored order. 'There will be no World War Three,' she said firmly, sitting angular and upright at her table at lunch the next day. She was a Catholic, so she would never lie. She was correct. There was no World War Three. That was that. We stopped thinking about our imminent extinction and moved on to the next drama: The Phantom Clothes Strewer of Ridley House. One of the great unsolved mysteries.

'Someone's been moving our clothes,' Chrissie said to Juno and Wisty, as the four of us marched along to Riding in our hacking jackets and jodhpurs, my hard hat still with the little V torn out of it where I'd hit the ground falling off Prince all that time ago in Cornwall.

It was a real November day. No sea, just a fog blanket. Blank windows all along the clifftop hotels. The stables were in a residential road, quite a walk from school. They must have been a coach yard at some point. It was a big paved yard scattered with straw and manure, with stables for seven or eight nags, most of which would have found their way into beefburgers these days. It exuded the usual horsey pong, which at that age you think is elixir. It was run by two men called Seelly and Blackie. Seelly was ancient and bow-legged and had probably been in the army, out in India. Blackie was a bit younger and had black hair going grey and a red face, but I was so man-starved he might have been Cary Grant.

'Our Games things,' I elucidated. 'Dressing gowns. Blouses and ties. Bras even. When you wake up in the morning they're all over the place. The Games pitches. On trees. In puddles on the cloakroom floor. And water poured on beds, too. It's been going on for weeks. Bretch is going potty.'

'Potti*er*,' said Chrissie.

'Perhaps you've got a poltergeist,' said Wisty.

'Oh – *what*?'

'Actually,' said Juno, 'I remember hearing about this Tyndale who woke up in the morning to find somebody had shaved her eyebrows off.'

'Golly,' said Chrissie. 'She must have been a very deep sleeper. I mean, wouldn't you have woken up and noticed at the time?'

'Well,' said Juno, 'there was a bit more to it than met the eye.'

'Eye*brow*,' I said.

'Shall I carry on?' she said, in her best 'I'm a Cranmer' voice.

'Sorry.'

'Everyone in her dorm was grilled. They all swore they hadn't done it. Then she woke up to find that her shirt and cardigan had had the sleeves cut off. The dorm-mates were sent to Jonah. Still swore they hadn't done it. Her parents came storming up to Felixstowe and threatened to bring in the police, and in the end the poor kid broke down and admitted it was her all along. Because she'd asked them again and again to take her away from this horrible place and they wouldn't listen. Anyway, she got what she wanted. They took her home with them the same day.'

When Chrissie and I got back from our ride, we told the others about Eyebrows Girl over our teatime toast and boiled eggs. Everyone made sympathetic noises and said, 'No! Poor thing!' and speculated who in Ridley could possibly be that miserable, but our thoughts soon switched to evening lessons – 'Another Maths test! Bound to be ghastly!' – and we got into our outdoor things and set off in the wind and rain to the school block.

'At least we've got Drama,' someone said, at which I remembered I was meant to bring in my wellingtons because we were rehearsing a skit called 'Mud, Mud, Glorious Mud', so I muttered that I'd catch everyone up and ran back down the path to Ridley.

The cloakroom seemed strange and eerie because it was empty and I didn't dare switch the light on because I wasn't meant to be there. Wellies were kept in a big wooden box in the corner, and I had to be quick because Maths was first thing, so it was all a bit welly-nelly ... I was chucking them on the floor in the frantic haste to find mine. It was no use. I'd have to have some light. And it was there, by the light switch, that the prefect found me.

'What are you doing?'

It was just like being accosted by a policeman. You automatically feel guilty even if you aren't. I went bright red and tried to explain, but I could see she was looking over my shoulder at the scattered wellingtons and could almost hear the cogs in her brain whirring.

After supper, I had to go and be grilled by Bretch. She was decent about it and I thought that was the end of the matter, but it was too late. In the febrile atmosphere, it only took one person in the wrong place at the wrong time to make everyone suspicious, and all of a sudden I was being looked at askance and sent to Coventry. How rotten people could be, Chrissie and I thought, because she'd told everyone it couldn't be me, because she was with me practically all the time – except for that one dash to the cloakroom, of course – and anyway, I wasn't remotely the sort of person who would creep around in the middle of the night hanging bras on trees.

The perpetrator became more daring, or desperate; stuff was moved in broad daylight. Then it happened one week-end when I was away on exeat with my parents. My trial was over. Everyone knew it couldn't have been me. But it had been horrid, absolutely horrid. Worse than all that stuff about World War Three, because I'd had a taste of how it felt to be unpopular. After a while the clothes stopped being moved, so I hope whoever was doing it had some help and care. We never did find out who it was.

Chrissie had turned out to be a fabulous dancer. Delicate in her footwork. Controlled in her movement. Just naturally sexy and sinuous. The strange thing was that the minute the music stopped she was crashing into things all over the place, as if she suddenly wasn't used to her body. Doors held a magnetic attraction for her, or perhaps it was the other way round, and she held the attraction for doors. She would only have to stand in one's vicinity and it would fly open and bash her. She sported bruises on her shins, bumps on her forehead, even one week a black eye that gradually turned the shade of Mrs Kahn's scrambled egg. And at the same time if any bug was going the rounds it would make straight for her, so when it wasn't a stinking cold it was feeling sick. Naturally, when German measles struck, she was one of the first to succumb.

More than half the school got it. Lucky pigs, no lessons for them. The San was already stuffed full, so dorms became isolation rooms and people lolled around all day and night, reading and listening to Radio Luxembourg and eating sweets, smug because they didn't have to go to Games and wouldn't have deaf babies when they grew up. Della won the jackpot. About a year before that, her mother had sent her to school with her big sister's vest on, and it turned out she was allergic to wool, because the skin on her chest came out in a vest-shaped rash. So a year later, when she dutifully went to Rayment and told her she was down with measles, a rather harassed Rayment said, 'No, dear, you've been wearing wool again, go away.' Then Della went home on exeat that weekend and the doctor was called about her wool rash. 'That's no wool rash,' he said, 'You've got German measles.' She was the luckiest pig of all. She had two weeks at home.

I didn't get it, not a single measle. What I did get was an awful letter about my mother.

Not until I was well into adulthood did I consider how unhappy my mother must have been, feeling lonely and unwanted and blazingly jealous of Jane. She was angry. A

Fury. It made her unkind. But who could she be unkind to? Not my father or Jane. So it had to be me. I was the youngest and smallest. The easiest target.

She couldn't stand me, it appeared. I watched other girls with their mothers – they would sit close, they talked about stuff, they shared a world. I was shouted at and criticised and called names. But my father would not come to my rescue. If I tried to stand up for myself, he would tell me to stop worrying my mother. He felt guilty. He was afraid of her temper, and he wanted a quiet life. I dreamed of him saying, 'What do you mean by saying all these untrue things? She's wonderful, she's the finest, loveliest, most beautiful girl in the world.' Or at least, 'Leave her alone, she's doing her best.' Then I would have felt much better because I had an ally. But obviously I was not worth breaching the peace for.

One afternoon Bretch, as usual, brought our letters into the commie when we came back from lunch and laid them out on the table by the door. There was one for me, with the postmark of my home town, but the writing on the envelope was unfamiliar. It was from a friend of my parents. She had noticed, she wrote, how my mother treated me, and asked if I would like her to intervene.

Awful, awful! I was so used to being treated unkindly that I didn't recognise kindness when it was being offered. What was this stupid woman doing, writing to me? Why shouldn't my mother treat me the way she did? I deserved it. I was bad and disappointing and ugly and useless. I had completely let her down. And besides, what would happen if I took up this friend's offer? My mother would be sure to find out. And there would be hell to pay.

And I remembered how she'd been when I was much younger. Just lovely. Playful and warm. She smiled a lot, and especially at me. Now she glared. But I wanted to keep her on her pedestal, even if that meant I had to be the bad one. I could take it, if it would help. I got rid of the letter as if it was a dose of poison and made myself forget about it. So successfully did I blot it out that I only remembered what had happened three years ago, after she died.

I wasn't the only one with mother difficulties. Juno's seemed even more troubled than mine. She drank, and had just fallen out of her car in Cranmer drive when arriving to take Juno out on exeat. So everyone knew. They had seen it. Those that hadn't seen it were told about it.

'My father's a magistrate and he drives around completely plastered a lot of the time,' I said, trying to be comforting, as we walked to Riding.

Juno didn't answer, and fatally I didn't leave it at that but went wittering on in a light-hearted vein about all the hilarious things my father had done while blotto, such as raising his hat to a lamppost and saying, 'Good evening, Madam,' and mistaking Rebel for a cushion and plumping him up, and then there was the time the doorbell rang and I answered it and it was a taxi driver who said, 'I believe this is your father,' and he was standing there grinning and so pie-eyed he couldn't even put one leg in front of the other to walk over the threshold. I had to prop him against the wall, fetch a chair and push him into it to sleep it off right there in the hall. And suddenly Juno roared, 'SHUUT UUUUUUP!'

We walked on, neither of us saying a thing. What kind of insensitive ass was I? My daddy is convivial. He likes to make us all laugh. He's never shamed me in public. And there's Juno, with her raving alkie of a mother, and here's her wound, and I've rubbed it red-raw. Ground, swallow me up.

And then Juno gave my arm a little friendly pinch.

'I say, my friend wrote and told me an absolutely killing story about her school yesterday.'

'What? Tell me!'

'Scandal. The Games mistress and the Games captain. Someone was sent up to the Games captain's room to get some scoresheets. A suitcase on top of the wardrobe wasn't closed properly – it burst open and all these letters fell out. Love letters from the Games mistress. So they read them.'

'No!'

'Oh yes! And the music teacher and one of the girls were caught on top of the piano. My friend thinks they were just fiddling, but they both had to leave.'

Let other pens dwell on guilt and misery.

# 18

# FILTHY BATES

I was very keen to get back to school for spring term 1963 because in the Christmas holidays I'd had my first kiss and I wanted to let everyone know about it. It was at a dance at the house next door, where they had the ballroom, and at midnight we had the Fireman's Waltz, in which you all trundled round and round, and then the music stopped, the lights went off and you had to kiss your partner.

The boy was called Nigel, and he was probably the smallest, most unappealing and desperate person there apart from me. The kiss just went on and on. I'd honestly had more fun cleaning my teeth. He obviously thought the same because after about a minute of bumping our lips together and pressing and snuffling, he said, 'Let's stop now, shall we?' And then we had to stand there in the dark listening to everyone else slurping and sighing and rustling each other's clothes till the lights went back on. There was another boy there who I fancied much more, so, when I wrote about it in my diary that night, next to Nigel's name I put a full stop that looked more like a comma and then the fanciable boy's name, and then a dash and a 'Wow!', so if anyone peeked at my diary they might think I'd been kissed by both.

Which is where I was happy to leave it for now. I didn't want to go on a date or anything, not that he'd asked. I could just picture it. Sort of. We'd have to kiss each other for ages again, wouldn't we? Then there would be a whole evening to get through in which we'd have to talk. It would be like sitting next to someone at lunch who you didn't have anything in common with because she wasn't in your form. All I wanted was to get back to school with my new First Kiss Brownie Badge of Womanhood, where I could savour my triumph from a long way away, and moan with the others about the exams they always made us take the very first week of term.

Why did they make us take them the minute we got back? Did they want to spoil Christmas and New Year by making us revise and worry and stay up late peering at our books? We wouldn't have put it past the old bags. We staggered out of the classrooms, grimacing and putting our hands to our cheeks. 'Maths was ghastly!' 'Geography was foul!' 'I'm bound to have failed!' 'I couldn't do a scrap! I had to waffle madly!'

Meanwhile, snow was falling, snow on snow. Snow on sodding snow, as Christina Gabriel Rosetti nearly said in 'In the Bleak Midwinter'. The Big Freeze was how it was described in the papers. All of Britain was paralysed. January recorded the lowest temperatures of the twentieth century and February was hardly any better. Anything less like spring you could not imagine. The sea was solid ice from Dunkirk to Herne Bay and someone drove a car along the Thames at Oxford. On our first Sunday back, piling into the cloakroom to put on our Harris Tweed coats for Morning Chapel, someone exclaimed, 'Oh, what's happening? Has cab overflowed? I'm paddling!'

Erica ran to fetch Bretch, and along she sailed to survey

the rising tide in the cloakroom, rolling her lips together thoughtfully before hurrying off to commune with Dan Dan the Boilerman in his Dan-cave. It turned out a pipe had burst and flooded the floor. What fun!

Dan was kept busy. A few days later, another pipe burst in the Lower Six dorm and drips came off the lights and ceiling in our commie. Then water started pouring down the walls and through the gap under the door into the corridor. We had to move back into the junior commie for tea, then moved operations into Ridley's little library at the far corner of the house.

You couldn't see out of any windows, as they were curtained by snow and ice. In the classroom we might as well have been back in the eighteenth century half the time because we had to work by candlelight. The electricity went on and off, and on and off, like the lights at Piccadilly Circus. We had one Bilge lesson illuminated by Bunsen burners. The northeast wind howled. Chrissie was commie captain that term, and one of her duties was to fetch Bretch's supper from Cranmer. It must have been stone cold when it got to Ridley, if it hadn't been blown off the plate on the way.

We were let back into our own commie at the end of January. It was still snowing. Lower Six got into a huge row because Bretch was eavesdropping outside their dorm door and overheard them saying she looked like a cab brush. She did! Just like one! It went all round House and soon the whole school heard about it. Round and round the dining room went the news. 'You've never heard anything so killing in your entire life . . . Balloon and Jo said Bretch looks like a cab brush!' We were in absolute fits.

That weekend we had a snowball fight after Chapel. A prefect sent us to Bretch who, after giving us a filthy row, said we could have another after lunch provided we wore macs and boots. It was absolutely sweet of her. We built a snowman and gave it a cab brush for a head.

No games, of course. The pitches had vanished. They lay somewhere under a giant white frozen marshmallow. We said hurrah too soon. Coulo made us practise lax stick work in the gym instead and gave very long lectures about tactics on a blackboard. Or we had to go for cross-country runs alongside the clifftops and beside the beach, the wind blowing, minus ten degrees, in our divided skirts. Though if you timed it right you could be a tail-ender, hide behind a beach hut and rejoin on the way back.

There was no let-up. Everywhere stayed white and snowing. When it wasn't snow, it was hail. I developed chilblains on my feet. Giant chilblains, as big and pink as carnations. All Rayment could think of was to cover them in her all-purpose goo. Who was the Middle Five sexpot now? Not me. I minced around, feet squelching in my shoes, itching and scratching. They were hot and painful, and I was very bad-tempered. But then we all were, stuck in the commie together for hours on end, Marlee blubbing in a corner because she wanted a friend to tell things to and she hated everybody because they were always foul to her, and Marion getting on everyone's wick because she kept going on about her hair being greasy. Greasy? She should try having my feet.

Marion stuck her nose in the air. 'You don't know your onions,' she said.

'What?'

'She means you're weird,' said Beth.

'And you've always been weird and you always will be weird,' said Marion. 'Your whole family's weird.'

I was going to smack her face but my hand hit my glasses on the way up and they flew across the floor and broke. I picked them up and put them back on crooked, which Beth apparently found the most hilarious thing that had ever happened in the entire history of the universe, so I slapped her horrid yok-yokking face instead of Marion's.

'Danny, don't be silly.' Chrissie grabbed my hand. 'Calm down.'

I stopped to think about it. No, I didn't want to calm down. 'You all get on my wick! *Waaa-haa-haaaa!*'

I ran out of the commie in floods. Then Beth ran out in floods. Cath and Chrissie followed me to the dorm and made soothing noises while Prue and Della went off to cheer Beth up, and eventually we all went back to the commie and got on with what we'd been doing.

But that wasn't the end of the *sturm und drang*. By no means. It was nothing compared to what happened next. *Erica and Bobbie broke up.*

The break-up between Erica and Bobbie was awful. A term-defining drama. Erica dumped Bobbie to go round with Lindy. They had a huge, hysterical scene in the dorm. At least, Bobbie was hysterical, then took to her bed. She pulled the covers over her head like a turtle and sobbed for five whole hours. It was horrible, like a divorce. Every night she cried and cried till the covers shook, while Erica, in the next bed to her, tried to pretend it wasn't happening. During the day Bobbie wore a vampiric look, with a ghastly pallor and her lovely soot-black hair all lank and her eyes red-rimmed, and she'd be waiting in Ridley drive for a couple to ask her to walk with them over to breakfast while Lindy and Erica strolled off into the distance. The dreadful thing was that although I was very sad for her an even stronger feeling was that I was glad it wasn't me.

'Oh, but Lindy, how can you go around with Erica, she's so bossy!' I wailed.

'If you can't beat them, join them,' said Lindy calmly.

# 19

# The Captain of the Seconds

The freeze of early 1963 hung on and on till February was nearly over. One day, though, came the sound of melted snow rushing down gutters, and dripping off branches, and car tyres sloshing along a wet Maybush Lane, and gradually the playing fields were visible again. *House Games would go ahead.*

House matches were staged every term. They had meaning. Blood would be shed, elbows deployed, sticks whirled. One Ridley got a lax ball in the eye, which nearly destroyed her sight. One year our Games captain staggered off the pitch able to waggle her nose between her fingers. Shots ricocheted from goalie's pad to foreheads. There was always someone being carted away to have stitches. But House matches carried on being held, because it gave opportunities to people who otherwise wouldn't experience the thrill of playing in a team. It was democratic. Everyone should have the chance to be miserable on the Games pitches.

But I wouldn't have been miserable. Secretly I craved to be good at Games. But I wasn't, not really. I ran around enthusiastically. I did not, unlike some of the others, hide in the wardrobe or under the bed. No names, no pack drill but, unlike one of my form-mates, I didn't get out of them by sticking a finger up a nostril and shoving it around till I got a nosebleed. But my legs were short, I ate too much and my glasses misted up when I was hot.

If you were good at Games, you could escape to another place for a few hours. You could meet another school and they'd all complain about how awful their school was. One of my friends boarded at a convent, one the day the hockey team had an away match against an approved school. My friend and her teammates were shown around and it was lovely. Sprung mattresses, single rooms, pretty curtains. Then the delinquent girls arrived for the return fixture. They were astonished. 'You mean,' they gasped, 'your parents actually *pay* to send you here?'

But I never got picked for anything. And then the list went up on the Ridley noticeboard for House Games and my name was on the team sheet. C for Centre: ME! I was captain. Captain of Ridley lacrosse seconds. I'd never been captain of anything.

My sporting debut was on a dank, blustery day. The touchlines were barely visible. On one side was what seemed like all of Ridley, out in force, the dull grey of macs and tunics and stockings livened up by our House colours of cornflower blue. Teddy bears had been press-ganged into supporting, dressed in tiny knitted blue jerseys and scarves; bunches were tied with blue ribbon; someone was wearing her (blue) dressing gown over her outdoor clothes. Even Bretch had swapped her brown winter suit for a navy Dannimac and blue umbrella.

I was on fire. The northeast wind blasted up the legs of my divided skirt as I sprinted behind the Cranmer goal, specs misted with effort, knees caked in mud and stained with grass, despite the fact that rain had been falling since face-off and that in between quarters I'd been trying to rinse them clean with the sleeve of my sweater. The detour took me on to the path by the fence that marked the end of our playing fields, where a steady stream of melted slush flowed towards the road and slopped over the top of my boots on to my lovely blue Ridley socks, although as those were already sodden anyway this hardly mattered.

We had been hanging on to a one-goal lead, and then Cranmer equalised. Heads went down. I was the captain. I had to galvanise my team. I was Danny Blanchflower in that famous sixth-round FA Cup tie against Sunderland, in the double-winning season of 1960–61: 'Now keep your heads and let's get going after a goal. We don't want that business down in our goalmouth again.' Well, I raised a clenched fist, anyway. 'Come on, Ridley!' I shouted.

Back on the pitch, I hurtled towards the crease with the Cranmer left defence, an enormous Upper Five with rollicking bosoms, hacking at my stick. This was it. This was my moment. This was when I performed the trick that regularly made Coulo flap her tracksuit top and twitch. I switched hands. It looked odd and ridiculous but it always worked. I was now cradling on the other side. My opponent couldn't reach my stick in time. The cry went up. *Shooooot!* And *whump* – my shot bounced into the net off the goalie's padded legs.

I had scored a goal. I had scored for Ridley. Two-one, two-one, two-one, two-one. And then the final whistle went. Ridley had won the Lacrosse 2nds Cup.

My last duty as captain was to raise my lax stick. 'Three cheers for Cranmer! Hip-hip–'

'Hurrah!'

'Hip-hip—'

'Hurrah!'

'Hip-hip—'

'Hurrah!'

Back at House, I swaggered nonchalantly into the kitchen to fetch a glass of water. Bretch was already there with the phalanx of prefects. 'Some have glory thrust upon them,' she purred. It was the only time Bretch was ever pleased with me. Three cheers for me! Hip hip hurrah! Etc.

It wasn't the restoration of Games that stopped us quarrelling, though. It was boys. Not visible boys. That wasn't allowed. It was virtual boys, in the form of letters. Getting a letter from a boy was the next level up in the Brownie Badges of Womanhood. You would go hot and cold all over because he'd signed his name with an x, and even more so each time the number of xxs per letter increased, not to mention when he sent one with a whole paragraph of just xxs, and when he moved on from Dear to Darling and then Dearest.

Sodding Erica was the first to get one. With a Harrow crest on the envelope. No xxs but signed 'Luv by the gallon'. She wrote back, ostentatiously. 'Can anyone think of any synonyms for sex and seduce?' she drawled, pen in hand. 'I don't want to repeat myself.' What bosh. They'd probably just sat out a slow foxtrot in a dim corner and fiddled around a bit.

But there was no getting away from it. She had entered another world and soon Lindy followed her with someone called Geoffrey. Geoffrey! What kind of Adonis calls himself Geoffrey? And then all the other girls who had older brothers started receiving letters with crests on the back, because these brothers had sex-starved schoolmates looking for girls to write to. Beth with her mattress-stuffing hairdo got a letter. Meanwhile, the Latimers were busily corresponding with a lot of Adrianos and Lorenzos and Benitos, after Sukie's friend Sian has gone on holiday to Italy and come back with a list of willing correspondents. How did they manage to smuggle them past Cawley? Easy. Sukie did Squash as an Extra. The courts were in the basement of the headquarters of Fison's Fertilisers, which had once been the Hamilton Hotel. It was near the seafront and about a mile away from Latimer. Sukie would post their letters to them on the walk down there. Hers was Roberto, who said he loved her.

And Cherry. Even Cherry was writing to a boy. Even though she still had no bosoms, let alone the curse. Her mother had sent her a bra, though she didn't need one. She wore it but the pouches stayed empty. And one evening at supper we had macaroni cheese, and Juno got up from her place and walked over to Cherry's table bearing a side plate on which was placed one piece of macaroni. Cherry's eyes opened very wide and then they both screamed the place down with laughter. Practically.

'I borrowed Juno's vanity mirror,' Cherry explained later. 'To look down there to see if there was any obstruction. There was a huge bit of skin like a piece of macaroni over *IT!* I am definitely *not normal*.'

And then everyone else was writing to boys and she was so desperate to get a letter from one too that she got one as a penfriend. 'But we can never meet,' she said.

'Oh, Cherry. Why not?'

'Because he thinks I'm a boy. I advertised in the *Eagle*, you see. I call myself Charles. It was just so I could say I've had letters from a boy. But you can see why meeting might be difficult.'

I had to act quickly. I was being left behind. Soon I would be a wallflower. Why hadn't I tied Nigel to a chair and threatened to make him kiss me again unless he exchanged addresses with me? In desperation I went down the penfriend route like Cherry. But I would not masquerade as a boy. The whole point was to find someone I could meet, so the *Eagle* was out of the question. Instead I placed an advertisement in the 'penfriends wanted' column in *Riding* magazine.

You had to say whether you wanted to write to a boy or a girl, and specify what region or country you would like your penfriend to live in. I made the mistake of leaving my advert in *Riding* out for all to see. 'Boy anywhere,' Cath read out, and then for days and days she and Beth kept calling me 'lovelorn Danny' and dissolving into giggles until I wanted to start smacking faces again. But I didn't in the end because one afternoon, when Bretch brought the letters in after lunch, there was an airmail envelope, redirected from home. It was from someone called Gunther, who enclosed a photo of himself in the outback. He was wearing some kind of Australian hat. Oh dear. I have to say, this Gunther chap was not what I had in mind at all. Could we make a go of it? When I'd stipulated 'boy anywhere', I'd meant somewhere like Colchester, or Esher, or even Solihull at a pinch. Somewhere that was accessible enough for me to pretend we had met at a dance. And anyway, Gunther was awfully beardy for someone purporting to be fifteen.

It so happened that soon after I received this missive it was time for our year to be given Miss Beynon's reproduction lesson, such as it was. Miss Beynon was scarlet in the face all the way through, very noticeable because of her carrot-head hair and its associated white, freckled complexion. Her reproduction lesson involved the drawing of blinds in the Bilge lab, and a white screen on which was projected a diagram of two stick people. They seemed to be lying on a table. Was that it? Then there was a picture of a willy. It was pointing straight down. How did the man do what Miss Beynon said he did if it pointed straight down? Would he and the woman have to form some sort of T-square? I was none the wiser. But I certainly wasn't going to form T-squares with Gunther. Into the wapey he went.

# 20

## CITIZEN KITTENS

As it happened, shortly after Miss Beynon's reproduction lesson, a sequel took place while Wisty and I were taking Rebel for a walk in Epping Forest.

What with Chrissie living far away in Guernsey, Wisty was the friend I saw most of in the holidays. We mixed hardly at all at school because she was a Cranmer, but we both did Riding and got chatting on those long walks from school to the stables, which was how we discovered we lived only eighteen miles apart – well within the reach of our mothers' cars – and almost from the start we spent a lot of time together outside term-time. There were other people from school who lived quite near me, but Wisty was the one I liked best. She had a gleam in her eyes; she was mischievous. Like Beth, but cheerful.

Wisty probably wasn't going to be Miss World – her nose was rather aquiline – but you could tell she would end up tall and dashing and would look good in big hats and high-heeled boots. She had creamy skin and thick, raisin-coloured hair, which tangled into ropes that flopped over her forehead. The colouring came from her mother, who was half-Turkish.

Often when someone had a foreign name it was quite embarrassing because it sounded horrid, like Bogwash or Splotzel, but Wisty's mother was Maja, pronounced Maya, and Wisty had that as her second name. Her first name was really Elizabeth, which one of her brothers (there were two: Roly, who was two years older than her, and Greg, who was two years older than Roly) couldn't pronounce as a kid. So he said 'Wizabeth'. Which turned into Wisty.

Much to my surprise our parents chummed up too, so the ferrying between each other's houses was often linked with pub lunches or drinkies, and they even made up foursomes for dinner dances, although, as Wisty's parents were sane and socially competent, I was baffled as to what they could see in mine.

I liked her so much! Not as much as Chrissie, and in a different way, because with Chrissie it was all about writing things and having private jokes and general propping each other up, whereas with Wisty it was doing things. At first that was mainly horsey stuff. We visited each other's riding school. Whole days of mucking out and grooming, with a picnic lunch of Marmite and lettuce sandwiches and Penguins, sitting on top of a pile of hay bales. Heaven. We watched the racing on *Grandstand* on Saturdays, and my father put on sixpenny bets for us. Her parents took us to the Royal International Horse Show at White City, and my parents took us to the Royal Tournament at Earls Court. We went up to London on the tube together to skate at Queen's ice rink in Bayswater.

I loved staying over at Wisty's house. They were like one of those dream families you read about, where everyone's always joshing each other and, while not sick-makingly huggy, there was a lot of arm round the shoulders and ruffling of hair. Wisty was allowed to be rude to her mother. One day she said, 'So what?' when her mother pointed out they couldn't have a tennis court in the garden because it would take up too much room and there wouldn't be any lawn left over for anything else. *So what.* I was aghast. I would *never* have got away with 'so what?'. Surely her mother would have the screaming abdabs? I waited anxiously for the storm. But Mummy just laughed. And her father sort of mock-cuffed the back of her neck and said, 'That'll be enough of that, young lady.'

Where were the dramatics? They weren't even cross. For all I know it might have been a front; they might have been masters of dissimulation and, when no one was there, brandished knives at each other, and kept a mad Turkish grandmother chained in the cellar and fed through a grille. You couldn't ever truly know what was going on in someone else's family. But I didn't really think any of those things. They were just lovely. Normal. With luck, contact with them might instil some regularity in mine.

They had an old fat Labrador, called Sheba, who was so broad from shoulder to shoulder you could rest your plate on her. She pottered, like a slowly moving coffee table. The hall was cluttered with tennis rackets and rugby boots and climbing gear because they were sporty and intrepid, and in the garden was a rickety greenhouse where Roly showed me a tortoise egg. It was on bedding made of gravel and straw, and a kind of cloudy white colour, as though he'd captured a miniature moon as it flew through the universe. But could it really be what he said it was? Did mother tortoise sit on the egg to hatch it? Surely she would crush it to pieces. Roly must be having me on. Not that I minded. I was alone with a boy, a real boy. Maybe he would suddenly take my hand. Then I thought, despondently, that he wouldn't be interested in me in that way. Not while I was wearing tartan trousers and a pale-blue hand-knit.

So, the sequel to Miss Beynon's lesson happened one weekend in the Easter hols of being fourteen, when Wisty was staying with me. Our house overlooked Epping Forest. You just crossed the road and there it was. It started with a long walkway of tussocky grass called The Glade, as wide as a dual carriageway, that unfurled for a couple of hundred yards before tracks led off to the left and right, the left-hand one being an extension of the green dual carriageway, the right-hand track leading to several exciting ponds where you could fish for tiddlers and collect tadpoles. The forest could be a spooky place, even in daylight, but the rustlings and cracking of twigs was more likely to be owls or lovers than escaped murderers, and what wonderful opportunities there were for a terrier of Rebel's inquisitive nature. He would bound off and that would be the last you saw of him. In the end you'd start to worry you'd never see him again, and you'd wander around calling his name for ages.

This time was like every other. Wisty and I were looking for him when we heard a noise in the bushes, so we followed it up and there stood a man with his coat undone, holding a sort of light-purple cylinder in one hand.

We couldn't believe our eyes. Surely not! We backed off and marched smartly away, as if we'd seen nothing, and just at that moment Rebel appeared, so we put him back on his lead.

As soon as we got to the bottom of The Glade, we turned the corner and ran as fast as we could to the road, where it met the sandy track and the forest-keeper's house.

'It was one, wasn't it?' said Wisty, when she'd got her breath back.

'I can't think of anything else it could have been.'

'Are you going to say anything?'

'Oh God, no!' I gasped. 'Are you?'

'What? And have everyone kick up a frightful stink? You're joking!'

We looked at each other. 'I hope they aren't all like that,' said Wisty, and then we got into absolute fits about it because it had given us such a shock, but all the same it had looked so funny. But worse might have happened and, by unspoken consent, we stopped taking Rebel for walks in the forest for a while.

In any case, fourteen was a kind of crossover age where we still liked doing some of the things we'd done at thirteen but discovered there was more to life than horsey stuff and swimming and skating. Now we both had Dansettes.

Mine was a hand-me-down from my sister, beige with two knobs at the front for volume and changing the speed of the turntable from 45 to 33 rpm, and a carrying strap. It did up like a little overnight case. Wisty's was even better. She'd got it for Christmas and it had an automatic record changer, which meant we could put a pile of 45s on the rod in the middle of the turntable and, with a bit of whirring and clicking, it would work its way all through the stack. So I would take my 45s to her house and we would sit on the floor playing 'Please Please Me' and 'From Me to You', and Billy Fury's 'Like I've Never

Been Gone', and the Four Seasons' 'Walk Like a Man', and 'Foot Tapper' by the Shadows. Over and over again.

While all this was going on, we invented a club called the Federal Union of Citizen Kittens. Club membership didn't involve anything; it was just an acknowledgement of our sophistication. I was getting quite daring in my writing. I had started a short story in which a character said 'sod'. And 'bugger'. But I'd never have said them out loud, let alone the F-word. At fourteen? In 1963? You just didn't, even if you knew what it meant. And I wasn't sure that I did.

Now that Epping Forest was off-limits, Wisty and I did a lot of wandering around Loughton High Street. This was a timeline of my childhood: the china shop, which sold the Beswick model horses I still collected; the church hall at the side of St Mary's, where I'd gone to Brownies (I was Sixer of the Gnomes, the only public office I was ever to hold); a café beside a triangular green where, when I was very young, my mother would take me for dainty afternoon teas featuring bone china and a tiered dish of Kunzle cakes. These were much nicer to look at than to eat. Once you prised off the decorations and peeled back the outer casing of chocolate you were left with a mound of sickly mock cream on a damp biscuit base. But why on earth would Wisty and I want to set foot in there? Our hangout was the Gaytime coffee bar, with its Formica tables, jukebox and its name spelt out in squiggly blue and red neon. They served coffee in Pyrex cups, which was very go-ahead for Loughton. My mother thought the Gaytime was the haunt of boys who rode motorbikes and girls with dyed hair, so we never let on we went there.

Our other new haunt was the record shop, which had LP covers stuck at angles on the wall behind the counter, an island in the middle where you could flip through LPs, and listening booths. I had been dying for ages to try a listening booth, but the prospect filled me with something like stage fright. Everyone in the shop except me was a proper teenager. The girls wore teenager clothes, while I was still in those tartan trousers and hand-knit woollies, because I let my mother choose my clothes, and I now understood they were all wrong and I needed nylons and flatties and a turtleneck top and a skirt that showed my knees. But now I had Wisty for moral support, and was able to ask to listen to 'Out of the Shadows' with reasonable confidence.

There was always the cinema, too. The Century, where the girl next door and I had been allowed to watch U films on our own, had closed down, and now we had to go to South Woodford, which meant dragging my mother out in her car or taking a stop-start journey by bus. But when you're fourteen going by bus with your friend is an adventure, and it would drop us off in George Lane, over the road from the Plaza or right outside the Majestic on the main road.

The Majestic was cavernous, with red plush seats and an upper circle. Great things had obviously been planned for it when it was built before the war but, with the coming of television, audiences had declined and, in the foyer, mysterious signs announced 'Banqueting Suite' and 'Ballroom', although there didn't seem to be either now. At the end of every performance the national anthem was played, so during the closing credits there would be the sound of seats going up and people nipping out and, if they were too slow, they would be caught by the first strains and have to stand stock still in the aisle.

The Majestic was where we saw our first James Bond film, *Dr No*. I was particularly excited by this because Wisty said that we'd be meeting Roly there. 'He likes you,' said Wisty. Perhaps he did, a bit. He did show me his tortoise egg, after all. But when we got to the Majestic I was terribly disappointed because he was with another girl. Why hadn't Wisty told me? But it seemed she hadn't realised either. The girlfriend had hair with a fringe and flick-ups and a short-sleeved turtleneck top and a skirt that showed some of her thighs. Which were long and shapely. She and I were separated by a year and, at a rough guess, one and a half stone.

Roly introduced me. I was dismissed with a glance. She turned and said something to Roly and laughed. I didn't think she was very nice. They lit cigarettes when the lights went down and, after a while, I could hear rustling and huffing. So I attended very closely to what was happening on the screen. If I was going to be a proper writer I would obviously have to put S.E.X. into my books, and I tried to reconcile the man with the purple pipe and what Sean Connery was doing with Ursula Andress, which seemed to be terribly effortless and *smoooooth*. It was much worse than not knowing what to do in the listening booth. Really, I hadn't a clue. It was like starting at a new school, or being plunged into a new world. I wished I knew someone who could tell me how to go about it.

After *Dr No*, it was almost time to go back to school for summer term 1963, so I didn't see Wisty again until I got to Liverpool Street to board the boat train. Of course, we smiled and waved, but she got into a Cranmer compartment and I tugged my suitcase a little further along until I found Chrissie and the other Ridleys. Soon we were all jabbering and shrieking about what we'd done and where we'd been and I barely gave Wisty another thought. She was a Cranmer and I was a Ridley, and in term-time the twain shall hardly ever meet.

# 21

# THE TEENAGE GENIUS

School seemed dull and regimented after the Easter hols. Instead of the cinema and the coffee bar and record shop, it was House meetings, locker inspections and a deadly lecture on schools in India, which the prefects made us go to, only just stopping short of driving us there at the end of a stick like cattle on market day.

'Life is drear and boarding school a drudge,' sighed Chrissie, as we toiled our way through tests in virtually every subject. I revised for Bilge in cab during break but it didn't sink in. Latin was all right, but Geog. was absolutely foul, and we were all bound to have failed. As for English Lit., I couldn't do a scrap of it, so waffled madly.

English Lit. was one of my least favourite lessons. We were doing *Pride and Prejudice* and had to submit to dear old Miss Evans, scratching herself and doing the crossword and droning on about Jane Austen's sense of irony while the tantalising *thwack-thwack* of ball on racket on the tennis courts went on right outside the windows. What a lot of snobs and prigs they were in *Pride and Prejudice*! Compared to Meryton, Felixstowe College was a hotbed of reds and anarchists. And frankly I would have chosen Wickham over stuffy old Darcy any day. At least he had a bit of go in him.

But why couldn't we study books that were relevant to Life As it Was Lived Now instead of ones by people who hadn't been alive for centuries? For light relief, I was busy working on *The Sandwich Stories*, a series of illustrated comic novellas with plots and characters that included not just some of my friends but also Bretch, Elvis and the Shadows. These were passed round to everyone else for their comments and suggestions, and we had our heads together over them in the library when suddenly there was a whoosh of air and a dark mass blotted out the light from the firmament.

How did Jonah manage to move so fast and so silently? Was she on castors? I went to move my hand over the drawing of Bretch scaling a rope ladder to the tower dorm for the purposes of eavesdropping. Too late.

'What are you doing?'

'W-working, Miss Jones.'

Jonah snatched up *The Sandwich Stories* and gave them a quick glance. Accompanied by a 'Mnph,' they left the library tucked under her arm.

What a disaster. Now I had to wait for my name to appear on The Jonah List. Out of what was obviously sheer sadism, two weeks were allowed to pass before the summons appeared on the green slip of paper outside the Bilge lab.

Girls to see Miss Jones

J. Welch

Back in Jonah's study again, with the Queen looking at me reproachfully from above the mantelshelf and my *Sandwich Stories* in Jonah's hand, folded back at the drawing of Bretch scaling the rope ladder.

'Why bring Miss Cross into it?'

In my dreams I would have said, 'Oh, come off it, you know very well. It's because she's got fuzzy-wuzzy hair and bottle-bottom specs and ski-sized feet and she's a perfect gift to satirise.' But I realised this question was what Miss Williams had told us was rhetorical, so I just looked at my feet as usual and mumbled, 'I don't know, Miss Jones.'

'You could be a likeable child if you weren't always trying to call attention to yourself.'

'Yes, Miss Jones. Sorry, Miss Jones.'

'Actually, Jonah was jolly decent, considering,' I said to Chrissie later that day, as we rushed to Chapel together for a last-minute practise of the lesson she had to read in Vespers that night. She was very nervous about it, and wanted to make sure the Bible was open on the right page. It was a good thing she did because the bookmark was in Joshua.

'It's a bad omen,' she said gloomily on the way out. 'I'm bound to pronounce Ephesus wrong.' At which we ran straight into Maggie, who gave us her choicest 'what-are-you-doing-in-the-Lord's-house?' face. 'Shouldn't you be at your clarinet lesson?' she demanded of me.

Oh heavens! I had completely forgotten that it had been changed from its usual time.

'Go and see Miss Cornford,' she snapped.

I trudged away to have my ear chewed off by Cornford, and thence to apologise to Mr Hailes, so I was late for Vespers and got a filthy glare from Jonah as I had to squeeze past rows of people to find a place while they carried on singing 'The Day Thou Gavest, Lord, Is Ended', thus calling attention to myself again.

At least I didn't miss Chrissie's lesson. Her hand was shaking so much she had to hold on to the rail in front of the lectern but she didn't make any awful bishes, thank goodness, and afterwards everyone, even the Ridley prefects, all crowded round to tell her, 'Well read!'

But the rapprochement with the prefects was short-lived. Not long after this, she forgot to collect Bretch's supper from Mrs Kahn, and only remembered halfway through Vespers. She slipped out and dashed over to Cranmer, where she met two of them triumphantly bearing the tray back to Ridley. Why not just pass the tray on to Chrissie? But no, they had to be foul to her. She had lost all rights to the tray. It was their tray now. And she was rude and bad and the most useless commie captain ever known to Ridley. How could they be so horrid to her? She was the politest, most decent girl in the world. Worth ten of those trainee battle-axes. What a ghastly term this was turning out to be. The prefects picked on us, the teachers gave us extra prep and Bretch wouldn't allow us to do *anything*. Could we go and dance in the studio? No. Could we go and play tennis? No. We made a bit of a stand and started hitting up against an outside wall, but unfortunately Gwen sent a ball through a window, so all our rackets were conflabbed, and while the batey bag was at it she had Lindy's and Beth's radios off them as well because they were playing them in the garden. So that was us down to two radios and we hadn't even got to the third week of term. And now it was Della's turn to be in trouble.

It was Saturday afternoon and we were playing skipping games on the hard standing outside the commie when there came a most tremendous roar and a screech of tyres. Who could it be? We abandoned our skipping ropes and dashed round to the front of House. What an amazing sight! An old MG Midget was parked in Ridley drive, and there was Della's big sister Jay, with her fair hair whipped by the breeze and her sunglasses perched on top of her head, and beside her at the wheel not a boy but a *young man*. I didn't catch his name because I was so taken by his trousers – which hadn't any turn-ups but were tapered at the ends, and were done up with a zip rather than buttons – but it was something suitable like Roy Ripping. Roy Ripping brought out a box of cigarettes then patted his pockets. 'Got any matches?' Chrissie and I beetled off to the kitchen and stole some, which he immediately pocketed (and we never saw them again). Anyway, it seemed that Roy Ripping and Jay wanted to take Della out to tea, but just at that moment Bretch emerged from the Covered Way and prepared to mount her bicycle, so Della belted up to her to ask permission. The answer was no, of course, and away Bretch cycled down the drive.

'Can I just sit in the car for a bit to see what it's like?' begged Della.

So she sat on Jay's lap and Roy Ripping gunned the engine and, with a puff of exhaust, the MG shot off down Ridley drive, straight across Maybush Lane and through Cranmer's gates, and turned in a mad circle and shot back out again all in one go, with Della screaming and laughing at the same time, and hanging on to the window handle for dear life, and then she staggered out with legs like jellyfish and tottered towards us absolutely lit up with fun and joy, while Roy Ripping and Jay roared off, leaving nothing but a little patch of oil on the gravel and a dull, still silence.

At which Bretch emerged from the caretaker's house at the end of the drive.

'She's been spying on us from the kitchen window!' hissed Beth.

We all tore inside and along the corridors but we could hear her behind us, so we belted into the dorm. Beth, Marion and Chrissie shot into the wardrobe, and the rest of us were diving under the beds when Bretch stormed in.

'Come on out, wherever you are.'

Sheepishly we emerged, one by one, feeling like burst balloons, and after that we had to stand in a line in the commie and be given a row.

'You're behind all the trouble in the house,' murmured Chrissie, *sotto voce*.

'You're behind all the trouble in the house!' raved Bretch. 'Julia Welch, it's no laughing matter!'

Of course, when someone says, 'It's no laughing matter,' when you have to be solemn and full of remorse, that makes you want to laugh even more, and Chrissie and I stared at Bretch's feet to try and steady ourselves, but they only made us want to laugh even more. But now Bretch was saying sweetly to Della, 'And what did you do after I went out?' when obviously the old bag knew jolly well, but she made Della confess all the same, so that was Della in floods, which left her completely washed out for the rest of the day.

Even though Erica got us singing 'One Petty Woman in a Tree' to the tune of 'Five Rosy Apples on a Tree' we were very subdued. This place was quite obviously in the charge of tyrants and madwomen. We were Middle Five now. Why should we submit to such pathetic indignities?

Jonah was right. I was famished for attention. Life was so frustrating and banal I began to imagine myself the subject of a TV documentary, 'The Teenage Genius', although I would only get as far as the trailer every time. My picture would appear on screen while a disembodied voice intoned: 'Danny. Mercurial. Enigmatic.' Then everything would vaporise and I would be back in the cloakroom whitening my plimsolls or lining up with the rest of the class in the gym for Drama, which that term was of crucial importance, as we had to perform something on Speech Day. Jonah was aiming high as usual, and this year we were going to have a money-spinning fête, combined with short drama performances enacted by every form in the school.

Our Drama teacher was known as Mops. She was modern in her approach, although old and small and wrinkled herself, with beady eyes and blackened, seaweedy hair. Her lessons took place in the gym and, as her clothes were strangers to the laundry, the entire place was filled within seconds with a terrible smell of stale sweat. Poo! Couldn't another member of staff have told her? They were probably too busy fleeing from her presence in the staff room, holding their noses. Mops's idea was that we should do something called 'The Breath of Life', which Beth immediately christened 'The Bad Breath of Life'. It was to feature scenes and poems portraying the emotions, and at the first rehearsal Mops tried to get us to play love scenes. To Erica's horror, Mops wanted her to kiss

Cherry. Cherry didn't mind but Erica was very upset at doing something so embarrassingly lezzy. The more uncomfortable she was, the more Mops insisted. And she would have to do it again and again in rehearsal, poor thing, and we couldn't stand the idea of Erica upset and uncomfortable every Friday morning in Drama, so we decided to think up an alternative. It had to be something that would appeal to Mops's modern predilections and, as we were all very keen on *Beyond the Fringe* and *That Was The Week That Was*, we came up with the idea of a revue, and set to work thinking up skits and composing topical verses.

As a nod to culture, the Cranmers were going to perform some scenes from Shakespeare, in modern dress, and Cherry and Juno had started their own pop group and would do one of their own songs. The Tyndales had a lovely dance and mime routine about a fortune-teller. Marion and Beth were doing a comic double act. Marion would wear her tunic in a gormless sort of way, and the costume cupboard up in the clock tower had yielded an ancient black shawl which, with a certain amount of adjustment, became McNulty's flapping gown. Armed with a ruler (McNulty had a tendency to rap people over the knuckles if they were wool-gathering) Beth became our Maths teacher: 'I say, I say, why can't penguins fly?'

'Oh – um – did Miss Beynon tell us in Bilge? Perhaps I missed that lesson. Is it because they don't have wings?'

'No, you eejit,' at which Beth would rap Marion's knuckles. 'Because they're chocolate biscuits!'

Bobbie, who was a brilliant mimic, was going to do some of her impressions of TV and radio personalities, including her famous one of Max Robertson commentating on the racing at

Snetterton. Snetterton was a funny name in itself, especially the way Bobbie said it. Della, who was still smarting about the spoilt visit from Jay and Roy Ripping, wanted to sit on a high stool and sing 'All Alone Am I', but we persuaded her that it might put a bit of a damper on things and instead I wrote her a skit on the BBC children's programme *Watch with Mother*. For the Latimers I composed a song and dance routine involving lax sticks and purple grease-painted thighs called 'Cradling', to the tune of Bud Flanagan's 'Strolling'. I had also written a humorous poem, 'Come To Sunny Felixstowe', with which we were going to close the show. In fact I contributed a lot of the sketches and, although I was too absorbed in our production for the Teenage Genius fantasies to resurface, I did think my mother would be proud to see it performed at Speech Day. Perhaps it would soothe the blow of my abandoning Chemmy if she could see my success as a writer.

There was a large L-shaped classroom at one side of the library and, because the gym was being used by the Wycliffes rehearsing 'Hansel and Gretel', most of our preparations took place in there. It was actually much better because it had lots of windows, which we would fling open when Mops's smell became overpowering. We were obliged, of course, to seek Jonah's approval for our revue, so Mops arranged a private viewing for her, and we cleared the desks to make space and found a stout chair, to which Mops escorted her. And so our revue began.

It was not a success. The *Watch with Mother* skit didn't seem so funny after all. Bobbie got halfway through her routine and then just dried at the terror of it all. Masses of ghastly things happened during the Tyndales' dance routine, i.e. they slipped, the record jumped and a bookcase nearly gave way. And Jonah just sat there, an industrial-sized basilisk. There was not even a twitch of a facial feature when Beth told the penguin joke, which had everyone in fits. She was inanimate. Had she died? I stared at her bosom to see if it was rising and falling, and it was. Jonah had not died, but we had. By now I was just longing for the whole ghastly thing to end, which was signalled by the rest of the cast creeping out, leaving me alone on our makeshift stage, almost face-to-face with Jonah as I delivered the last verse of our closing number:

> *So if you want to see a concert,*
> *Or need a place to go,*
> *You'll always get a welcome*
> *At Sunny Felixstowe.*

At which, as arranged, there came a tremendous banging on the classroom door and the entire cast shouted, 'Let us in! We're soaked!'

Jonah rose and, with a grunted, 'Thank you,' left the classroom. We had to wait for our next Drama lesson for the verdict when, with much hand-wringing, Mops broke the news that we would not be performing our revue at Speech Day because it made fun of Felixstowe. So much for the Teenage Genius. It had simply not occurred to me that last year's sopping 'Hiawatha Wedding Feast' would be a sensitive subject with Jonah.

So now we were back to 'The Breath of Life', and in the meantime all the other forms had bagged the interesting things to organise at the fête, and we were left with the produce stall. But actually, that turned out to be good fun. After having nothing to do for the last few weeks of term, we spent the whole evening before the fête making toffee apples (scrumptious), icing cakes and filling flans, and in the morning we buttered sandwiches for the teas to be held in Ridley gardens and arranged our display of bottled fruit, fresh farm butter and twenty-two different kinds of jam.

And the fête really was awfully jolly, with the stalls decorated with brightly coloured streamers and striped sunshades and laden to overflowing with goods aplenty. Younger brothers and sisters were having a go on the pony rides, while fathers showed off their bowling at the coconut shy, and the bottle stall sold hundreds of tickets, and everyone looked so gay and happy in their red blazers and summer dresses. And throughout it all the sun was shining fit to burst, so the poem about the rain would have been flopped completely anyway. Nobody would have got the point of it and I would have looked awfully silly. It would have been a disappointing end to my dreams of literary stardom. But I *would* be a writer. People *would* take some notice. One day. One day.

# 22

# SEX AND KIRBIGRIPS
# AND ROCK 'N' ROLL

Summer hols, 1963. My sister and her fast businessman got married. They were off to start a new life in Australia, which plunged my mother into gloom, as the original plan was for the happy couple to buy a house within motoring distance of ours. She had dreamed of frequent visits and being a mother-in-law of the most useful possible variety and, when the time came, a granny available for childcare duties, which she would have loved. And she would have been terribly good at it, too, because with small children she was in her element. Instead her older daughter, her favourite, was going to be the other side of the world.

We went to Heathrow to see them off.

'It's such a long way,' my mother said dolefully.

'You can put my pony fund towards the fare and go to see them,' I said gruffly. I had forty-eight pounds saved, enough roughly for a leg and a half. Perhaps the tail, too. My mother affected not to hear, because to have her unlovely, unpleasing younger daughter offering all her worldly goods to help her get to Australia would have forced her to rethink her view of herself as a tragic victim.

Thank heavens, though, I was able to get away from it all. I was off to Guernsey to stay with Chrissie. The sun shone, we sailed across the turquoise sea to Sark, and I was able to forget everything except swimming, sunbathing, shopping and eyeing up boys. What a lovely mum Chrissie had. Warm and happy, and she made me feel so welcome. Why couldn't mine be like that? Why did my home life have to be such an attritional muddle?

But perhaps, when I got home, things would be better? No such luck. There was a right old ding-dong going on in head office. My father had bought both my mother and Jane new cars. While trying to park in our drive, my mother had driven her Vauxhall Victor into the back of Jane's Wolseley Hornet. Stepped on the accelerator instead of the brake. According to Freud, there are no mistakes. All is intentional. My mother had rammed Jane's backside.

'Hello, I'm back.'

'Jane and your father are carrying on!' shouted my mother. 'You stick up for me!'

Why should I? I thought. You never stick up for me. And anyway, I didn't want to be put into a position where I had to champion one parent against the other. I was looking forward to seeing my own bedroom again and reacquainting myself with my model horses and back issues of *Horse & Hound*, and I dragged my suitcase into my bedroom. My mother followed me in.

'You needn't unpack.'

I was to be got rid of again. The last thing she wanted around was this fat, awkward gooseberry. I was to go to Brittany for two weeks with another friend and her family.

'Your mother is imagining things,' my father bleated. 'I don't know why she keeps going on like this. We could have such a happy home.'

Adults. Huh. Why were they so incompetent at managing their lives? I hoped my parents would get divorced and that my father and Jane would get married and I could live with them. Then, I thought gloomily, my father would never let that happen. I'd be stuck with my mother.

My father obviously felt very guilty about all this carry-on, because I was bought a horse. My love, my friend, my thoroughbred Welsh cob cross. He was bay with a white blaze down his nose shaped like a diamond, and an aristocratically dished head, and a little feathering of hair around his heels, which came from the plebeian Welsh cobby side of his family. I called him Applejack, since a new song had just been released called 'Tell Me When' by a band called the Applejacks. What made the name additionally attractive was that I found 'applejack' a very romantic word, like 'moon' and 'gillyflower'. It was also a kind of cider, and I liked drinking cider. Drinking was grown up, and cider tasted much nicer than horrid, tart gin.

Applejack was not my only new possession. I also had a boyfriend. Shortly after the binning of Gunther, I'd had a letter from another boy. This one sounded nice. He lived in London and we exchanged letters all through summer term. He sent me a photo. Was it really him? It was. I met him at the end of the hols. Tall and blond. A bit of a hunk, actually. As far as I could tell, because I wasn't wearing my glasses. We sat in my bedroom and played singles on my Dansette. 'That's the type we want,' said my father, after he'd gone, and my mother said he was 'manly'. Life was looking up.

So, back to school for autumn term 1963, with Applejack travelling to Felixstowe in a horse box to the riding stables where he was to be kept at livery. My new boyfriend, handsome and nice though he was, came rather a poor fifth in my pantheon of passions that term. Applejack was first. My parents arrived within three weeks to take me out on exeat and I abandoned them all afternoon to plait his mane, polish his hooves, untangle his tail and bring a shine to his lovely bay rump. Second was John Lennon. I had settled on him as my favourite Beatle rather than Paul. I felt he had a superior mind. Third was Blackie the riding instructor, on whom I'd suddenly developed such a violent crush that he started bringing his wife to the stables as a safeguard whenever it was my afternoon for Riding.

In fourth place was Jesus Christ. Our year had been confirmed *en masse* at Easter, which had been terribly exciting, like getting married. Rellies and godparents sent us little cards – 'Congratulations on your Confirmation'. We treasured our crucifixes, showing them to each other, each thinking ours was the nicest and most holy.

The confirmation ceremony had taken place at a church in town because the college chapel was too small to fit in all the fond parents. Veiled, in our tussores, we queued in the aisle, stepped up and knelt – two at a time to speed the process up a bit. When the Bishop's hand descended on my newly wigged hair I waited for the hoped-for bolt of heavenly goodness to shoot through me, but nothing happened. He might as well have been patting a Labrador. Disappointing. Still, we could now go to Communion. Going to Communion meant you were grown up. So did being an Upper Five. We could also at last attend the make-up and etiquette lectures in the library.

Ladies from Lucie Clayton, all hats and cashmere, with perfectly shaped eyebrows and lipstick-free teeth, and smelling of Joy and Madame Rochas, gave us hints on grooming and posture, the use of good cosmetics and personal hygiene. We had a lecture on dress materials from a Mr Weblin of Harrods. He described briefly the manufacture of various fabrics while we studied samples, and then gave hints on buying our own material. Another Harrods person produced a tweed suit, and showed us some of the accessories that could be worn with it. A Balenciaga original! The winner of the Golf Cup, a lithe blonde, got to model it. I sat there and dreamed it was me. But nothing like that would ever happen to me. She looked gorgeous. She always did. I would gaze at her when she played lax. She was a winged Mercury, flying towards goal, natty in her white Aertex and grey divided skirt, with her neat bust and trim ankles, and her short, feathery hair. Almost gamine. Perhaps just a hint of a moustache, which was probably part of the attraction. I could never be like her. My short legs would never get any longer and, however hard I tried not to, I still ate too much. And then there were the glasses. Would I never be attractive? I began to think I was from a different species.

Friday 22 November 1963. Dreadful news. Someone had tried to assassinate John F. Kennedy. We heard as we came back from a form hockey game. Upper Five A vs. Upper Five B. The As won. Chrissie played right half for the first time and did jolly well. As we were slinging our hockey sticks into the container in the cloakroom, someone came belting in.

'Have you heard? President Kennedy's been shot!'

'Oh, don't be so silly!'

It was only when we got to supper, and everyone there was talking about it, that we realised it was true. He had been taken to hospital, apparently. Gravely wounded, but we thought they were trying to save him. I imagined America's finest surgeons at his bedside, repairing the damage, putting the president of the free world back together again. He would slowly get better. I had no idea his brains had been shot through and Jackie, in her sugared-almond-coloured suit, had crawled across the car to fetch a piece of his skull that had gone flying. Picking things up off floors and returning them to their proper place was instinct-ive behaviour in a wife and mother. He was already dead when they reached the hospital. I went to bed still thinking he was alive and then, in the morning, we were told the truth.

How glamorous he had been. How young. All over the Western world, streets would be half-empty and subdued. But we had a trip to Colchester Natural History Museum and Zoo arranged and life had to carry on.

The streets of Colchester were rather unsatisfactory, as plenty of people were about doing their weekend shopping as though nothing had happened. How could they be so insen-sitive? I kept trying to think about President Kennedy but it was hard to be solemn on an empty stomach, and earthly considerations like dying to go to cab had to be taken into account. After the talk on natural history, we went to the zoo and had lunch there. It was bangers and mash, and we played 'Please Please Me' and 'I Saw Her Standing There' on the jukebox, and started bopping. Marion affected to be furious. 'You haven't any respect for the dead,' she intoned.

After supper, we were allowed to watch a tribute to Kennedy on TV, which stunned us into silence for a while. But difficult decisions had to be made. Should we cancel the midnight feast we had planned in the dorm for that night? Everything was stored in a cardboard box inside the wardrobe. We had a packet of Dad's Cookies, sardines, hard-boiled eggs, crisps, wafer biscuits, a big bar of Cadbury's Fruit & Nut, tins of cling peaches and Nestlé's Milk, and some dates, which came in a small but heavy half-brick, wrapped in cellophane with a yellow palm tree printed on it. We decided to go ahead with it. We didn't think JFK would have minded. It was all so awful but we were alive and so were John, Paul, George and Ringo.

Strangely enough, the term JFK was assassinated was also the term of bed-hopping. It started with an approach: 'We were wondering if you'd lie on top of us so we could find out what it's like to have a man on top of us.'

We were in the nine-dorm that term, the one that ran the length of the Covered Way, bridging the oldest part of Ridley and the pre-war extension. The dorm had a hospital look, with the beds set out in a line. That night we waited a while after Lights Out, and then beds were left for other beds. It didn't feel sexy at all, but I was pleased with myself that I'd accomplished it. None of us spoke of it afterwards, and it wasn't until fifty years or more had gone by that I mentioned it to Cherry. 'Oh, we did that lying on top of each other thing,' she said. 'Immie, Hilly, Juno and me, when we were in the four-dorm. I had no sexual feeling at all! Do you think someone talked to someone or were we all doing it at the same time? Morphic resonance, as Rupert Sheldrake would say.'

We worked out that the timing was almost identical, within a week or so of the Kennedy assassination, so the question had to be whether the death was some sort of catalyst. But perhaps that was just a coincidence because, not long after, Annie told me about her year's 'rather dodgy love-ins'.

'It was only that one year,' she said. 'Strangely, it was also confirmation year. In the dorm, we all did Bible-reading fellowship. All competing to see who was the purest. Then we would probably have a midnight feast. The seven-dorm was where we'd have our trysts. Between four and six of us – it varied. We'd spend hours enacting whatever we thought might occur between a couple in bed. There must have been couplings going on all over the place.'

They were confirmed in 1964, a full four months after the assassination. So I don't think John F. Kennedy can have been instrumental.

In the real world, skirt lengths were on the rise. We hitched up our tunics by folding the tops over our girdles, though Maggie or Cawley would yank them down by the hem. There were rebellions against wigged hair. We were aiming for the Cathy McGowan look. *Ready Steady Go!* went out on ITV on Friday nights with the line, 'The weekend starts here!' and everyone apart from swots and wets crowded round their House TV to watch, fantasising for half an hour that that weekend wasn't going to consist of Prep, Games, Chapel and a lecture on the Architecture and Grounds of Stowe School. The theme tune was Manfred Mann's '5-4-3-2-1', the opening bars of which were 'Five ... Four ... Three ... Two ... One!' followed by a harmonica riff by their lead singer, Paul Jones. What a dish he was. As were Allan Clarke of the Hollies and Mike Smith of the Dave Clark Five (*boomp, boomp*, glad all *over*).

Lucky Cathy McGowan, who had weekly access to these gods. She was *Ready Steady Go!*'s presenter: a gorgeous, lanky 21-year-old with long, straight black hair and a fringe that reached past her eyebrows. Long hair and fringes sprouted all over the school. Jonah went to war, because hair meant sex. Memos were pinned to House noticeboards:

I am increasingly depressed about hairstyles in the School generally, and while taking parents round yesterday I saw many girls trying to revise with their hair hanging all over their faces. I realise this is more obvious when girls are working than it is when they are walking about, but please could you have a hair inspection before examinations begin and insist that girls wear Kirbigrips or tie back their hair?

R. M. Jones

The alternative to Jonah's Kirbigrips was to wear your hair in bunches. We had to line up for hair inspections in Cranmer's front hall at the start of every term. One poor girl had an Alice band. Jonah called her out in front of the whole school. 'Turn round. Turn in front of everyone. Do not wear that thing ever again.' As though it was a thong or tassels on her nipples.

The Hair Inspection of Autumn Term 1963 took place in Cranmer front hall after lunch, since all girls and their House mistresses and the two alpha matrons, Poulson and Pipe, were already in situ. We had to file past them. They fired off catty comments and divided us into categories. There was the OK group, who were free to go. The Some Hope brigade was sent to one end of the hall. Chrissie and I were Beyond Hope. We had to go to the other end of the hall, where Bretch made us part our fringes in the middle and anchored them with Kirbigrips. Not only did I have Kirbigrips, I had to have bunches, too. Rubber bands were provided. They stuck out like Mickey Mouse ears. It was not the look I was after. I wanted Cilla Black meathooks, those long wings of hair that curved around her chin as she sung 'Love of the Loved' on *Thank Your Lucky Stars*.

But Cilla's hair obviously did what was expected of it. Mine was maverick. It wasn't curly, but nor was it straight. It just went the way it wanted to go, whatever I tried. My fringe would always go wavy and stick up at the ends, even though I wetted it and anchored it to my forehead at night with Sellotape. And a fat lot of good those beauty lectures were doing me. I was so broad in the beam, so wobble-thighed, so speccy. If I left my glasses off I had to screw up my eyes and, even then, anything more than ten feet away was a blur. In the Christmas hols I went to a dance held by Della, where Cath's brother danced with me once and then not again, and no other boy did either. I sat upstairs in the loo for hours and hours.

Juno recommended the Mazola diet. One tablespoonful of corn oil a day. 'It really works,' she said.

'How would you know? You've always been a broomstick.'

But this was a new, cool Juno. Still a tall, fair-haired broomstick, but no longer a gawky, stoopy one. She'd stopped not quite knowing what to do with her legs. She still had a drunken mother to cope with, but now she also had an older woman in her life. This was someone called Jean, whom she had met at her stepbrother's wedding reception at the Hurlingham Club in Fulham and who had taken a liking to her. Jean had trained at Lucie Clayton and was twenty-three. She wore Mary Quant – skinny-rib sweaters and geometric patterns – and had a fur-collared winter coat in Red Fox, which *Vogue* had pronounced that season's colour. Her shoes were from Bally and Charles Jourdain – those black loafers with the gold chain across the instep. She didn't have a diet, she had a *régime*. She went to the Establishment Club and let Juno read her copy of *Private Eye*. Jean and her boyfriend turned up at Felixstowe in an Austin Healey Sprite and they drove up and down the seafront with Juno sitting on the ledge at the back, and no one even noticed, because you could get away with anything in Cranmer. Well, almost; you still couldn't use the main staircase. But I was heartily sick of Jean already because it was the adult world, and someone had opened a door for lucky Juno to let her in.

But at least I had John, Paul, George and Ringo. A gang of us went to see them on their Christmas tour in January 1964. The Astoria in Finsbury Park was a huge, grimy palace that stuck out on the corner of Seven Sisters Road and it was filled with more girls than I'd ever seen in one place; more even than at the finals of the Schools Hockey Tournament at Wembley; enough to fill thirty chapels. It was a girl Hajj. They just flocked. I saw girls there whom I'd met on school trips, and girls I knew from other schools. We heard 'Roll Over Beethoven', 'All My Loving', 'This Boy', 'I Wanna Be Your Maaa-aan'. 'She Loves You', 'Till There Was You', 'I Want to Hold Your Hand', 'Money' and 'Twist and Shout'. Actually, we didn't hear much because of the screaming. I didn't see much either. I'd left off my glasses (I couldn't let John or Paul see me in specs) and squinted like mad. I couldn't scream. Why could they all scream while I couldn't? Perhaps I saw some sort of Jonah hologram out of the corner of my eye, wearing her poker face. Or heard some inner prefect: 'Will you stop making that disgusting noise!' But it was marvellous, marvellous, and so far, far away from Chapel.

My parents let me hold a party at the end of the Christmas hols. We didn't have a ballroom like next door, but men from my father's works cleared all the furniture out of the dining room and there was enough room to stick a group in the window bay. They were called Formula Four. I'd seen their advert in the local paper. They weren't the Beatles but they were a proper group with drums and amps and they had the hair, at least. My parents footed the bill.

I wore a sleeveless satin dress in dark turquoise, tactfully given a drop waist by my mother's dressmaker. 'You look attractive,' said Della, sounding surprised. She was going to stay the night. So was Chrissie, who had flown over from Guernsey. My father had driven up to Victoria to meet her. Why did I never think at the time of all the effort my parents put in? My mother made up bed after bed in the spare rooms because Gwen was going to stay the night too, and so were the First Proper Boyfriend and his mate ('Both dishes!' commented Chrissie), and then, there she was, making tea and crumpets while we sat in the living room watching the wrestling on TV. And then more tea when Prue and Bobbie and Wisty rolled up.

Thank heavens. I'd been feeling nervous all day, because however many parties I held I always worried that no one would come. And then the doorbell just kept ringing. Boy after boy, girl after girl. One minute we were standing in a little circle, smoking and drinking punch, which had also been made by my mother, and then we were standing in an ever-larger circle and then the dancing started and we were off. So were the lights. From time to time my father would open the door and switch them on, and as soon as he left they went off again. And the racket the band made. Till one o'clock in the morning. What a trial it must have been for my parents.

Who had to be on duty the following day, too, because clearing up had to be done (I lifted not a finger) and people had to be driven to stations or dropped off back at their homes – so many of us in my mother's car that Della had to sit on my lap. And it just went on, the whole of the rest of the week. Chrissie was staying with me till term began. We were driven to cinemas, and collected from cinemas. We had meals made for us while we sat in my bedroom and played records. We monopolised the television, because the Beatles were on *Sunday Night at the London Palladium*. My mother drove around repatriating things borrowed for the party.

One morning, on behalf of the family firm, she had to go to the West End headquarters of a company that specialised in an item of technology called an Epivisor, and of course she was thrilled to have the responsibility of judging its suitability and to be acknowledged as a company director. If there had been more of that, I'm sure she would have been much happier. She took us with her and, after she had concluded the business meeting, we went to Harrods where she treated us to a smorgasbord. On we went after that to Bond Street, so we could gawp at the shops. And in the days that followed she drove us to Wisty's, so we could read magazines in Wisty's bedroom and go shopping in the local high street, and boy spotting. She bought us pub lunches. She drove the two of us back to Felixstowe. I took it all for granted. I never once thanked her. What a spoilt pig.

# 23

# HELP

In spite of my defects I had by now stockpiled four boyfriends, including an American bishop's son who lived in Belgravia and somebody I got off with on an educational trip to France in the Easter hols of 1964. What an experience that was. He had the hugest tongue you could possibly imagine, and the flappiest and the wettest. Flob, flob, flob. It was like snogging a rubber glove. Still, now I'd done French kissing and that was what counted. But perhaps Chrissie and I should have been more covert about our boy spotting. My mother had festered malevolently about the goings-on at the party in the Christmas hols. It wasn't until summer term that I discovered she had struck out behind our backs.

Apart from our first term, when we had no say in the matter, Chrissie and I were always in the same dorm and our beds were always next to each other's. But now my mother had put a spanner in the works. When we arrived at Ridley, Chrissie came dashing up to me. 'Danny, we've been put in separate dorms!'

We looked pleadingly at Bretch, who was in her defensive stance, one long arm straight across her midriff like a tiller. 'I was asked to,' she said stiffly.

'Julia, I want you to know I had nothing to do with this,' said my mother in a very stilted voice. What a liar. It turned out she had written to Jonah, complaining that while Chrissie stayed with us during the holidays she had been 'making eyes at the coalman', and asking for us to be separated.

Such a horrid day. In floods, both of us. Plenty of shoulders were offered to cry on. We begged Bretch to change us back, and she said she would as soon as she could, as it had made us unhappy. So there was that to cling on to. But not much else. Chrissie was hauled into Jonah's study to be told she was uncouth and uncivilised. Rotten for her. So unfair. I was left trying to cope with the knowledge that my mother had written that poisonous, ludicrous letter. She had given no hint to me of what was afoot. I had been stabbed in the back. By my own mother. I felt responsible for her behaviour. I was so ashamed.

I had a lot of growing up to do before I had any insight into what she had done. She was an unhappy woman, and when you're unhappy and see happy people you can really want to lash out. I think she felt threatened and left out by the closeness Chrissie and I shared. She was also at a time in life when a woman, frankly, may not be quite sane, and having to deal with two exuberant teenage girls and their burgeoning sexuality must have been dreadfully hard.

But how were we going to get through this? We had O Levels coming up. O Levels were going to be a miserable time anyway. Life would be no fun at all. Swot, swot, swot, day after day. Summer passing unnoticed. The girls splashing about in the sea weren't going to be us. It was all about revising to the very last minute, propped up against the bolted door of cab at two in the morning. And now no Chrissie. Perhaps no Chrissie forever more. She was so unhappy she asked to leave.

Jonah and Bretch were both on her back. The venom was directed at her, not me, and all because of my mother. You're unruly, you're sulky, young ladies don't behave like that, you're this, that and the other (insert pejorative of choice), bark, bark, bark. It got to the stage of her parents giving notice. In the end she only stayed on because she wouldn't have been able to do A Level Spanish at a school in Guernsey. But her parents stood up to Jonah. If she stays, you're not to be nasty to her anymore, was the gist of the message. It seemed to work. The verbal horse-whippings stopped, anyway.

I just felt more and more depressed. I was going to have to forget all this had happened, the way I forgot that awful letter in Middle Five. It was the only thing to do. She was my mother. But I covered the front of my summer dress in biro, as if I wanted to scribble myself out. No one noticed.

Annie was miserable, too. I didn't know, as she wasn't in my form. And anyway, she'd always looked so happy, the classic naughty schoolgirl. She had been happy, for the first half of school. The second half was awful. She was young for her year – still ten when she was sent away. And then everybody except her started growing up, and all the pranks and the midnight feasts got left behind, and one day, when she was in Middle Five, playing jacks in the commie, the cool girl in her year said, 'I'm not surprised you're no good at it, with big hands like yours.' What fourteen-year-old girl wants big hands? And then came the solution. She and another girl were outside hitting tennis balls against the commie wall. The other girl announced she was on a diet. That's what I'll do, thought Annie. I'll join her on a diet.

She started getting a bit thin. And a bit more thin. Upper Five was a really rotten year. She was in the Tower with a girl who bullied her. The bully was the girl with the mostest. She had a big sister, she was good at sport, in all the teams, she'd had a boyfriend in Middle Five. It was a verbal drip drip drip. Waking her up at night. Annie got even thinner. Anorexic maybe, though it wasn't really known about in those days. She was just so miserable. She was going to have to do Languages for A Levels instead of Geography. She didn't find Miss Wrinch's lessons boring like the rest of us. She loved them. But she was going to have to take Languages, because her mother wanted her to go into the Civil Service, and in those days you didn't have much say. Oh, this is how it's got to be, she thought. Not eating was a cry for help. Oh, please won't someone notice me? No one did.

Sukie wasn't eating, either. She'd arrived when we were in Middle Five and was put in Latimer, poor thing. She'd lived in Kenya, where her dad was a solicitor, and had been at a boarding school in Nairobi. Dancing was her passion. She went into Nairobi on the back of a truck every Saturday, to ballet lessons with a woman called Madame Zerkovich. Madame Z was small and dark with a big stick that she used to hit you with if you didn't get your legs right. 'Open!' 'Hands!' Sukie loved it. But her mother was petrified her school was going to become multiracial, because they had one African and one Indian there, so her aunt on her father's side — she was her godmother as well — very kindly said she'd be her guardian in England if they wanted to send Sukie to school over there.

Prospectuses arrived – all those extraordinary, wonderful houses she'd never seen but had read about in Enid Blyton and Angela Brazil books. It was all quite exciting. In the last week in August she was put on an aeroplane under the auspices of an eighteen-year-old girl who said she'd sit next to her and look after her. She arrived in Gatwick and was met by this frightfully smart cousin of her mother's who lived in Ormonde Gate, Chelsea. Everything seemed very grey. Driving up through the suburbs from the airport, she said, 'Why are all the houses joined together?' because she'd lived in Kenya since she was two and had never seen terraces before.

The frightfully smart cousin handed her over to the aunt, who took her to Harrods for the uniform. Sukie was absolutely flabbergasted. She'd never owned so many clothes in her life. Suddenly she had liberty bodices, which she'd never heard of, and white linings and a grey dress to change into in the evenings. She'd never worn stockings and a suspender belt before.

The aunt drove Sukie to school for the first day of term. She was a mousey little thing with specs, and quite anxious. It was all so new. First they went to Latimer, but were sent down to Cranmer more or less straight away to meet Jonah. She'd never seen Jonah before. With that great big desk overlooking the sea and that imposing bosom, booming, 'Welcome! Welcome to England!' she was just something out of Angela Brazil. Even the aunt was a little intimidated.

They went back to Latimer, where the aunt arranged for Sukie to be allowed to keep her trunk at school over the holidays because she wouldn't be going back to Kenya. She was one of the very few girls permitted to do that. She met Cawley, who seemed very old.

'Not allowed to use the front stairs, you know!' Cawley squawked.

'Oh, all right,' Sukie stammered.

The aunt couldn't wait to get away. Sukie was handed over to Mary, and the first thing Mary said was, 'I was born in Nairobi and I told the others you wouldn't be black.'

Not many laughs in Latimer. They were too scared. They didn't have midnight feasts, as Pipe would have been on them. She wasn't homesick, because she knew there was nothing she could do. In fact, she only went back to Kenya once the whole time she was there. Her father had no money. Mummy wrote a lot. So it wasn't too bad. She just got farmed around various relations.

Not being able to go home for half term, though, that was horrid. She did feel sad then. For her first half term, she stayed with her aunt, but she had to stay in Latimer for her second half term because her aunt's son had got typhoid from the water while skiing in Zermatt. The school opened the library for her. She read. She walked. And went for three meals a day with Miss Pipe, the matron – in Pipe's dining room. Pipe was furious because it meant she didn't have any time off.

So in Upper Five Sukie got anorexia. It started when Nancy, the American girl, arrived. Nancy had green contact lenses and a boyfriend in Vietnam. Her guardians lived on the Isle of Wight and had a butler, so there was a lot of angling for invitations to stay in the hols. At the beginning of term, at Weighing, Sukie and Nancy were both nine stone. Oh God!

So fat! She and Nancy decided to go on a diet. Nancy's lasted a day, Sukie's till she left school.

She was dancing a lot, hours a day. She needed to be thin, because she was doing ballet. She made a list of everything she'd eaten. If she'd had just one roll then she wasn't allowed to have anything for lunch. If they had semolina, she'd get a great big dollop of jam, say, 'Mmm, delicious,' swirl it around and leave it. Her periods stopped for the whole of the three years she was there. The not eating, the dancing, the fright. She had to keep pretending to be off games. She had a stack of STs she had to give away.

She was always a goody-goody, because she was petrified of being shouted at by Cawley. God, Cawley could shout if you didn't do something right. You could hear it all over House. Sukie was so scared she didn't have the chance to laugh. Her little sister came the year after her and cried for three weeks; wouldn't even eat her birthday cake. She had Sukie's arms round her every day. Cawley and Pipe were so cruel. Sukie dropped from 9st 2lbs to 7st 2lbs.

'You're losing too much weight,' said Sister Berg. And did nothing.

I wished my own misery had whittled me down so conveniently. Instead I stuffed my face. That summer hols of 1964 I made my first pilgrimage to Biba, which I'd read about in *Honey* magazine, where a pink-and-white-check dress had been featured. Biba was in Abingdon Road in Kensington and did not look like a clothes shop at all. The outside was painted black. Inside, music played and clothes hung from bentwood hatstands. In the dim lighting, and without my glasses, it was not always possible to tell which garments were wrapped around a human form and which simply hung from the hatstands, particularly as the colours were on the 'subfusc' side. Prune. Dead daffodil. Pin-striped mud. Floorboard. Dried blood. Aniseed ball. Neither were they absolutely me, measurement-wise. The sleeves were cut very tight and I would hear little ripping noises if I moved my arms too energetically. But they were a revelation, and I loved them.

# 24

# THE BICYCLE THIEVES

Back to school. We were in Lower Six, and had returned to sensational news. Cherry got the curse. Finally. It happened while Juno was staying with her in the hols. Oh, and Juno's mother was doing better. Some kind of rehab had been organised through Cherry's father, the canon. A religious place. Monks involved. Golly. But a corner had been turned. Three cheers for Cherry and Juno.

And three cheers for Lindy. She was made Head of House. But the dramas and crises that came her way! Burton the maid threatened to walk out because Beth and a Middle Five had left the cloakroom in a mess, so Beth and the Middle Five had to write letters of apology to her. Meanwhile the exterior of Ridley was being given a new coat of paint. The grey stucco was disappearing under a coat of Suffolk pink. Ridley blushed, and you couldn't blame it because it turned out the new girl in our year, a sweet but rather droopy girl called Geraldine had developed a *tendresse* for one of the painters, and Bretch gave Lindy a filthy row for not telling her but Lindy didn't even KNOW!

And more cheers still. Oodles of cheers. Chrissie and I had

passed our O Levels, and were allowed to share a dorm again. Now it was A Level time, and I was definitely going to do Latin. Our teacher was a MAN, a great big scruffy bear of a man, Mr Robinson. Not a fierce bear; Rupert rather than grizzly. He told jokes. He'd turn up with sweet in his pockets and always, always, a bit of food down his front. None of his clothes matched. Most of it needed cleaning. You could while away the lesson by getting him to talk about his travels by car through various parts of the Middle East. And now he was the Physics teacher as well. Cherry was delighted. The last one had been this amazing army commander who made it clear that it was beneath his dignity to teach Physics to girls because they hadn't stripped down a motorbike by the age of twelve. But now he was gone, and Jonah got Mr Robinson to do it along with Latin. He had this old car that he drove round and round the Games pitches, blowing his horn to teach them the Doppler effect. All that and chocolate too. Just adorable. I never wanted to do Physics but I was definitely going to take Latin. But I hadn't known what else to do.

More specifically, I did not know what to do about Miss Williams, our English teacher. Miss Williams was small and dumpy, wore rather tight tweed suits and had muscly legs. She wore her hair in a French plait that was never quite under control, and her eyes gleamed. A very good teacher and an interesting character, with a sort of subversiveness, as if she didn't care what 'they' thought of her. She was tremendously encouraging to me and I did enjoy her lessons, but she was a bit too grown-up for me, frankly.

It started when I was in Lower Five, and sitting on The Williams Table. I was at one end, and she was at the other.

'Someone on this table got a hundred percent for their essay,' she murmured.

I realised it was me she was talking about. How exciting! But I had to appear modest, and concentrated on my chicken mush while she just went on and on about my essay to the girls at her end of her table. Far better than anyone else in the school could write . . . one tiny grammatical mistake but she couldn't bring herself to deduct a single mark . . .

By this time I was blushing and feeling terribly uncomfortable and just wished she'd handed me back the essay in class and let me glow in private.

My life with Miss Williams continued in this rather peculiar way. She expected high standards from me but I didn't always live up to expectations. One minute I was being made to feel I was really special, and the next there was a put-down and I'd feel dreadfully silly. Perhaps she was a bit silly herself. Look what happened when Gill's father died. Gill's father was a really nice, gentle, kind man, a local GP. He did house calls. Everybody in the community knew him, and he knew them. A gem. He went into hospital to have a back operation. Gill was thirteen at the time, in Lower Five. It was a spring day and she'd woken up in the nine-dorm thinking, Oh, Daddy's coming out of hospital today.

Everyone had gone back to House after lunch. Gill heard the phone ring outside Bretch's sitting room. She was coming downstairs at the time and didn't really register anything at all. She went into the commie and then someone was sent to fetch her. She walked into Bretch's room. Enormous Jonah was almost hiding behind the door – a mountain. Gill looked up at its peak. 'I'm terribly sorry,' Jonah said, 'your father's died.' He'd gone for a walk in the grounds, and said he didn't feel very well. It was an embolism. The funeral was on a Tuesday. Gill and her sister Elizabeth returned to school on the Sunday after. A letter was waiting for her. 'It arrived for you after you'd gone,' said Bretch, 'and I recognised your father's writing.' Gill took it and turned round, then ran right into her best friend, Alexa. Alexa's arms were clamped to her sides because, of course, you never hugged anyone back then. 'Oh. Hello,' said Alexa in a clipped way. Gill clutched the letter. She just had to get away, find a cab empty somewhere so she could read it in private, but Alexa was chasing her around the corridors, not realising Gill wanted, *needed*, to be on her own because she didn't want anyone to see her crying.

The next morning, Gill had an English Lit. lesson. Miss Williams brought in a pile of dark-green, A5-sized books of short stories and handed them round. They were books of short stories. She told the class which page to turn to.

'Gillian,' she said, 'you can read the first two pages of this story for the class.' The title of the story was 'His Father's Funeral'.

Anyway, back to Williams and me. She so encouraged my creative writing. She kindly read and critiqued, in her spare time, the poetry I wrote, and it wasn't a matter of just one or two, there were terms when I couldn't go half a day without dashing off a sonnet or some multi-page epic in free verse. Beside the margin of one I pressed on her, she'd pencilled 'sounds sexual'. She was right. It was, *and I didn't even realise*. I'd unknowingly written about S.E.X. And I'd heard that one of the A Level set books was *A Passage to India*, and that meant Williams would talk about S.E.X. In class. 'Snakes.

Caves. You know what that means, don't you?' Yuk. So I stabbed Miss Williams in the heart by dropping English and, along with Latin, I did French and Spanish with the glorious Miss Sanford. And Russian. We now had a teacher of Russian! The only girls' boarding school in the country to have one! Another first for Felixstowe College!

It was a two-year crash course. Mrs P was a Russian married to an Englishman. Inevitably we called her Rosa Klebb. Her lessons were dreadfully boring. Four consecutive 35-minute periods every Thursday evening. We studied the clock closely. But heigh-ho. What did that matter? Now we knew how to write 'I love you' in the Cyrillic alphabet.

And halfway through Lower Six, I wanted to write 'I love you' in every possible language. I had stopped stockpiling boyfriends. I had been hit by first love. He was wonderful. A scholarship boy, swotting for Oxbridge, about to carve his way in the world just as my father had. He made me laugh. He made the sun more brilliant. He made the rain retreat into the sky. And my mother told me I could not have him because he came from the wrong side of town, where all the council houses were. He must be common. I should have more pride. She didn't love me, but she wanted to stop me having someone who did.

The soundtrack was Radio Caroline, broadcasting offshore *all day*. We woke up to its call sign, 'This is Radio Caroline'. Instead of singing our hearts out in our gigantic new chapel ('Now Thank We All Our God'; 'Immortal Invisible'; 'The Day Thou Gavest, Lord, Is Ended'), we were bopping and swooning in the commie to Unit 4 Plus 2's 'Concrete and Clay', Francoise Hardy with 'All Over the World', Jackie de

Shannon and 'What the World Needs Now Is Love'. And for me, 'Poor Man's Son' by The Rockin' Berries. I was not going to give that boy up.

During the summer term, my mother went into hospital to have a hysterectomy. My father and I went to visit her and, after ten minutes or so of dreary chit-chat, she started crying. It was sudden. A shock. My mother never cried. She only did anger. 'I feel as though I'm in prison,' she wept.

Neither my father nor I moved. Then he said, 'Er, go and comfort your mother, dear.'

So I put my arms round her and made 'there there' noises – all a bit awkward and pertunctory – while he just stood there. It wasn't me she needed. Why didn't *he* put his arms round her and comfort her and love her? The poor woman.

But I still carried on seeing that boy.


It was the last night of summer term, the last night we'd ever spend in Ridley, and the prank was going to be the best ever played in the history of the school.

As far as Della was concerned, it served Bretch right for telling Della she was going to be made Games captain, which didn't happen because of some breach of rules. So Della was out for revenge, and as she was leaving at the end of that term she was going to town.

There had been an undercurrent of excitement in the Lower Six commie for days. After supper (baked eggs followed by pink blancmange, which nobody but me liked so I ate everyone else's as well), we casually headed off to the dorm, one by one, so as not to arouse suspicion. Bretch had been in a filthy mood with us for days, not talking to us, making us wash our own tea things on Sunday, getting Lindy into floods when she tried to sort it out and saying that we weren't prepared to give up much for the House when we wouldn't take the juniors on a walk because we wanted to work. They didn't even want to go on a walk! Silly bag.

The raid was scheduled to take place under cover of darkness, but by the time we were ready to go for it a pale sun was already shouldering its way above the horizon. Some of us were in the downstairs six-dorm, so getting out was simple enough. Just open the window and climb out. We'd been doing it for years. A dawn breeze made our dressing gowns flap as we made our way on tiptoe across the patio. Down the stone steps on to the lawn we crept, then scurried around to the front of Ridley.

Bretch's bike, the object of the exercise, was propped against the door to Dan Dan The Boilerman's cellar as usual. It was a boneshaker, a familiar sight during summer term, as Bretch glided on it along Maybush Lane, straight-backed, specs glinting. With the skirt of her shirt-waister flapping, she exuded a kind of innocent gaiety. Little did she know. It was a risky job, but with the attraction that it has never been done before. Operation Boneshaker. Target: to put Bretch's bike on the cloakroom roof.

It was just after five a.m. Beth, who was Head of Manoeuvres, pointed silently to the cloakroom, and Cath, Della, Bobbie and Prue crossed the drive and disappeared behind it, giving the window of Bretch's bedroom a wide berth. Bretch's bedroom was the potential flashpoint. All part of the thrill. Beth and I glanced quickly at each other. We'd come this far. We could not now give up. We stepped gingerly past her window, taking

care that our slippers didn't crunch on the gravel. We grabbed
the bike but had to carry it across the drive because it rattled a
bit when the wheels went round. A pedal barked my shin and
I bit back a yelp. Hobble, hobble, wince, wince.

We joined the others behind the cloakroom. Stage One
accomplished. There was a brief pause while Bobbie passed me
her hanky – 'I haven't used it,' she whispered – and I blotted
the blood from my shin. Now for Stage Two.

There was no dispute about who should climb on to the
roof. Beth stepped out of her slippers, wiped her palms on the
sides of her dressing gown and grasped the drainpipe. Planting
her toes on the bolt that fixed its lower end to the wall, she
hoisted herself up, one foot feeling the lumpy pebbledash for
a toehold. There was none till five feet up, where the cab
window ledges started.

Beth dropped to the ground again. We conferred.

Della bent over into the brace position and Beth climbed on
her back. She grasped the drainpipe with one hand and placed
a foot on the ledge. We caught our breath. Up the drainpipe
she climbed, inch by inch, crevice after crevice. The skin of
her bare feet must be sore by now, I thought. She must be
getting tired. But there was no question of her doing anything
but keep going. She pulled herself on to the roof, to a collec-
tive exhalation of relief from those of us waiting below, and
reached down.

Della and Prue hoisted the bike into the air, and Beth
grabbed the handlebars and heaved it on to the flat surface of
the roof.

'Move it towards the other side or she won't see it,' whispered Della.

And so it was done. Beth slithered back down the drainpipe and we all patted her on the back.

It had taken the best part of half an hour, long enough for us all to feel hungry. We made a detour to the Ghost Walk where Prue, the designated quartermaster, had stashed apples, a bag of Fox's Glacier Mints, two sticky willies saved from breaktime, pieces of chocolate crunch smuggled over from Thursday night's supper at Cranmer, some large crumbs formerly known as fruitcake, and our midnight feast tipple of choice which, now we were in Lower Six, was Drambuie. The paper bag in which the food had been kept had mostly disintegrated in the dew.

We ate and sipped to the soundtrack of a gentle rustling, as summer rain landed on leaves. A few drops fell lightly on our bare ankles and the tops of our hands. The sea was beginning to sparkle, and the air so clear that we could see the portholes of the ships heading for Harwich and Europe. We waved at whoever was behind them. Then we crept back to the dorm and, through the window, tumbled inside.

The following year Annie's form put a scarecrow in Bretch's bed. One could not be anything but impressed by how they overcame the logistical difficulties involved in capturing Worzel Gummidge and sneaking him into Ridley undercover. Was their prank superior to ours? Decide.

# 25

## THE LAST HURRAH

Well done, Chrissie! She had worked awfully hard in Lower Six and now she had won a sixth-form scholarship. Super for her not to be in Jonah's bad books any more. I didn't mention it to my mother, who would have wanted to know why I hadn't been awarded one.

How grown-up going into Upper Six seemed at first but, as the weeks went by, it wasn't as thrilling as I'd hoped, because though we were in our own Upper Six Houses, and had bicycles to ride and could wear our own clothes at weekends, we were still at school. We could go into town whenever we wanted, but I didn't want to go into Felixstowe, with its dreary shops and flat horizon. I wanted London – Carnaby Street and the King's Road, and lunch at Cranks health food restaurant. And we still weren't allowed to talk to boys because, if we did, the old bags who spied for Jonah would get on the phone to her about it and you'd have your home clothes taken away till the end of term and be put back into your grey afternoon dress.

But still. There were advantages, no denying that. We had our own kitchen and fridge. And bedsits, not dorms. Chrissie and I shared a room in Coverdale. The beds had sprung mattresses, which was bliss after four years of horsehair pallets. The common room was more like the sitting room in a flatshare, with coffee tables, comfy chairs, a Dansette record-player and, in one corner, a treadle sewing machine. We had our own cheque books; our parents were instructed to make us an allowance, which was meant to last an entire term. There was a good fabric shop in town, and I ran up mini-skirts with the material I bought, so I soon went through my allowance, what with the accompanying purchase of a pair of white calf-length boots. I had seen a photo of Jean Shrimpton wearing them. On me, they didn't look the same.

I was forever trying to keep to a diet, but it was so difficult. That fridge was my downfall. I believed that yoghurts contained no calories and could therefore be consumed six at a time. We could cook our own meals at weekends, and we took it in turns. Chrissie and I dished up cod steaks with tomato and onion sauce, mushrooms, fried onions and sprouts. It ended up on the soggy side, but no one died. What a relief!

The House mistresses were genteel widowed ladies. Mrs Parker was Hooper's. She had bandy bow legs, poor darling, and livened up her sponge cake with whisky in the butter icing. She drank quite a lot. But she was a lovely person, a cut above. So was Mrs Swain, a sweet, very unobservant lady who was nominally in charge of Coverdale. Her son worked for the *Daily Telegraph*, and there was great general excitement when he came to visit. She had lank, greasy hair and would shuffle around in the evenings in a scruffy dressing gown and slippers, and waft in and out discussing knitting patterns. 'Now, dear, I need to talk to you about something. Dear, would you come and see me.'

Otherwise she'd listen to the radio in her room. If you offered her a cup of tea, you'd think you'd offered her the world.

Oh dear. How some of us took advantage of that poor woman. You could get away with anything. I would hang out of the window smoking Gauloises, then spray talc around to mask the smell. There was a pay phone in the hall, and two girls broke into it with a hairpin. There was a lot of money in there. They couldn't possibly take it. They went to Mrs Swain and told her what they'd done. She was absolutely flummoxed. What should she do? She sent them to Jonah. Jonah was flummoxed too. Why did they do it? 'We wanted to see if we could,' they said.

I filled in my UCCA forms. Next year I would be free. But I wanted to be free *now*. I felt I was stuck on a station platform. I was waiting for Life, but the train was delayed. I had a portable typewriter, which must have been a nightmare for everyone on our corridor, as I bashed away at it all hours, finishing my second novel. I skipped lessons and didn't once go to Communion.

Our new chapel was at least four times as big as the old one. It had chandeliers and altar rails and hanging baskets. And a giant cross, plumb centre at the end of the aisle. The biggest, most splendidly decorated school chapel ever built, surely. Old plain-and-simple Reverend Percy Warrington must have been looping-the-loop in his grave. It was a statement. Just when the world outside was getting sexier and ruder and much more fun, here was this hangar of a place to pack in even more virgins singing their hearts out. Meanwhile, the old chapel became a lecture hall. And it was where we held the Sixth Form Dance.

The Sixth Form Dance had traditionally relied on boys being bussed in from nearby schools such as Felsted and Framlingham College, and had been held in the library, but this year was going to be different. Jonah had consented to us having our own invitees. A very sophisticated Cranmer had also arranged for a rock band called the Wild Oats to supply the music, and another Cranmer's daddy supplied beer and wine. The bar was where the altar had once been. Meanwhile, Jonah established herself in the porch to make sure there was no hanky-panky.

The day before the dance, I'd had an interview at Bristol University. I was on a high. I'd been offered a place. I only needed two Bs. We spent all afternoon getting the lecture hall ready and then primping ourselves. I'd invited my boy from the wrong side of town but he wasn't able to come. I was a bit disappointed but some other boys from home stepped up. Chrissie and I waited at Coverdale for ages for them to arrive. They didn't come and didn't come, and then Jonah rang to tell us to go down to the lecture hall, so we did. What a haze of noise and drink. Did Jonah know that someone was already throwing up in the shrubbery? My boys eventually arrived in their car around 10 p.m. They'd got lost. Or so they claimed. The one I had earmarked for myself promptly went off with a stunning Tyndale, but I was so relieved they'd turned up and my face had been saved that I didn't mind in the slightest, and I found another partner. We had to say goodnight to Jonah at the end and thank her for letting us have the dance, and then some of us jumped into one of my friends' cars and went roaring around Felixstowe for a bit. It was after two in the morning when we climbed back into Coverdale through

a window. But it was Cherry's night, really. She got off with
a boy. A real boy. And he was going to take her out in the
Christmas hols.

'He's a bit spotty,' she said. 'But, well, been asked. Held a
sweaty hand. And now I've done some French kissing. I am
a real woman at last.'

If you were going to try for Oxbridge, you were meant to stay
into Third Year Sixth. For some reason Jonah decided I should
take the exam for New Hall, Cambridge, a year early. 'They're
bound to like you because you're mad,' she said. So around the
time I had my interview at Bristol, I took New Hall's entrance
exam as well. And now they wanted to interview me.

The Bristol interview had been great. My mother had
written to Jonah insisting she be allowed to accompany me.
Jonah stopped me in the library to tell me. I explained that I
was going out with a boy of whom my mother didn't approve,
and that she probably thought if I went on my own to Bristol
I would somehow arrange to see him on the sly. That hadn't
even occurred to me. I just wanted to go on my own. Jonah
understood immediately. She wrote back to my mother. I
don't know what was said but I was allowed to go unaccompanied the night before with my overnight case, containing
the outfit I had bought for the occasion – a green and black
checked shirt from C&A, a lovely sludge-green miniskirt
from a new boutique called Foale & Tuffin, and a pair of black
kinky boots. I stayed at a place called the Clarendon, half
hotel, half service flats, which was close to the Wills Building,
where the interview was going to happen.

Sitting down to supper and ordering on my own felt

stupendous. I had liver and bacon with mashed potato, followed by steamed pudding with custard. Not quite up to Mrs Kahn's standard, but delicious all the same. The next morning, I was interviewed by the professor of philosophy, Stephan Korner, and an assistant professor, David Milligan. Stephan Korner was small, with grizzled hair, very courteous. How lovely it all was. The high-ceilinged room, the stained-glass windows, and two MEN. Men who were interested in what I was saying, who treated me as someone on their level. Not scary old biddies picking me up for this and that and telling me what was wrong with me. This was where I wanted to be. This was where I was going to be. When they finished interviewing you, you had to go and sit on a bench outside and wait while they deliberated. And the door opened moments after I had sat down and I was called in again to be offered a place . . . and then I went home bursting with happiness and all I got was, 'Don't say yes till you've been to Cambridge.'

No chance of my being able to do this one on my own. This was the big one for my mother. As my parents drove me to Cambridge, I felt as if I was dragging an enormous weight behind me. She had such hopes of me. Of being able to say, 'My daughter, who's at Cambridge . . .' The trouble was that having been told I was clever from a very early age I assumed that was all there was to it, and thought I didn't actually have to work – which was not a clever conclusion at all. My chosen degree course was Moral Sciences and I had been given three books to read over half term. I flipped through them. They were deadly dull, so I'd given up and decided I'd wing it, as usual. Not preparing properly; it is still my fatal flaw.

The interview was a complete disaster. I remember being

told at one stage I was very young and wouldn't it be better to wait until next year, which was their way of letting me down gently. Back at school a few days later, in the library, Jonah brought me the letter with the New Hall crest on the envelope and stood there while I opened it. 'I've not got in, Miss Jones,' I said. She sort of grunted and hurried away.

Psychologically it was a huge moment for me. I had disappointed the two most significant women in my life. I felt I was no longer of interest to Jonah. My mother was foul to me, as was I to her because, of course, I was more like her than I would ever want to know. I wanted to break things. Chrissie and I fell out. She had told her mother about me and my Poor Man's Son, and about my mother's disapproval.

'I hope you don't mind,' she said.

Yes, I did mind. I was furious. It wasn't that I minded her telling her mother. What made me angry was her telling me she'd told her mother. Rubbing it in that hers was nice and mine was nasty.

I couldn't stay at odds with her for long, but then I was dumped by my Poor Man's Son. And the novel that I had dispatched to a publisher landed back with a thump through the letterbox. I thought I was going to be a writer. Now I had another rejection. I was ragingly angry, morose and completely self-centred. The boys I'd invited to the Sixth Form Dance wanted to make a return visit. Chrissie was far too sensible to get involved but two other girls came with me.

Oh what a night! They had booked hotel rooms. Did they actually think . . .? How could I have been so naïve? (Very easily, is the answer, given that my teens had been spent in a closed single-sex society.) I was in above my head, and I made one of the boys drive me back around midnight. I don't know what happened to the other two, because we never talked about it. There was a terrible school meeting the next day, at which Jonah asked the three girls who were seen out the previous night to stand up, and we were rounded up and despatched into the Red Hall.

'You'll all be expelled, of course.' I hadn't been on the end of Jonah's full fury before. She wasn't someone who shouted and raved. It was controlled fury. Far more terrifying. Would I be put in the San like the jam-eating nymphomaniac, waiting for my parents to come and take me away? But a few days later she wavered. I wasn't to be expelled. I could stay on to take my A Levels. She would not have me back for Third Year Sixth, though. She would arrange for me to take Cambridge entrance at a London day school.

So off I went to take an entrance exam for yet another school. And did not do well. A few days after I returned to Felixstowe, Jonah intercepted me in the library.

'Don't shout the place down, but you haven't been accepted. They didn't like your French paper.'

'I think,' I said, 'that it was really that they didn't like me.'

Good. I was off the hook. I wouldn't have to go to a day school to take Cambridge entrance. Bristol, here I come.

I was wrong. Jonah did another about-turn. I had come to see the error of my ways at last, she thought. I had realised I wasn't a nice person. The first step to reform. I could return for Third Year Sixth and try for Cambridge again. My mother phoned, crowing with delight at the news.

But I dug my heels in. I couldn't bear it any longer. I wanted to get out into the world, have fun. I didn't want to go to

Cambridge. I didn't want to spend three more years of rules and curfews and formal dining, of living with other women and being taught by old biddies. And even if I did stay on at school and take the entrance exam, it would all be a waste of time. There was more chance of the sea turning to tomato soup that my being offered a place.

So I took my A Levels, the end of summer term approached, and I was back in Jonah's study for the last time.

'Goodbye, Miss Jones.'

'I'm sure your mother would be a lot happier if you got a first,' she said.

'Yes, I'm sure she would be if I gave her the moon in a golden carriage drawn by unicorns as well.'

I didn't really say that.

Off I went to Bristol, with my mother shouting that I was a failure. But I wasn't. In my third year I won a prize, the *Daily Telegraph* Young Writer of the Year Award. Entrants had to produce an article about 'Britain Today', and I wrote about student life and love and sex and drugs and abortion, and my entry was the winner. It was published in their colour supplement and it so happened that, not long after it appeared, Chrissie went to an Old Girls' Weekend.

'Did you see what your friend wrote?' Cawley screeched at her. But what did I care? She was a mad old bag and I was a writer.

# 26

# THE GREAT FIRE

If you've been paying attention, you'll remember that above our library was a clock tower, reached via a set of stairs that led from the Red Hall. On the way you would pass Jonah's daytime office, where her P.A. would sit busily typing out The Jonah List and all the rants about hair, and from whence Jonah would make her lightning hit-raids to quash any misbehaviour in the library. Further up was a maze of little rooms where we went for Elocution, Shorthand and Typing and wigging. You could hear the whirring of the clock mechanism. It was the Hogwart's bit of the school and, one night in September 1973, it all went *whoosh* and *whump*.

It was so easy to get into our school and set fire to it. There was no security to speak of in the grounds. The Great Fire of Felixstowe College was front-page news: 'Arson Probe After Girls' School Blaze'. Second lead in the *East Anglian Daily Times*, only conceding prominence to 'Guerrillas Shoot Arab Jet Hostage'.

The photo that went alongside the report showed the library after the fire had done its worst. The doors to the Red Hall had been blown out and metal frames and roof girders exposed. Where windows had been were gaping holes and everything that hadn't been turned to cinders was peeling or hanging. It was horrible, horrible, our beautiful library, just gone. All because some young lad had kicked off after a row with his girlfriend.

Strictly speaking, the Great Fire doesn't belong to our school story because by then we'd all left and were already scattered round the world. In another way, it belongs absolutely, because it was the end of *our* school, *our* memories. And in any case, in a place where the biggest drama to date had been the time Mrs Kahn burnt the curry and we all had to eat it anyway, this was it, the ur-drama, the ultimate Big Thing (apart from closing down) that happened to Felixstowe College.

It was early September 1973, a week before the start of term, and Miss Manners, Jonah's successor, had just returned from a holiday in Austria with her great friend, the historical novelist Mary Stewart. When she wrote about the fire in the school magazine, the prose took on something of the fraught, swoopy tone of romantic fiction.

'Long before I reached the gate,' she wrote later, 'I could see the angry glare in the sky beyond the science block. Panting and out of breath, silly tears dazzling my eyes, I came round the corner from the music school on a nightmare scene.'

The library block was beyond saving. The parquet floor turned into a flame carpet, the glass dome disappeared in a brief shower of hot crystals. Six thousand books went, five classrooms, the Upper Six commie, the office that was Jonah's lair, the wigging rooms, the drama room with all its costumes, the sixth-form studies, Bretch's typewriters, eight cabs, the

complete school records, hundreds of textbooks, piles of
A Level work, all the stationery.

I had no idea that it had happened. It was just after the
start of the 1973–74 football season, my first as a reporter.
Saturday 8 September, Crystal Palace vs. Middlesbrough.
The day is engraved on my memory because after the match
I was given a lift back to Fleet Street by my childhood hero,
Danny Blanchflower, who by then was a journalist on the
*Sunday Express*.

Meanwhile, Maybush Lane was blocked with fire engines
and Miss Wrinch, while the wreckage was still smouldering,
tippy-toed through the doorway that was no longer there to
rescue the A Level work. This wasn't just duty. Nor was it the
desire to be the heroine of her own school story, 'Miss Wrinch
Saves The Day'. This was her goodbye to the building made
by her father.

In spite of the encroachment of her illness, the first signs of
which were that dreadful faint into the rice pudding, Wrinch
had gone on serenely teaching Geography, carrying out her
role as Deputy Head, first to Jonah and then to Miss Manners.
*The Story of Felixstowe College* recorded that her one ambition
was to see her father's library restored:

> [. . .] and it was with great joy that she installed herself in the
> new Deputy Head's room. With the school back to working
> capacity in its new building, she felt that her task was done
> and prepared to retire in July 1976, calmly making plans
> for a future which, in her heart of hearts, she must have
> known she would never see . . . A few weeks before, she
> had addressed the school in chapel, speaking bravely of the

illness she was fighting, and certain of the divine strength that was supporting her. It had become only too apparent during the last year that this was an heroic struggle.

She died, with typical consideration and lack of fanfare, *after* the end of autumn term.

At least she got a proper, very Felixstowe send-off, in the big new super chapel: the overwrought holiness, the prefects in billowing robes, the teachers po-faced under their hats, the incantations and recitations. And all the other stuff that, once you've escaped from it, makes you think, Oh dear. But Lois Wrinch has always stayed in my mind. A few years ago I took part in the 'Three Peaks in 24 Hours Challenge'. You might have heard of it. The object of the exercise is consecutively to climb, for charity, the three highest mountains in Britain, linking them all with mad drives from Scotland to the Lake District to Wales. We summited Ben Nevis in a roiling mist, we did Scafell Pike in dawn's early light, and I thought of Miss Wrinch and my Geography exams all the way up Snowdon. 'Wales is a very mountainous country with some peaks up to over 3,000ft high'. I would have been awfully grateful if she had appeared alongside me and handed out one of her glucose tablets.

# 27

## VALETE

Or goodbye, in Latin.

*Daily Telegraph*, 27 June 1994

## FALLLING ROLLS MARK END
## OF PUBLIC SCHOOL

An independent school for girls is to close because of financial problems. Felixstowe College, in Suffolk, which charges £3,500 a term for boarders and £2,500 for day pupils, blames falling numbers and the burden of paying for a new sports hall.

The school, founded in 1929, had at its peak 300 senior girls and 90 in its mixed junior school. The number of seniors has fallen by half.

Headmistress Mrs Bridget Patterson said, 'We thought that numbers for September were going to be enough, but we have had some withdrawals. There are not enough boarders coming in at the bottom end of the school to keep it viable.'

> Parents received letters about the closure on
> Saturday. A group of them are to discuss a rescue
> package.

Nothing came of the rescue package discussions, Q.E.D.
When I went to Felixstowe to interview Elizabeth Manners
in 2011, it was to meet a woman who had done thirty years
of seething about her successor, Miss Guinness.

'I was going into Marks and Spencers one day,' harrumphed
Miss Manners, 'and there she was at the door. "Welcome!" she
said. "Welcome?" I said. "You've just welcomed me to Marks
and Spencers!"'

The trouble was that Jonah, as that wonderful Old Girl
Janet Copland said, 'got the hell out'. Miss Manners did not.
She stayed on in Felixstowe, a figure of note in the town, a
personality, serving on the local council, appearing on BBC
Radio 4's *Any Questions*, a woman of strong opinions, some of
which concerned what was happening to Felixstowe College.
Miss Guinness was charming, gentle, devout, and unfortunate
enough to be in charge of the school when the decline started.

'Before I went there, they'd been boarding girls out in the
town,' said Judy James, who arrived in 1989 to be the last
House mistress of Ridley. 'In the early 1980s it was still very
difficult to get into. It was burgeoning. Then it *went*, like a
house of cards.'

There was the credit squeeze. Fewer parents could afford it.
The reduction in the armed forces meant a draining away of
girls on subsidised fees. Felixstowe's remoteness was another
problem; its catchment area was reduced by zillions of gallons
of sea and its poor transport links became a problem once

greater contact between parents and children became the norm, and many schools allowed weekly boarding. Then there was the kind of education that was being offered. Under Miss Manners's regime, the school had become more academic, less of the 'College for Young Ladies' that Jonah had been so keen on. Miss Guinness had taken it back to its more ladylike days. But times had changed.

'They weren't renewing with people coming in,' said Judy James. 'Boys' schools were very active recruiting and promoting, had better facilities and didn't cost much more. Mothers were now choosing where daughters went, not fathers, and often they'd been at convents and wanted somewhere that was more fun.'

Which, by the 1980s, meant boys. With hindsight, the beginning of the end was one year into Miss Manners's reign. It was as far back as 1968, when Marlborough College became the first major public school to go co-ed, starting with its sixth form. By 1989 it was fully co-educational; alumnae include the Duchess of Cambridge and political wives such as Samantha Cameron, Sally Bercow and Frances Osborne. Some schools cottoned on quickly to the trend. Boys' schools began admitting girls first into their sixth forms and then throughout the school. St Felix followed, opening its doors to boys.

Miss Manners capitulated, agreeing to go down the co-educational route. Only one boy was interested and he soon lost enthusiasm when he found he was the only one. Another of Felixstowe's failings was that it was on the sea, and was difficult to get to from London. Gradually the number leaving became greater than the number joining. Things were grim in the last few years.

They relied more and more on girls from overseas and, in the final years, Felixstowe had more or less become an international school. It was not what some parents sent their daughters there for. Felixstowe was expensive to run, too. Those letterheads – thick grey, red, embossed; indicative of the expense and quality of running the school. They couldn't change them. People would have known immediately. *Whooooa!* They're going to close!

In an attempt to halt the decline, headmistresses were removed and installed and removed again. Time started going backwards, the building up of the school in reverse. Houses closed. Hooper went, then Monkbarns, the Lower Six house bought by the school during Miss Manners's time. Tyndale became the Prep, which flourished then died, so that was the end of Tyndale.

'In the last two years, they cut down on cleaners,' said Judy James. 'They no longer came in every day. On Sundays we had to clean the house; we had squads. Money got tighter and tighter. The sixth-form house at the end was very wild. There was a pregnant girl there, from Singapore. She was very pregnant when she came to sit her exam. She needed the qualifications.

'Wycliffe was there for my first two years. Then they decided to bring the young ones in, which was very hard for them. By this stage they had to have mixed-age forms – little ones with the next year up. Would there be enough of us to make a team for House Games? We could see the numbers falling and many of us had been looking for jobs for a long time. Ridley was going to close next.

So the writing was on the wall. Felixstowe had certainly

transformed into being a totally international school. 'In Ridley I had Chinese, Japanese, Kenyan, Nigerian, Brits, Belgians, and an American from one of the bases. One girl's father died in the middle of everything, which didn't help. Then they discovered he'd been evading taxes. We had to ask her to leave. She was a very disturbed child. That's the trouble with a falling roll; you were so pressured by the head to keep someone on. But if you do, you'll lose more than one child.

'The staff were totally cloud cuckoo: "They won't close us." Having come from business it was quite a shock to me to see how unworldly they were. One of the biology staff was made redundant and the staff room virtually disintegrated. A lot of schools were in trouble at that time. It was Felixstowe vs. St Felix. There was one too many, and St Felix stayed open.

'When it closed, the staff had gone to pieces; it was the House staff who found other schools for the children. Some girls were about to take GCSEs and we had to find somewhere quick. We took a whole busload down to Westonbirt; a big bus of Nigerian and Chinese girls, predominantly. "There are cows! They've got a church in the grounds!" One Chinese girl said, "Mrs James, there are dead bodies buried there!" It was a culture shock. Our chapel didn't have graves.'

Felixstowe College was sold for £6 million. Westonbirt took the contents of the library and Harrogate Ladies' College the music equipment. Trophies and shields were auctioned off. All that was left were bits and pieces, including some com-memorative tea towels left over from the wedding of Prince Charles to Lady Diana Spencer. Considering how Felixstowe College began, when Uplands School was razed by fire in

1927, there's a symmetry about what happened next. The bits and pieces went to an Old Girl who ran a prep school. They were lost in a fire.

In 1995, not long after the closure, Helen went over to Felixstowe to see a family friend. 'I walked into the place and it was as though there had been a bomb dropped on the country, as if everyone had left in the wake of a disaster. I could go everywhere. The gym was covered in graffiti, the wooden floor was torn up and the windows broken. In the Chemmy lab, stools were lying on their sides and work unclaimed by the girls was scattered on the floor. And the music school was all shattered windows and graffiti. I spent an hour there in floods of tears. I could not believe it; it was the sacrilege of it all. After everything it had meant, and everything everyone had done to make it happen. All destroyed.

> By the rivers of Babylon we sat and wept
> When we remembered Zion.
> Here on the poplars
> we hung our harps.

'Psalm 137 (I looked it up) ... one of those beautiful collections of words which Sir William Walton included in his wonderful oratorio, 'Belshazzar's Feast'. A school friend and I, for two years, used to queue from 2.15 in the afternoon to go and hear it at the Proms. We always ended up on the front rail.

'The psalm is very apposite, and weep I did.'

# 28

# OLD GIRLS

There's something about going back to your old school; a peeling away of the layers of adult experience. My mood is ping-ponging between excitement and apprehension: wanting to go back and not wanting to; curious to see all the places I lived and learned in; scared, as if someone is waiting there to pass judgement. Finding myself back in Jonah's study, staring at my shoes and blushing as Jonah grunts, 'People are saying you're conceited.' I am still that child.

It's a beautiful spring day, and the train journey into Suffolk hasn't been much different from the ones I took half a century ago: Liverpool Street, Chelmsford, Colchester. We pass through Constable country and stop at Manningtree, where I almost expect the two blonde sisters, farmer's daughters, to get on; they did something sexy with their hats. Now here's Ipswich, where, in O Level year, before we changed on to the branch line, I would make the transition from London teenager in the ladies' waiting room. Off with the Mary Quant keyhole skirt, black skinny-rib sweater and Mansfield granny shoes. On with the grey afternoon dress. Scrubbing away my make-up at the very last moment.

The near-empty Felixstowe train – single carriage these days – rattles through the flat Suffolk countryside. This isn't the first time I've been back. I went to Jonah's memorial service in 1985. Much nearer to the moment I'm in now, I visited Elizabeth Manners, in her flat. What remained of the old place was some half a mile away. I retraced my steps to my car without looking. The home I grew up in, the *Observer* building that was my first place of work, the hospitals my children were born in: all my life landmarks had gone. I hadn't wanted to see what had happened to Felixstowe College. I wanted it to still be there, at least in my mind's eye.

Felixstowe station is a husk of its former self, now so hidden among its surroundings the impression is that somebody stole it. But once I find my way outside, everything is familiar straight away: the muted colours of the buildings; the way the roads run in parallel curves to the sea like an auditorium, each house a seat. The Orwell Hotel, where my parents used to stay on exeat weekends, is still on the corner at the top of the high road. Meringues with strawberries on top! Going to the Hamilton Road shops! Watching *Juke Box Jury* in the residents' lounge! (Seeing my parents for the first time in a month possibly wasn't as important as it should have been.)

I set off for the seafront, past the Spa Pavilion and the pretty villas and the municipal flowerbeds still planted on the same steep bank with what may well have been the same red and blue hardy annuals. A hundred yards away, Chrissie is waiting in her open-top BMW. The plan was to have a proper English picnic on the beach before taking a tour round whatever is left of our school, but within seconds comes one of those sudden east-coast downpours. I run the rest of the way and fling handbag and thermos on to the passenger seat and myself on top of them.

The North Sea occupies the entire horizon. 'It's exactly the same colour as it was the day we got here,' observes Chrissie, unwrapping egg and cucumber sandwiches and sausage rolls. 'Cold cocoa.'

I embark on the task of pouring tea from the thermos without emptying it over my lap, and think briefly of our friendship, the one that started in the first week of our first term, and then I think of us writing poetry and stories together, and swooning over the Beatles, and sharing the terror and hilarity. I remember us being new members of an old club – the other eight Ridleys who had been there for two years already. I can see them all now, in the junior common room on that very first evening, inspecting us. Erica, pretty and charming with a grown-up tinkly laugh, performing the introductions; Bobbie, dark and good-natured with milky skin; Cath, with that gorgeous copper-beech hair; Beth and Marion who were woman-shaped already; little Della and Prue; Lindy, the English rose with a core of steel; Marlee, skinny with enormous glasses. I remember us escaping from the junior commie for a midnight feast on a balmy autumn summer night, and dancing to Chubby Checker's 'Let's Twist Again' in the Middle Five commie . . .

The wipers are squeaking against the windscreen. It's stopped raining and the endless sky of the North Atlantic has turned from gunmetal to a gauzy grey through which the sun is trying to announce itself. Time to get going. I pour the rest of the tea into the road and we set off towards the familiar view of Cranmer on its clifftop.

We round the corner into Maybush Lane and walk a little way up the drive. To our left are some new iron gates and a sign: Ridley House.

'Ohhhh.'

The Covered Way has gone, obliterated at one side by a large extension that juts out into what used to be the turning circle for parents' cars. There is a gap where the other end should be, and then a whole new house, an ungainly replica of Ridley, like the plain adolescent daughter of a beautiful mother.

Then we walk a little further along the drive, turn and look to our right. We stare, mute and aghast, at the scene before us. The new chapel is still there, at the end of the old Ridley driveway, but our lovely Art and Dance studio has gone. The rest of our school, too, has vanished. We blink in amazement, as our gaze travels over the altered scene. Housing developments have replaced the school buildings and they stand on top of playing fields where once we galloped around with our lax sticks, the wind whipping up our divided skirts.

More memories. The term Cranmer caught fire. The seat was the little kitchen on the top floor, installed there for the making of tea and a boiled egg before Communion. It was around midnight, and people were lying awake chatting after coming back late from a ballet trip to London when they heard the noise. *Crackle, crackle, crackle.* And when they got up and opened the dorm door, it was to find the whole corridor full of smoke and the kitchen turned into a fire-breathing dragon. And no one knew where the fire alarm was, so they ran up and down the corridors banging on doors. 'The house is on fire! This is not a prank. Repeat, this is not a prank!' They had to wake up Jonah, who stood in her dressing gown, head full of Kirbigrips, shivering on the lawn with everyone, watching the Fire Brigade.

And more memories still. Coming back from Cranmer after lunch and spending most of the time just laughing. And getting into fits in the dorm, and Bretch telling us to shut up, so we did, and just looked out of the window for a while, then went into hysterics again over nothing.

And the hot, hot summer of 1963, when the sky was raining ladybirds. The whole sky. Full. Thousands and thousands of them. Millions. All over the Games pitches. Swarms of the things. You could come out of the classroom and put your hand out and catch them.

And the time the Duchess of Gloucester arrived by helicopter and landed between Ridley and the gym. The whole school turned out, in boaters and Sunday dresses, to greet her. The term when we celebrated bonfire night and the army did the catering and burnt the soup. The time we were banned from using Ridley's back lawn because some girls talked to boys over the wall. The time we were split up and had to go in separate dorms.

Chrissie, being from Guernsey, always seemed a tiny bit exotic, more French than English. Some years back, on holiday in Brittany, I noticed how many of the women reminded me of her: broad-shouldered, deep-bosomed, narrow-hipped. I don't see her any different now. A smiling face, fine crinkles at the corners of her eyes; they were there even then. I remember the way she pushed her glasses back on to the bridge of her nose when she was discombobulated about something. She laughed when I reminded her about that.

'I was the little fat girl with glasses. At my primary school people were mean to me. I was often left out of things because I was fat. There's a bitchiness current in little girls. It might have been one of the reasons I was keen to go to boarding school, to get out of it.'

'But there were mean girls at Felixstowe too,' I protested.

'I seem to remember people were really mean about some of the fat girls,' she said, 'but nobody was really horrid to me. And Marlee was incredibly thin and people were nasty to her as well. I always tried not to be mean because I was aware I was a good target.'

It's true; in all the years she's been my friend, I've never known Chrissie do anything mean, though she can be deliciously beady in private when her guard is down. By the time we were seventeen, we had other friends as well, but our bond has never gone away. Even though months, sometimes years, go by without seeing her, once I am with her I talk more freely and unguardedly to her than to anyone else.

Looking back, I was really lucky to have found such a friend. We just clicked. She was funny, kind and intelligent. Oh, the fun of having someone to mooch with, sleepy-eyed, over to Cranmer for breakfast; to stagger away from the music school with after Theory of Music with Miss Cornford; to sympathise with when our names appeared on The Jonah List; to comb the dictionary for rude words with (to be fair, we were inclusive on this issue and invited Della to join in. She repaid our faith in her by discovering *fart* and *fornication* while Chrissie and I had only progressed as far as *catamite* and *cohabit*).

We wrote stories and poetry side by side. I recall an epic of free verse called 'Catching the Silver', of which Chrissie said in a letter to her parents, 'The title was better than the poem'. We watched *West Side Story* together five times, once in a French cinema (*without* subtitles) on a school trip to Menton; it inspired our *roman-fleuve*, 'Saints and Sinners', which we wrote in alternating chapters. I took Saints and Chrissie took Sinners. We went swoony over film stars and rock stars and then real boys together. Our friendship featured intense analysis, familiar to anyone who has been a teenage girl, of What He Said and What He Meant; ludicrously tiresome (to adults) running jokes and arcane catchphrases, just the first word of which would convulse us all morning (particularly potent when whispered in Chapel). Reading the diaries she kept from the second term of Middle Five onwards, reliving the times we spent together, is wonderful. People moan now about having been sent to boarding school and come out with all sorts of stories about how their lives were thus blighted, but I could never feel that way because if I hadn't gone to Felixstowe I would never have had the chance to experience such a glorious friendship.

A while back, I appeared on a BBC Radio 4 programme about boarding school and positively choked up when it came to talking about having her as a friend. I have never liked anyone so much. To have that experience, of having someone who knows exactly what you mean without your having to explain; of trusting someone with all your thoughts and ideas (and some of mine were floridly exuberant and left field), and knowing you would never be made fun of or criticised, was wonderful. Our friendship was my defence against the vicissitudes of boarding school life: the soul-blistering tickings-off; the agonies of being dumped by letter by a boy; humiliations so intense that you only admitted them in solemn vows of eternal secrecy; mean prefects and mad teachers, against whom we were a two-girl fortress.

I've never found starting to write a book easy. When it was all beginning, she was the first person I rang, and she promptly emailed me a list of names and addresses of some of our former school friends. While I was reading it, I had the same feeling as I'd had all through our years at Felixstowe: I had somebody *with* me. I wasn't alone in the world.

'You had to have a friend,' says Chrissie. 'A friend you'd chosen rather than being thrown together as the last two left.'

'Yes. You kept me going, I would have drowned without you.'

'That's funny,' she says. 'I always leant on you as the strong one.'

I try to tell her what our friendship has meant to me, and thank her for all the joy it has given me, but it's threatening to get a bit weepy. Chrissie's mouth is turned down at the corners and I've got something in my eye. We hurry back to Ridley and the chapel. A woman comes to the door as we stand outside, giggling at the memories, at Cawley and Maggie crossing themselves, counting how many times Elly-J said 'and', and organising whose turn it was to faint and be carried out before the sermon.

The door opens and a woman says, very severely, 'We do computer programming work very quietly in here,' which just sets us off again and, as we walk along the path below Cranmer, it gets colder, windier and wetter – Sunny Felixstowe at its worst. We think of those cloaks blowing around, letting in the cold air as we trooped down the road from school to Cranmer for supper. We think of Karen, the scandalous matron, bolting out of the dining room to throw up in the tamarisks. We think of Bretch pedalling along Maybush Lane on her bicycle, swaying from side to side.

We are in hysterics.

# NEWS OF OLD GIRLS

## MY RIDLEY FRIENDS

Freedom at last. We went to university or art school, or trained as secretaries or nurses or teachers; we shared flats and went to parties, and wore what we wanted. Some of us found jobs and others travelled. We all got married – those I know about, anyway. I couldn't track everyone down. Beth was last spotted at London University (as it was known then) in the late 1960s. We think she might have gone to South America. The trails on Bobbie, Erica, Marlee and Marion went cold early on, too. Geraldine, who had the fling with the lad painting Ridley, is just a jaw-dropping memory for everyone.

Della left at the end of Lower Six. 'I couldn't stand it any longer. I really couldn't. I still have nightmares about it now. I wasn't homesick. I didn't like home much either. I think I was waiting to grow up.' She went to art school but spent her working life as a librarian. Now she lives by the sea on an unspoilt part of the east coast and is married to one of the nicest men you could hope to meet. She has a son and a granddaughter and looks as attractive as ever. I went to visit her and we were joined by Cath, who lives not far away and whose gorgeous copper-coloured hair is now discreetly blond. Cath had a successful nursing career, which continued until she married. Now she has retired she can indulge her great passion, breeding collie dogs. It was wonderful to see them both again, as it was Lindy and Prue. In some weird way, they all look the same to me now as they did at school. They always will.

## Annie

In spite of her misery in Upper Five, Annie did outstandingly well at O Level. She wanted to leave and do A Levels at Chelmsford High, but her mother wouldn't allow it. Nor would she allow her to take Geography and Biology, her favourite subjects, because she wanted her to go into the Foreign Office. So Annie wasted a year doing Languages, which she didn't really want to do. She left after Lower Six and went to France to learn the language, and from there she went to live with a marquis and marquesa in Madrid. Theoretically she was studying A Levels on her own. She went back to Felixstowe to sit the exams and spent the night in the San. It was horrible. She was part of it but not part of it. She got two Ds.

Nobody specifically suggested university. They didn't know what to do with her. 'There was a feeling that the kind of girls who went to uni were the ones who played golf and learned to drive,' she says, 'and I had never had much to do with them. I wish I had. I felt nobody was interested in me, and I sunk.'

So, off she went to train as a secretary. One day her first boss asked her to sew a button on his shirt, and then he said, 'Well,

I'm wearing the shirt, so you'll have to sit on my lap to do it.'

This would not do. Back to Spain she went, ending up as the dolly bird on the beach teaching fat Germans to water-ski. So different from anything that had gone before. So many things to do. So much fun. She had a ball! You could do anything! She'd been so miserable, and now life was like, 'Hey!'

'I ended up working at Ford, in Warley, near Brentford, which was lucrative but incredibly dull. Then I ran the postgrad medical centre in a hospital in Essex. My dad was a GP, so people knew me. There were parties, boyfriends. I'd already decided, I'm used to dealing with doctors, don't fight it any longer, so I trained as a nurse. Got married, had kids, blah blah blah.'

Sometimes, when I was asking my friends about their Felixstowe lives, they would tell me the funniest anecdotes which, for one reason or another, couldn't be fitted into the story. One concerns the time that Annie went back to Felixstowe for the day with her three girls, then aged nine, seven and five. It was a beautiful day – the sun was shining, the sea sparkling. Naturally the girls wanted a wee, so she took them to the Ridley toilets. When they came emerged, Bretch was standing outside, eavesdropping. *Plus ça change!*

Annie sent me a list of what she had taken from taken from school: 1) Am very independent and can cope with most problems. 2) I still enjoy tennis and other outdoor activities. 3) Am very seldom cold. 4) I appreciate the things I actually learned. 5) I will eat anything.

'They weren't the greatest days of my life,' she says, 'but it made me who I am.'

## Helen

It was 1967 and Helen had no intention of being in the school after Jonah left. She wanted to do A Level Music and needed to do it in a music environment so, after spring term, Lower Six, she went to Cambridge Tech before going on to the Royal College of Music. She finished there in 1972. But she had been playing the piano since she was four. She'd had double piano with Miss Cornford every week, learned the timpani and the recorder for school plays, the clarinet because they wanted her in the orchestra, the guitar and the organ because she was the school's musical Jill-of-all-trades. She'd had enough of music for a while. And she liked straight lines and fiddly bits, so she went to work in editorial and design for the Antique Collectors Club. Then she got married and had two daughters. But she still finds herself waking up from a dream in which she's been galloping around Ridley, in that cloak with its holes where the pockets should have been for you to put your hands through. In the gales and the wind and the fog for six years.

'My music and its profound influence in my life – with dear Cornford's help, of course – has now come full circle. I have a flourishing private practice teaching singing and piano to adults and schoolchildren, which for years I swore I would never do! I love every minute of it. To have an aptitude for music is one thing, but to go to a school where it was nurtured and encouraged so much, where there were endless opportunities to go to two or three celebrity concerts or civic concerts every term, where the teaching was exceptional, that was indeed special. I shall forever be grateful to Cornford, the music school and Jonah.'

Helen's sister Lydia, who sang so beautifully at the nativity concert at the end of my first term, took up her place at Cambridge. Somewhere along the way her heart took a detour: love, marriage, children. She only got a 2.2 because she didn't keep her eye on the ball; she'd just got engaged. That didn't matter really; she always found work she wanted to do. All Cambridge Voices' recordings, the Rodolfus choir, Herald Records, doing all their CD covers. Every year she held an Epiphany party, to a time-honoured formula, with the family and all the music people she was involved with. Saturday supper, people sleeping on floors. The party started again on Sunday morning.

In 2006 the parties stopped for good, when Lydia died of endometrial cancer. She had flatly refused chemotherapy. Before she died she received hundreds and hundreds of letters and emails. Her sons read them to her. Her memorial service was at St John's, Cambridge, where her working life had been spent.

I told Helen about the notes of the song, the voice I'd heard at the end of my first term, the one that still sings in my mind's ear. 'It was a girl's treble,' she says. 'It was like that right to the end.'

## Gill

Jonah might have gone, but she saw to it that 'her' girls were all right, and Gill left in 1968 to study English at Bristol University. After that, she wanted to travel. She did not become the first female pirate, the ambition she had confided to Jonah during her entrance interview, but something even better: she became a national windsurfing champion in her adopted country, Australia.

'The YMCA used to run all these courses,' she says. 'I was

thirty-three and hadn't done much sailing. I just did it because I could get a discount on the class. It very quickly became obvious that I was one of the only females in Western Australia who could actually do it, and I won a National.'

She was selected for the 1984 World Championships. They were held in Largs, in Scotland. She did not come back with a medal but found a husband. 'We were all shivering, and Hugh said, "Who would like to put their hands in my pockets?", and I was the only one who did.'

## Caroline

Caroline, who was so homesick on first joining, was not encouraged by the school to follow her natural bent as a practical, nurturing person. In consequence, she was 'hoicked out' after O Levels. Her mother had told her that if she didn't know what else to do she should learn to cook, so first she went to Eastbourne College of Domestic Economy, where she was taught to just decorate everything with parsley, and then to Cordon Bleu. Being in London, doing what she turned out to be terribly good at and enjoyed doing, was life-changing.

'It was creative, like lighting a touch paper – the drinking, the smoking, the colours, the fun, the boyfriends – it was just magic, wasn't it? I've never understood how people can say schooldays are the happiest of your life.'

She went on to cook for Henry Kissinger, Agatha Christie and Margaret Thatcher. She lived in with Peter Sellers at weekends, and among the guests she cooked for was Ringo Starr. 'He was a very well-brought-up lad, and came in to say thank you.'

After that, life was marriage, children and lots of cooking. She worked between each of the kids. Marriage had its ups and downs, and after she was divorced she became production manager of *County* magazine and organised concerts, art exhibitions and conferences. A few years ago she started a new career as a maternity nurse. She is proud of what she has achieved, considering she was not regarded as bright enough to do A Levels, and thinks that whoever says you can't qualify for anything over the age of fifty-nine is talking rot.

## Cherry

Cherry was offered a place at St Hilda's College, Oxford, to study medicine but turned it down to train at the Royal Free Hospital in London, where she met and married a fellow medical student. She has a son and a daughter, both of whom also work in medicine. She was a consultant paediatrician for many years but later fulfilled her ambition to work overseas for Médecins Sans Frontières, an independent humanitarian organisation providing medical assistance to people who would otherwise be denied access to healthcare.

## Wisty

Wisty did her degree in Spanish at St Andrews then took a year out to go travelling, which turned into a lifetime. She met and married her husband in the USA, where she breeds and shows Appaloosa horses.

## Juno

Juno left after her first term in Upper Six and spent six months in France as an au pair, then returned to England and became a beauty consultant, which she continued with after marriage and children. She was successfully treated for breast cancer in her late forties.

## Sukie

Sukie left after Lower Six because her father could no longer afford the fees. Her ambition was to be a lawyer, but a Latin O Level was required back then and she failed it twice. So she gave up that thought in favour of the Foreign Office.

'Why do you want the Foreign Office?' asked Bretch.

'Because I'd like to go abroad.'

'Well, you won't go abroad till you're at least twenty-one.'

Oh God, that's forever, she thought. So her mother found her a job through *The Lady*, looking after three little boys in Kent who ate more at one meal than she did in a week. Then she went to St James Secretarial College, and that got her a job abroad – she worked for a dermatologist in South Africa. She then came home and married a naval officer, and had a daughter and a son. And at the age of forty-three she went to university at last, did an LLb and became an academic lawyer, teaching at Southampton Solent University. 'It was,' she says, 'a lovely ending. I've had a lovely life.'

## Joanna, Gay and Rosie

Joanna achieved good grades in her A Levels, but no one encouraged her to go to university. Instead she was offered four choices of career: nursing, occupational therapy, teaching or secretarial. She was accepted by a teaching college in Lincoln, a poor exchange, she felt, for her first choice of a life with the under-graduates at Cambridge by going to Homerton, or her second choice, a life of nightclubs in London by going to Roehampton. So she turned it down but did get her wish by being accepted at the 'Ox and Cow' secretarial college in Oxford. She met lots of suitable young men and eventually landed her first job, Secretary to the President of Corpus Christi. Mummy was terribly pleased when she married a Guards Officer because Felixstowe's education in the social graces meant she would know what to do as the wife of a Commanding Officer.

After two years at the Institut Francais in London, Gay qualified as a bilingual secretary and worked with a large American legal firm for a handsome young French lawyer, unfortunately already married. She met Jamie, her future husband, an accountant at Deloittes in Paris. Soon after their wedding they left for Tehran, but after two-a-half years they had to flee the country because of the Iranian revolution. They eventually moved back to England and have three daughters and three grandsons. Gay always loved music, her piano lessons with Cornbags and singing in the Chapel choir, and she has ended up as a piano teacher. She says, 'I also sing in many choirs!'

Undecided when she left school as to what she should do, Rosie was sent, like Joanna before her, to the 'Ox and Cow'. 'My mother never hid the fact that she felt it gave us a chance to find a "suitor". I met Ashley a year later, when I was nineteen, and he asked my father for my hand in marriage in 1975 but my father refused. My mother had decided he was unsuitable as he was still a medical student and had no means!'

Meanwhile, Rosie trained as a nurse at Westminster Hospital. She qualified in 1978 and took up a post there as

Staff Nurse on a Cardio-Thoracic ward before joining Ashley at the Royal Sussex County in Brighton where she worked in A & E. 'When Ashley was accepted as a doctor by a hospital in New Zealand he proposed to me so I would be able to work there with him for a year. We married three weeks later and flew to Auckland.'

They returned to England and their first son was born the following year, in 1982, and their second son in 1984, by which time Mummy had come round to the idea that Ashley wasn't such a bad catch after all.

## Liz Bruce

As a Latimer, with Cawley as her House mistress, Liz was more or less forced to do Science A Levels. Her grades were good enough to win her offers from Nottingham, Sheffield and Leicester: 'I still remember going for my interviews and feeling very alone sitting in various London stations on my way up north for interviews, wearing a mini-skirt and freezing.' After all that, her family moved to Australia and she ended up at Sydney University instead, doing Chemistry. Which she never actually used because she *hated* Chemistry.

'I never had a feel for it. In fact, I feel very strongly that Cawley had a very negative influence. We were never encouraged to study the things we actually liked.'

After university she married and had a daughter and a son. 'I've lived in Canberra for decades and am very happy. I ended up running a plastic surgeon's practice, which was terrific.' And nothing to do with Chemistry.

## Sue Robinson

Practically the last thing Jonah said to Sue was, 'Elizabeth [Manners] has chosen you to be Head Girl. How ridiculous is that?'

It was the end of summer term 1967, and Miss Manners was due to take over that September. Lower Six had been a mixed year for Sue. Her father's latest armed services posting had meant a move from Aden to Northern Ireland, and it was around that time that her mother, to whom she was very close, began a series of surgeries for breast cancer. For the first time, school became something of a haven. 'Friends. Fun. I could get away from the anguish.'

Manners expected quite a lot from her prefects. She wanted them to be a real presence in the school. 'More approachable. Less of the spy; more guiding, helping, supporting younger pupils. Be kind to them. So she was trying to eradicate bullying. But I think that had an impact on us from an academic point of view. We weren't in lessons, and it was our final year.'

Sue was studying for A Levels in Chemistry, Physics and Double Maths and, along with her responsibilities as Head Girl, there was plenty at home to be worried about. Christmas was horrid. Her mother was in hospital for most of it. In the Easter holidays, she found out her father was having an affair. The neighbours in Ireland told her.

'I absolutely went for him. I was furious. Not that he was having an affair, but that it was public knowledge and that my mother knew. And that he couldn't cope with her being mutilated. Plastic boobs and whopping great steroid doses. He expected his wife and daughter to be good-looking. Represent what was best. I wasn't sorry for him, which perhaps I should have been.'

She had been offered a place at Birmingham to do nuclear physics. 'Three Cs. I screwed them up. Cs for Maths and Chemistry, D for Physics and E for Further Maths. I did really well in General Studies but that was no good to anyone, was it?'

She did re-sits at Cambridge Tech., where she changed her mind about Birmingham and applied to Homerton to read Maths, Cert Ed. and the Cambridge Tripos part, B. Ed. She had also embarked on her first serious relationship and, in the middle of it all, got pregnant.

'My mum was in a hospice. My dad did the never-darken-my-door-again thing, and refused to fill in the grant form. I was accepted by Homerton then, through very kind people there, and got a place at an unmarried mothers' home.

'Mum died in July 1969. She never made it to her forty-fifth birthday. Three months after she died, my father married someone three months older than me and I never saw him again.'

Sue's son was born in her first term at Homerton. She was allowed off sport and PE because her tutor reckoned labour was enough.

## Our Teachers

### Jonah

At the end of the summer term of 1967, Jonah left the stage. Her parting gift from the school was a model of a whale, with a miniature Jonah inside. Her retirement home was a bungalow outside Swansea, overlooking Caswell Bay: 'Pronounced "casual", as in your shoes,' said Jonah. Here she flung herself into working for the Red Cross and at the Women's Institute's Denman College. Her big treat was having a television in her bedroom. She liked to wake up to find David Frost at the end of her bed.

Jonah died in January 1985. Her death notice in that year's school magazine says that it was 'peacefully in hospital after a very short illness', although it's hard to think of Jonah doing anything peacefully.

### Bretch

Bretch retired in 1989, the last of 'our' teachers to go. It was very hard for her to leave Ridley, her home for almost all her adult life, and she only moved out the day before Judy James and her family arrived.

### Maggie

Maggie carried on as Tyndale House mistress and teaching until December 1979. Many of 'her' girls invited her to their weddings and visited her in her bungalow in nearby Kirton after she retired.

## Cawley

The last time I saw Cawley was in the Christmas vacation after my first term at Bristol. Chrissie had stayed on into Third Year Six and, mini-skirted, I went back to Felixstowe accompanied by boyfriend *du jour* to see her. As I chatted to Chrissie outside Hooper, a familiar squawk was to be heard. 'Julia Welch, what do you think you look like? I can almost see your bottom!' Cawley had obviously shot out of Latimer to see what was going on.

Cawley died in 2002. Her funeral was at St John's in Old Felixstowe. High Church, of course. Penny Stevenson, who Cawley was kind to in 1949, went, but she was more or less the only one. A lot of people who might have been there, her favourites, didn't turn up.

## Coulo

When I began researching this book, it appeared that all the women who had taught me had died. Frustrating. Then a chance conversation with a former school friend on Facebook revealed that Coulo, our former Games mistress, was still around, living at a great age in a residential care home. Not just that, but she loved to receive letters and phone calls. I wrote, explaining what the book was about, and asking if an interview would be possible. Two evenings later, my phone rang. It was her. We chatted, it was lovely, her voice was no different. I half expected her to say, '*Shoo-ooot!*' We left it that we would speak again on the phone when I had got to further grips with the book. A few weeks later, it was too late.

Another door opened. Unlike our other teachers, Coulo

was a mother. I emailed her son, Richard, who kindly offered to give me an account of his mother's life. He also sent some wonderful photos, including one of her as a beautiful, sophisticated young woman. I have had to compress, and leave out a lot, of Richard's account. It really deserves a whole book in itself, as packed with drama, loss, heartbreak and success against the odds as any Penny Vincenzi novel.

She was born Diana Meller in Leighton Buzzard on 14 October 1916, in the middle of the First World War. Her father, Bob, went to Harrow, and then Trinity College, Cambridge, before qualifying as a doctor and serving in the navy; her mother, Florence, trained at Bart's and nursed the Turks during the Bulgarian Turkish war of 1912–13. Her parents met in Khartoum, and she had two younger siblings, Jo and Billy. After the war, the family moved to Hampshire and then, when Diana was ten, to Felixstowe, where she continued to live for forty years.

In 1929, Di, Jo and Billy were playing in a sandpit belonging to a nearby construction site when the sides collapsed and they were buried. Diana managed to dig herself out, and then her sister Jo, but Billy died. He was eight years old. His name was never mentioned in the family again. Richard thinks Billy's death may have had a lasting effect on his mother, as she was always reluctant to talk about people who had died.

Diana was nineteen when she went to Bedford College to train as a PE teacher. In the holidays she would go skiing in Bavaria, and on one of those expeditions she met Richard's father, also named Richard. He was an alumnus of Jesus College, Cambridge, a keen rower and captain of the boat club, and went on to qualify as an architect. At the outbreak of war, he volunteered for the navy. That August, Diana and Richard were married. In November 1941 he set sail from Malta on HMS *Neptune,* along with two other cruisers and an escort of four destroyers, to try and sink a convoy of merchant ships carrying forty-five Panzer tanks and other much-needed supplies from Italy to Rommel's army, in North Africa. As they approached Tripoli, the *Neptune,* which was leading the squadron, sailed at full speed into a minefield and was severely damaged. After hitting a further mine later in the night, it sank. Richard was among the 766 of the crew of 767 who died. Seventeen days later, on 6 January 1942, Diana delivered her son. With baby Richard, she returned to live with her family in Felixstowe and went back to work, by which means she was able to put Richard through school. And that is how she came to be our Games mistress.

## Me

As for me, I took a degree in Philosophy from Bristol University then joined the *Observer* sports department. I was the first female ever to report football in a national newspaper. Everyone said it was a brave thing to do but, quite honestly, if you've spent five years with Jonah, Cawley, Bretch and Maggie nothing is ever going to terrify you again. Since then I have written books and scripted films and television plays, and have achieved my other ambition, which was to get married and have lots of children. Like Sukie, I can say I have had a lovely life.

And what became of my parents and braw Jane? They simply went round as a threesome well into old age. Jane was the first to go, and my father and mother both missed her very much. My father died a few weeks before his eighty-ninth birthday, and all my mother's courage and determination came to the fore as she rebuilt her life as a widow. In her final decade she moved to Scotland to live near my older sister. Well into her nineties, she would return by plane to visit me in London, full of beans at the excitement of the journey. I was very proud of her. My nephew, Matt, was something of an honorary son to her and they loved each other dearly. He was with her when she died at the great age of ninety-nine and a half. Her last words were to her two great-granddaughters. They were, 'What did you do at school today?'

# The School Hymn

Dr Savill, Chaplain, 1989
Tune: Doncaster, S. Wesley

'Ne Manus Offendat' – Cranmer
  *Let not your hand offend*
  *But rather let it serve*
  *The cause that has no earthy end*
  *Bring love and truth and birth.*

'Honour before honours' – Ridley
  *A glorious goal ensures*
  *The way is glorious too;*
  *Honour alone our place secures*
  *To your own self be true.*

'Vincit omnia veritas' – Latimer
  *So hear the joyful sounds*
  *'Truth conquers in all things'*
  *For eager hearts and open minds*
  *With them can take wings*

'Utmost to the highest' – Tyndale
*For hearts and minds and wills*
*Must fully face the tests*
*Demanding all those perfect skills*
*The highest aim expects*

'Fide Constantia' – School
*Endurance, faith and love*
*Rich qualities of life*
*Will help the spirit from above*
*To harmonise all strife.*

Old Girls/all
*From age to age passed on*
*These virtues shall not fade*
*Truth, honour, faithfulness and love*
*Of these the school is made.*

# ACKNOWLEDGEMENTS

I would like to thank all my friends for giving such generous help with my research and for telling me so many wonderful tales about life at Felixstowe College. Although some names have been changed and situations 're-described' to protect the privacy of those involved and to help the story rattle along, this is a faithful account of our experiences and I have never had so much fun writing a book before. Friends from other boarding schools also beguiled me with anecdotes, and I'm grateful to Lindsey Bailey, Peggy Bailey, Penny Perris, Sally Louis, Linda Mallory, Sue Lloyd, Gillian Bull, Caroline Elliott, Jenny Sinclair, Carla McKay, Annie Caulfield and Jill Drewett, all of whom succeeded in keeping me in fits. Thanks also go to Robert Kirby and Ariella Feiner of United Agents, who helped me believe this was a story worth telling, to Kerri Sharp, my editor at Simon & Schuster, for her passionate championship of the book, to Margaret Angus and Jane Claydon for their fascinating background information about boarding schools and lacrosse in particular, and to my husband, Ron, and sons, who for the last two years have performed the essential duty of cheering me on.

# ABOUT THE AUTHOR

Julie Welch was Fleet Street's first female football reporter and is well known for her screenplay about her childhood following Spurs in the 1960s, which was turned into a TV film, *Those Glory Glory Days*, by David Puttnam. She is also the bestelling author of numerous titles including *The Ghost of White Hart Lane* (with Rob White), the story of Spurs legend John White.